TOWARD
INTERNATIONALISM

Readings in Cross-Cultural Communication

SECOND EDITION

Louise Fiber Luce
Elise C. Smith
EDITORS

NEWBURY HOUSE PUBLISHERS
A Division of Harper & Row

Library of Congress Cataloging-in-Publication Data

Toward internationalism

    Bibliography: p.
    1. Intercultural communication. 2. Cultural
relativism. I. Luce, Louise Fiber, 1935–
II. Smith, Elise C., 1932–
GN496.T68 1986   303.4'82   86-12599
ISBN 0-88377-123-3

Cover art by Hardy House
Cover design by Carson Design

NEWBURY HOUSE PUBLISHERS
A division of Harper & Row, Publishers, Inc.

Language Science
Language Teaching
Language Learning

CAMBRIDGE, MASSACHUSETTS

Printed in the U.S.A.
63 25294

First edition: April 1979
Second edition: August 1986
6 8 10 9 7 5

To our parents
Guy Fiber and Mildred Johnson Fiber
for their love and support over the years

Credits and Permissions

The authors wish to extend their thanks for reprint permission to • **American Anthropological Association.** "Body Ritual Among the Nacirema" by Horace M. Miner from THE AMERICAN ANTHROPOLOGIST, Vol 58, No. 3, copyright ©1956. By permission. • **The Asia Society, Inc.** Pp. 4–30 "Asia in American Textbooks," 1976. By permission. • **Dean C. Barnlund, author.** *Public and Private Self in Japan and the United States*, pp. 66–90 and pp. 176–177 relating footnotes, copyright ©1975. By permission of the author and the publisher, The Simul Press, Inc. • **The Bobbs-Merrill Company, Inc.** Pp. 147–167 from AN INTRODUCTION TO INTERCULTURAL COMMUNICATION by John C. Condon and Fathi S. Yousef, copyright ©1976 by The Bobbs-Merrill Company, Inc. By permission. • **Center for Applied Linguistics.** "Kinesics and Cross-Cultural Understanding by Genelle G. Morain from No. 7 in the series *Language and Education: Education and Practice*, pp. 1–27. By permission • **Center for Global Perspectives.** Pp. 8–12 "Cross-Cultural Awareness" from Robert G. Hanvey, AN ATTAINABLE GLOBAL PERSPEC-TIVE, copyright ©1976. By permission • **Reprinted by permission of Harvard Business Review.** "Negotiators Abroad — Don't Shoot from the Hip" by John L. Graham and Roy A. Herberger, Jr. (July–August 1983). Copyright ©1983 by the President and Fellows of Harvard College, all rights reserved. • **Intercultural Communication Network.** "Culture Shock and the Cross Cultural Learning Experience" by Peter S. Adler from READINGS IN INTERCULTURAL COMMUNI-CATION. Vol. II, pp. 6–21, copyright ©1972. By permission. • **National Textbook Company.** Pp. 97–114, line 22 from LIVING IN LATIN AMERICA by Raymond Gorden. Copyright ©1974 by National Textbook Company. By permission. • **Norton Press.** Pp. 67–95 from *The Sisterhood of Man* by Kathleen Newland, copyright ©1979. By permission. • **Brent D. Ruben, author.** "Guide-lines for Cross-Cultural Communication Effectiveness," pp. 470–479 in *Group and Organization Studies*, December 1977, 2(4). Copyright ©1977 by International Authors, B.V. Reprinted by per-mission of Sage Publications, Inc. • **Edward C. Stewart, author.** *American Cultural Patterns: A Cross-Cultural Perspective*, pp. 26–44. Copyright ©1972 by Edward C. Stewart. By permission. • **Constance A. Sullivan, author.** "Machismo in Its Cultural Dimensions," pp. 1–12. By permis-sion. • **Lorand B. Szalay and Glen H. Fisher, authors.** "Communication Overseas," pp. 1–27. By permission.

Contents

About the Editors

Louise Fiber Luce is an Associate Provost and Professor of French at Miami University, Ohio. During her 25-year career in education, she has taught courses in French language and literature at the university graduate and undergraduate level and at the junior and senior high school level; taught English as a foreign language at the Lycée Molière in Paris; served as faculty member of NDEA Summer Institutes for teachers of FLES; been adviser and consultant for FLES programs in Ohio and Michigan; served as codirector of the French Language Summer Program at the European Center (Luxembourg) of Miami University; and published (*ADFS Bulletin, French Review, Foreign Language Beacon, Accent of ACTFL*) and lectured on foreign study for American students, methodologies for intercultural contact in the American classroom, and innovation in foreign language learning. Funded by a grant from Miami University, she has recently developed a course in Cross-Cultural Communication for undergraduates of several disciplines in the College of Arts and Science. She holds a B.A. degree from the University of Michigan, an M.A. from Middlebury College, and a Ph.D. from Northwestern University.

Elise C. Smith has served for 6 years as Executive Director of OEF International (formerly the Overseas Education Fund), a nonprofit organization that focuses on small enterprise development and job skill training for women in Third World countries. She has had extensive contact with foreign students, in both Latin America and the United States, having taught English as a foreign language at American University, Syracuse University and University El Rosario, Bogotá; she was program director for the Council on International Educational Exchange serving Colombia; was evaluator of ESL junior college programs for the Colombian Ministry of Education Agency and supervised workshops on cross-cultural awareness; and has served as resource person and consultant for the Mental Health Advisory Committee of the Department of State. She holds a B.A. degree from the University of Michigan and an M.A. from Case-Western Reserve University, and was a Rotary Fellow at the University of Strasbourg, France.

About the Authors

Peter S. Adler has worked and published widely in the cross-cultural communication field. In particular, he is respected as a significant contributor to our understanding of the dynamics of adjustment to new cultural environments.

Dean C. Barnlund is professor of intercultural and interpersonal communication at San Francisco State University. He is coauthor of *Dynamics of Discussion* and author of *Interpersonal Communication and Public and Private Self in Japan and U.S.* His theoretical and research articles have been published in journals of anthropology, psychology, sociology, medicine, psychiatry, and communication. He is currently completing studies of communicative styles in Japan, Greece, and the United States.

John C. Condon, professor of communication, University of New Mexico, has been involved in intercultural studies for over 25 years, including 12 years of teaching and conducting research in Latin America, Asia, and Africa. He has also worked with refugee organizations in the United States and in the multicultural setting of the southwest. Dr. Condon is the author of more than a dozen books on intercultural relations and serves as a consultant for many businesses, professional, civic, and humanitarian organizations in the United States and abroad.

Glen H. Fisher, Ph.D., is adjunct professor of international policy studies at Monterey Institute of International Studies and a consultant to government agencies and business and academic groups and author of two books on international communication, *Public Diplomacy and the Behavioral Sciences* and *International Negotiation: A Cross-Cultural Perspective.* He was a foreign service officer, delegate to the U.N., dean of the Center of Area Studies at the Foreign Service Institute, and on the faculty of the Georgetown University School of Foreign Service.

Raymond L. Gorden is professor of sociology at Antioch College. One of his prime areas of study has been nonlinguistic behavior as a barrier to communication, particularly among Colombians and young Americans living with Colombian families in Bogotá. He is the author of *Living in Latin America.*

John L. Graham is assistant professor of marketing at the University of Southern California Graduate School of Business and research associate in the school's International Business Education and Research (IBEAR) program.

Robert G. Hanvey is a consultant and specialist in educational curricula. He is especially interested in the development of educational programs that promote international awareness. He is the author of *An Attainable Global Perspective.*

Roy A. Herberger, Jr. is professor of marketing and the dean of Southern Methodist University's Edwin Cox School of Business. Previously he served as the associate dean for academic affairs at the Graduate School of Business at the University of Southern California and as director of IBEAR.

Horace M. Miner, professor of sociology and anthropology at the University of Michigan, is the author of several monographs and books. He both edited and contributed to *The City in Modern Africa,* In addition, he has done research on the ecology of change among the Hausa of the Anchau Corridor, Nigeria, on a National Science Foundation Grant in 1970–1971.

Genelle G. Morain (Ph.D., The Ohio State University) is associate professor of language education and romance languages, University of Georgia, and a member of the ACTFL board of directors. Dr. Morain's articles on culture have appeared in *Foreign Language Annals* and in *The Britannica Review of Foreign Language Education* (Encyclopaedia Britannica, 1971) and *Essays on the Teaching of Culture: A Festschrift in Honor of Howard Lee Nostrand* (Advancement Press of America, 1974).

Kathleen Newland is currently on assignment in Japan as aid to the rector of U.N. University. She was a senior researcher with Worldwatch Institute, Washington, D.C., and has written on human resources. Trained in political science and economics at Harvard and Princeton, her articles on women, on population, and on employment have appeared in magazines and newspapers around the world.

Brent D. Ruben, Ph.D., University of Iowa, is professor and director of the Ph.D. program, School of Communication, Information, and Library Services, Rutgers University. He is author of *Communication and Human Behavior* (Macmillan, 1983), and author or editor of *Interdisciplinary Approaches to Human Communication* (1979), *Beyond Media* (1979), and other books, book chapters, and journal articles centering on communication theory, communication education, and intercultural and health communication.

Edward C. Stewart is affiliated with the Department of Communication, International Christian University of Tokyo, Japan. He received his Ph.D. in Psychology from the University of Texas. His research and interest have been in the area of culture, especially American culture, and the development of simulation as a method of education and training for intercultural communication. He has worked with the Peace Corps and the Business Council for International Understanding, and has taught at several universities.

Constance A. Sullivan is associate professor and chair of the Department of Spanish and Portuguese at the University of Minnesota (Twin Cities). She received her doctorate in Spanish literature from the University of Illinois (Urbana-Champaign) and has published articles on twentieth-century Spanish literature, Spanish proverbs, machismo, and feminist approaches to analysis of Hispanic literatures and cultures.

Lorand B. Szalay is director of the Institute of Comparative Social and Cultural Studies, Inc. He received his Ph.D. in Psychology from the University of Vienna. His professional interests include social psychology, communication, analysis of subjective culture, and psycholinguistics. He has taught at George Washington University, American University, and the University of Maryland, and is the author of many publications.

Fathi Yousef is associate professor of communication studies in the Department of Speech Communication, California State University, Long Beach. Dr. Yousef has an extensive background in education and industry. His areas of specialization are intercultural communication, verbal and nonverbal behavior, and organizational communication.

The Asia Society's study on Asian stereotypes in U.S. textbooks reflects its purpose as an organization. Its goal is to deepen American understanding of Asia and to stimulate trans-Pacific intellectual exchange. It also offers services to educators to help strengthen school resources on Asian peoples and cultures.

INTRODUCTION

Cross-Cultural Literacy: A National Priority

Louise F. Luce and Elise C. Smith

Since *Toward Internationalism* first appeared in 1979, reality has surpassed the expectations of even the most audacious predictions. Global interaction, whether political, economic, or educational, has intensified so dramatically that, as a nation, we have begun to understand the significance of cultural pluralism and its impact on national affairs and daily life. Among the problems of international complexity facing our country today, the random examples of foreign import restrictions, crushing debts of Third World countries, fishing rights, oil reserves, the Greenpeace movement, and the weak competitive position of the United States in international trade are all too familiar by now. They touch not only diplomats and public officials but also the auto maker in Detroit, the textile worker in Massachusetts, and the housewife in Memphis. Clearly, even those events which once appeared limited to distant nations' internal affairs increasingly have repercussions on larger economic and political ecologies. The direct impact of this reality on every level of American society has led to a dramatic increase in public awareness at both the national and local level of the ever-growing imperatives of global interdependence and international cooperation among nations.

Thus a fundamental question is at stake today. Simply stated, how can a nation and its institutions better assist its citizens to comprehend global issues? How can it help the individual citizen to understand the implications of international policies which directly or indirectly touch his or her life? Surely we have arrived at a time of more profound global consciousness raising in this country. Today an enlightened policy for international cooperation demands not only international negotiations and formal terms of treaties; it requires the public's comprehensive awareness of and empathy for the variables of national cultures, especially as they move toward a single unitary global economy. At the present time, a growing commitment exists both here and abroad for nonspecialists, ordinary men and women, to acquire the insights and skills of cross-cultural literacy. In fact, other industrialized countries are far ahead of the United States in making that commitment a reality.

Cross-cultural literacy means that our citizenry knows how culture influences perceptions and actions. It no longer accepts cultural stereotypes and clichés about other nations. It recognizes that American culture takes its place beside other national cultures as one construct within the spectrum of human societies. Most importantly, cross-cultural literacy requires that Americans know how to read the cultural cues of other nations and decode their meaning. Within this decade, cross-cultural communications skills will become increasingly an indispensable tool for every citizen. Cross-cultural literacy must be a priority on our national agenda as we approach the end of the decade of the 1980s and near the 21st century.

In the past few years alone, a new surge of energy, purpose, and specificity has come to bear on cross-cultural research and training. An international community of psychologists, sociologists, linguists, anthropologists, diplomats, and businessmen and women are sharing in ever more aggressive and creative efforts to refine cross-cultural communication strategies. The need for such strategies is eminently apparent. The gradual erosion of the American influence overseas has given way to multinational and international interests, especially in the areas of science, business, and technology. Not only is there greater interaction between nations on crucial global economic and political issues, as we have already noted, but new, evolving trends in our own country lend further weight to the growing imperative for cross-cultural literacy. We need to examine these trends found within the United States, since they are critical to the formulation of current U.S. public and foreign policy.

Looking first at demographic trends within the United States, three areas of change have dramatically affected the place and importance of cross-cultural literacy for our citizens. First, there is the growing population of legal immigrants as well as undocumented refugees arriving here. Their points of origin—Southeast Asia, Cuba, Haiti, Central America—will bring a higher ratio of different races and cultures into the country than the previous influx of northern and southern Europeans, whose value systems were relatively similar to our own. A strong need already exists for social service personnel with cross-cultural communication skills to assist refugees with their transition into American culture. Once the adjustment has taken place, the immigrants will increasingly become an economic force in the country, with their numbers competing more aggressively for the job market. Policy makers must learn how to address issues now from several cultural perspectives, if fair and equal consideration is to be given to all interest groups.

Yet another demographic change is the growth of minority populations within the United States today. Like the immigrant and refugee groups, native Chicanos, Puerto Ricans, and Asians are also having a significant impact on our education and economic programs, from bilingual education and job training to bicultural programs in the arts. One can correctly speak of a dynamic synergy at play with our more traditional, prevailing value orientations. The political process itself cannot remain indifferent to the cultural diversity these minority populations represent, as the 1984 presidential election amply demonstrated.

A final demographic trend within the United States to be reckoned with relates to the fact that women are now entering the work force in significant numbers. Of equal importance, moreover, they are a new constituency who share concerns across national boundaries. Since 1975 the United Nations Decade for Women has served as a catalyst for them, providing an international forum for the free exchange of ideas and aspirations—in Mexico City in 1975 and in Copenhagen in 1980. The Decade for Women drew to a close at an international meeting in Nairobi, Kenya, in 1985, but the document, "Forward Looking Strategies," which was developed at the meeting, will have a long-term impact. The U.S. government and U.S. private voluntary organizations have already made extensive commitments to the outcome of the meeting, recognizing that women's issues are in fact issues of political and economic significance that transcend national frontiers.

Because of American population trends and social changes affecting refugees, women, and minorities, new demands will be placed on government officials, voluntary organizations, educators, businesses, and individuals to communicate in different modes with these new and expanding constituencies.

For yet another persuasive argument in favor of cross-cultural literacy in this country, one has only to look at the international marketplace.

With the revitalization of U.S. entrepreneurship, midlevel and small businesses (the heart of U.S. business growth) are now marketing new services, new products, and new information systems both at home and overseas. We are moving into an era where four out of five new jobs in U.S. manufacturing are generated as a direct consequence of foreign trade. Newspapers speak daily of foreign investors in the United States, more foreign businesses locating in the United States, more joint foreign and U.S. business ventures both here and abroad, and, finally, more U.S. investments overseas.

Multinational businesses and international markets will inevitably change the nature of communication skills, drawing more from a cross-cultural frame of reference. Upcoming new job markets in the software and service areas have expanded beyond the United States to the global market. From this perspective, the need will increase for training of service area practitioners in cross-cultural skills and additional foreign language study.

The business community and the policy makers in Washington are coming to realize that there is no way to compete effectively within the global economy without strong cross-cultural understanding. In other words, they must create an environment receptive to global trade and development. To do so, they need a citizenry that has achieved a capacity for cross-cultural literacy. Clearly, as Americans also realize that their future economic security is linked inextricably to the economics of other parts of the world, they too have become advocates of global education and intercultural communication skills. Greater sensitivity to other cultures and their values and greater awareness of varying modes of communication can lead, at the most pragmatic level, to more jobs for American working people. This is not a negligible argument for increased intercultural competency.

The incentive to achieve cross-cultural literacy in this country is nowhere more evident than in the education sector. By the mid-seventies the *Chronicle of Higher Education* had already recognized that another growth industry in this country was the education of international students, especially in technical areas, within our own university system. The influx of foreign students continues to grow today, generating considerable income for the strained budgets of our colleges, universities, and technical schools. As for our own students, in a recent College Board Report (May 1983), as well as in the report of the President's select committee on foreign languages and international studies (1979), there is a call for more foreign language study and greater competency in global area studies. Already one finds increasingly ambitious cultural components in instructional materials for the foreign language curriculum. Indeed, our interest in internationalizing the elementary and university curricula has led to several initiatives within the past few years, initiatives that might well never have come about without a clear mandate from the government that set cross-cultural literacy for its citizens as a national priority.

The Biden-Pell Amendment to the International Security and Development Cooperation Act of 1980 passed in Congress is part of that mandate. In this instance, it is legislation that implements a program to educate Americans on world hunger issues. In yet another program, five regional foreign language and area studies resource centers across the United States have been established through funding initiatives of the federal government. Other prominent national organizations are finding cross-cultural literacy and global education projects of equal interest. For example, many members of the Council on Foundations as well as the National Endowment for the Humanities have clearly stated their interest in supporting creative programs to increase global understanding. Likewise, national church organizations and private businesses are persuaded that it is in their interest to fund programs here and abroad that deal with global issues and communication across cultures. A few examples of such programs include forums between U.S. and local businessmen in Columbia, South America; community action programs in the slums of Argentina; small business training for Laotian women refugees in Minneapolis; and, as a last example, joint meetings of Mexican women farmers, U.S. migrant farmers, and key U.S. citizen groups to examine the role of women as food producers.

In November 1983, over 120 private voluntary agencies that work in international development set out a "Framework for Development Education in the United States." As stated in the Framework, the national development education strategy seeks to "build a committed constituency for development both here and abroad by presenting the facts that document global interdependence, mutual interests and the inextricable link between local and global problems and their solutions." Such development education "stimulates individual and community action aimed at improving the quality of life and eliminating the causes of poverty."

An important next step occurred at a meeting held in West Virginia in July 1984. A high-level group of U.S. educators, government, and voluntary organizations set forth the first programmatic activities of the Framework to be implemented by the formal education sector.

The impact of this historic new thrust on development education will be increased exchange across cultures of ideas, methodologies, and

government and community development responses to basic development needs, such as child care, nutrition, health, grass roots small
businesses, and appropriate technologies. This is another area where
cross-cultural literacy will be vital.

Yet another measure of the impact of internationalism on our
priority for cross-cultural literacy can be found in professional organizations dealing with intercultural research, training, communication,
or education. What are they talking about? What are their immediate
and long-range concerns? Two such groups are the International
Communication Association and the Society for International Education, Training and Research. A quick scrutiny of the programs of their
recent national meetings shows that their interests interface with the
developments in demography, education, and economics that we have
already examined. Their topical agenda includes refugee transition
training, ways to institutionalize cross-cultural literacy, global security,
global environmental interaction, transfer of technology, global
communication, cross-cultural negotiation and conflict resolution, the
integration of language and intercultural training, youth exchanges,
and global education in the U.S. schools. It is difficult to overlook the
implicit message found in the frequent use of terms like transition,
transfer, integration, or interaction. They speak to synthesis and the
transcendance of former unidimensional, unicultural modes of
communication.

The expanded role for cross-cultural literacy is also seen in new
constituencies joining the professional dialogue of cross-cultural
trainers and researchers, thus broadening networks and creating new
alliances. The Society for Intercultural Education, Training and
Research, the National Association for Foreign Student Affairs, or the
International Communication Association interact now with the Joint
National Committee for Languages, the American Association of
Colleges, the Council for Graduate Schools, the Council for Languages
and Other International Studies, or the American Council on Education. Humanists are also extending their interests to include cross-
cultural study. A recent instance occurred at Stanford University's 1984
Institute for Intercultural Communication where there was a workshop
on the program titled, "Exploring Intercultural Perspectives through
Fiction." Its focus? To use literature as a tool for teaching cross-cultural
communication concepts and issues, including cultural values and
assumptions, when analyzing dialogue, narrative point of view, literary
genre, and problems in translation for a cross-cultural perspective.
While such an orientation to literature is not yet commonplace, a

breakthrough has clearly been made.

Just as there are new constituencies in the intercultural field, so too are there new materials being produced for use in the classroom from the elementary school through the university. New graduate degree specializations are now designed for the foreign student adviser, for the intercultural specialists in counseling, educational exchange, and study abroad programs. A growing number of MBA programs now specialize in international business and include a rigorous foreign language component and overseas internships. Within the business world, consultants have designed programs to help select those employees best qualified for overseas assignments, to help the employee, the spouse (not necessarily the wife anymore), and children to adjust effectively to the overseas assignment and to cope with reentry upon their return. There are also programs to train stateside personnel to work harmoniously with their foreign national counterparts assigned to businesses in this country.

The several new developments in world affairs and the national interest in cross-cultural literacy that we have just reviewed offer compelling evidence for the wave of the future. At the 1983 meeting of the National Association for Foreign Student Affairs, the keynote speaker was Kingman Brewster, the former president of Yale and former U.S. Ambassador to Great Britain. At that meeting he set the stage for global education and cultural competence in the coming years when he observed, "The interdependence of the world is a fact. What to do about it is the problem." We have already begun to find solutions to the problem. Global understanding of issues and cross-cultural literacy are both a national priority and a national mandate to action.

ADJUSTMENT TO
NEW CULTURAL ENVIRONMENTS

The three articles in this section focus on different aspects of adaptation to new cultural environments. Robert Hanvey, in *Cross-Cultural Awareness*, addresses adjustment to new cultures. He discriminates between degrees of cross-cultural awareness and the means by which they are achieved within a given society. He further posits a correlation between the personality type of traditional modern and postmodern peoples and the quality of the empathy each is able to bring to the cross-cultural situation. Peter Adler's analysis of culture shock is well known in the cross-cultural communication field. In his article, *Culture Shock and the Cross-Cultural Learning Experience*, he discusses first three traditional models of culture shock which emphasize predominantly negative aspects that occur in early phases of adaptation. Then Adler proposes a different model, positive in nature. He perceives culture shock as a cross-cultural learning experience leading to deep personal growth. Such meaningful growth can result in greater cross-cultural awareness and increased self-awareness. This positive approach also presents a challenging model for the development of new training techniques and simulation exercises to facilitate adaptation to new cultural environments. Finally, Brent Ruben argues in *Guidelines for Cross-Cultural Communication Effectiveness* that effective communication skills are the key to adaptation and coping with culture shock. Communicative competence is especially essential to overseas technical advisers and teachers who need to successfully transfer knowledge and technology. Communicative skills lead to successful adaptation as well as professional success and personal growth.

(For further discussion on adjustment to new cultural environments, see S. Bochner, C. Dodd, P. Harris, N. Adler, M. Hamnett in the bibliography.)

Cross-Cultural Awareness

Robert G. Hanvey

From Robert G. Hanvey, *An Attainable Global Perspective,* 1976. Reprinted with permission of the author and the publisher, Center for Global Perspectives, New York (218 East 18th St., New York 10003).

Cross-cultural awareness may be one of the more difficult dimensions to attain. It is one thing to have some knowledge of world conditions. The air is saturated with that kind of information. It is another thing to comprehend and accept the consequences of the basic human capacity for creating unique cultures—with the resultant profound differences in outlook and practice manifested among societies. These differences are widely known at the level of myth, prejudice, and tourist impression. But they are not deeply and truly known—in spite of the well-worn exhortation to "understand others." Such a fundamental acceptance seems to be resisted by powerful forces in the human psychosocial system. Attainment of cross-cultural awareness and empathy at a significant level will require methods that circumvent or otherwise counter those resisting forces. Let us think afresh about what such methods might be, with a full recognition of how difficult the task will be and a corresponding willingness to discard ideas that don't work.

DOES UNDERSTANDING FOLLOW CONTACT

One of the cherished ideas of our own times and of earlier times is that contact between societies leads to understanding. The durability of this notion is awesome considering the thousands of years of documented evidence to the contrary. Consider the following example. When the

13

French began to explore North America they came into contact with a number of aboriginal groups. At various times they attempted to muster the males of these groups into fighting units. The Indians clearly had no aversion to fighting; they were warriors, skilled in the use of arms, proud of triumphs over an enemy. But they would not take orders. French commanders had no control and the so-called chiefs of these groups depended on persuasion, which might or might not be successful. Every individual Indian warrior made his own decisions about whether to join a raid or war party, worked out his own battle strategy, and left the fray when he chose.

This kind of contact between the French and the Indians provided the French with detailed information on the ways of their Indian allies—information they noted scornfully in their journals, sometimes sputtering in rage and frustration. But the behavior they described was incomprehensible to them. By virtue of the concrete experiences that the French had with the Indians, the French had rich data—but no understanding. The French were able to see Indian behavior only in the light of their own hierarchical social system, where it is natural for the few to command and the many to obey. Social systems that worked on other principles were literally unimaginable.

Of course, now we are more sophisticated. What happens when the nature of the contact between groups is not one of exploitation or domination but rather one of sympathetic assistance, and where there is at least some preparation for the cultural differences that will be encountered? Here is an account of Peace Corps experience in the Philippines:

> Most human relationships in the world are governed by a pervasive fatalism, in the Philippines best described by the Tagalog phrase, *bahala na,* which means, "never mind" or, "it will be all right" or, "it makes no difference." Americans, more than any other people in history, believe man can control his environment, can shape the forces of nature to change his destiny. That peculiarity, which is essentially Western, is quintessentially American.
>
> Most of the peoples of the world also value dependency and harmony relationships within the in-group. Rather than stress independence in relationships—freedom from restraint and freedom to make choices—they emphasize reciprocity of obligation and good will within the basic group and protection of that group against outsiders. It is the group—family, tribe or clan—which matters and not the individual. In the Philippines, this phenomenon is perhaps best described by the term *utang na loob* which means a reciprocal sense of gratitude and obligation.
>
> The value of independence in relationships and getting a job done makes us seem self-reliant, frank, empirical, hardworking, and efficient to ourselves. To Filipinos, the same behavior sometimes makes us seem to be unaware of

our obligations, insensitive to feelings, unwilling to accept established practices, and downright aggressive. . . .

Nearly all volunteers had to struggle to understand and deal with Filipino behavior that, when seen from our peculiar stress on independence in relationships as opposed to Filipino *utang na loob,* was deeply distressing. . . . Filipinos wanted to be dependent on others and have others dependent on them; they were often ashamed in the presence of strangers and authority figures; they were afraid of being alone or leaving their families and communities; they showed extreme deference to superiors and expected the same from subordinates; they veiled true feelings and opinions in order not to hurt others or be hurt by them. . . .

It is one thing to study and understand *utang na loob.* It is another to have a principal treat you as a status figure and to insist that you tell him how to run his school, or to have children in your class cower in what seems to be shame, or to have neighbors who care much more that you should like them and that you should have a pleasurable experience than that you should get your job done.

Filipinos, with their incessant hospitality and curiosity, repeatedly made it plain that for them the main job of Peace Corps volunteers was to enjoy themselves and to enhance pleasure for those around them, an approach to life best described by the Filipino phrase, *pakikisama.* . . . Nothing was more difficult for volunteers to understand or accept than that Filipinos wanted them for pleasure in relationships and not to achieve the tasks to which they had been assigned. . . .

It was not just the Filipino's stress on *utang na loob* and *pakikisama* which interfered with getting the job done. It was also *bahala na,* the widespread fatalism of the barrio which showed itself in the lack of emotion at the death of little children, the persistent and nearly universal beliefs that ghosts and spirits control life and death, and the failure of Filipinos to keep promises and appointments. Why should the job matter when fate governs human existence? . . .

During the first two years, four volunteers resigned and twenty-six others were sent home, usually by mutual agreement, because they were not able or willing to cope with the extraordinary psychological burdens of being Peace Corps volunteers. Some volunteers developed a "what's the use" attitude and failed to appear at school, or made short unauthorized trips away from their barrios. Withdrawal was sometimes followed in the same volunteer by extremely hostile behavior against the Philippine Bureau of Public Schools, Washington, and the Peace Corps staff. Some volunteers, particularly those in the first group, wished there was some honorable way for them to cut short their tour of duty without an overwhelming sense of personal failure.[1]

The American Peace Corps volunteers, like the French officers of the 17th Century, could not escape the powerful influence of their own culture, especially since that culture was so deeply embedded in the very definition of the mission. The task was to render assistance. And success was measured by some kind of closure, "getting the job done." Filipino behavior stood in the way of getting the job done. There were distractions, delays, and detours. And the positive reinforcements that a busy, efficient American would have received in his home setting were nowhere to be found. The result: puzzlement and frustration equivalent to that of the French in their relations with Indian groups.

ACHIEVING UNDERSTANDING

But some volunteers did solve the cultural puzzle.

> A male volunteer from South Carolina, D was as much admired by Filipinos and volunteers as any volunteer in the project. Almost from the first, he accepted people for what they were, learned the dialect, made friends, and seemed to enjoy that more than anything else. After two years, he wrote, "I consistently believed and followed a life based on getting away from all identity or entanglement with the Peace Corps. My reasons were . . . to figure out a little bit about what was going on in the Philippines, to see what was really significant in my own place, to try to understand life here, and to learn to function in a way that could be meaningful to me and the community. I burrowed into life here unmindful of anything but my community and involvement and survival. . . ."
>
> Although everyone had thought that he epitomized the ability of a volunteer to live deeply in the culture after just six months, he wrote toward the end of his third year, "I have continued to change here and have now sort of reached a point of being able to feel with others. This is different from understanding how they feel. I am able to be a part of them as they do things with each other and me . . . " (Fuchs, p. 253).

D was a success in both Filipino and Peace Corps terms. So was another volunteer.

> A male volunteer from Massachusetts ran what appears to have been highly successful in-service training classes on English and science for teachers. He also had effective adult education classes and a successful piggery-poultry project. He seemed to blend into his community almost from the beginning, becoming one of the first volunteers to learn the dialect from his region and use it extensively. He enjoyed serenading at night with the gang from the *sari-sari* store and drank tuba with the older men who, as he put it "had the pleasure of learning they could drink the American under the proverbial table" (Fuchs, p. 250).

These two cases teach us some useful things. Both volunteers genuinely joined their communities. They learned the language, sought to "burrow in." Most importantly, they accepted the Filipinos on their own terms and made friends with them, presumably long before their own understanding of the local culture had developed. D wrote, "The people are different, but willing to take me in. . . ." Somehow or other, the Filipino traits that so frustrated other volunteers were not an obstacle to these two. Instead, these two accepted not only the worth of the Filipinos but the worth of their ways, enough to practice them joyfully. And out of that long practice came D's remarkable statement that he was now able to feel *with* others.

Did the two volunteers "go native"? In a sense. Perhaps the most important respect in which this is true lies in the acceptance of the worth and authority of the local community's standards of conduct. These volunteers *participated* in Filipino life. That participation was reinforced in two ways. First, it must have been intrinsically enjoyable to these particular young men. It was satisfying to drink tuba with the local males. Second, that participation must have won social approval from the Filipinos *and that approval must have mattered* to these volunteers. Conceivably the approval of Peace Corps staff became less important (remember that D chose to shake off "entanglement" with the Peace Corps) as the approval of the local community became more important.

The sequence of events seem to go like this:

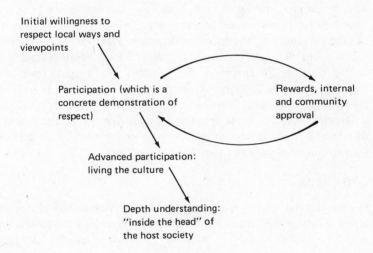

Initial willingness to respect local ways and viewpoints

Participation (which is a concrete demonstration of respect)

Rewards, internal and community approval

Advanced participation: living the culture

Depth understanding: "inside the head" of the host society

It is worth noting that it was only after three years of intense, 24-hour-a-day experience that D felt that he was inside the Filipino head, seeing and feeling in Filipino ways. This, of course, should be no surprise, especially to Americans with their centuries of experience in the difficulties of immigrant assimilation. Stories of immigrants are replete with the difficulties of adjustment, the persistence of old-country ways and attitudes, the stress between parents and the children born in the new country. Many immigrants never made the cultural shift emotionally, even after decades of living in the new setting. But many did.

RESPECT AND PARTICIPATION—MISSING ELEMENTS

What the Peace Corps examples—and the American immigrant experience—show us is that it is not easy to attain cross-cultural awareness or understanding of the kind that puts you into the head of a person from an utterly different culture. Contact alone will not do it. Even sustained contact will not do it. There must be a readiness to respect and accept, and a capacity to participate. The participation must be reinforced by rewards that matter to the participant. And the participation must be sustained over long periods of time. Finally, one may assume that some plasticity in the individual, the ability to learn and change, is crucial. In general, the young will be more flexible and able to achieve this.

This kind of cross-cultural awareness is not reached by tourists nor, in the days of empire, was it reached by colonial administrators or missionaries, however long their service on foreign soil. In American schools, despite integration and black and Chicano study programs, whites do not achieve such an awareness of minority world-views. The missing elements are respect and participation. The society offers limited gratifications for reinforcement of respect for minorities—and very limited penalties for disrespect. And it offers absolutely no rewards to those of the white majority who might seek to participate in minority behavior patterns. The situation for the minority groups is somewhat different; there are social rewards for participating in the majority culture and many individuals shuttle more or less successfully between the two worlds or work out some kind of synthesis.

OPTIONS

If cross-cultural awareness of a profound sort is extremely difficult to attain, what are the options? Are there lesser varieties of awareness that might nonetheless be said to contribute to a global perspective? Are there better methods than have typically been employed to reach awareness? Is the goal itself worthwhile; i.e., does cross-cultural awareness matter?

Let me talk to that last question first. Yes, cross-cultural awareness does matter, for the following major reason if for no other. Several million years of evolution seem to have produced in us a creature that does not easily recognize the members of its own species. That is stated in rather exaggerated form, but it refers to the fact that human groups commonly have difficulty in accepting the humanness of other human groups.

We call a group of primitives in northern North America Eskimos; this name, originated by certain Indians to the south of the Eskimos, means "Eaters of Raw Flesh." However, the Eskimos' own name for themselves is not Eskimos but in Inupik, meaning "Real People." By their name they provide a contrast between themselves and other groups; the latter might be "people" but are never "real."[2]

This practice of naming one's own group "the people" and by implication relegating all others to not-quite-human status has been documented in nonliterate groups all over the world. But it is simply one manifestation of a species trait that shows itself in modern populations as well. It is there in the hostile faces of the white parents demonstrating against school busing. You will find it lurking in the background as Russians and Chinese meet at the negotiating table to work out what is ostensibly a boundary dispute. And it flares into the open during tribal disputes in Kenya.

It must, once, have been an adaptive trait. Perhaps, in ways that we now tend to deprecate, it still is. We call it chauvinism rather than self-esteem. Clearly, there are positive effects associated with a strong sense of group identity. Loyalty is a virtue everywhere, disloyalty abhorred everywhere. The inner harmony of groups is strengthened if aggression can be displaced, diverted to external targets. And if aggression is to be justified, then it helps if the enemy is not quite human. It helps even more if the enemy can be shown to be engaging in practices that are so outrageously different from one's own that they can be credibly labeled inhuman.

There was a time when the solidarity of small groups of humans was the basis for the survival of the species. But in the context of mass populations and weapons of mass destructiveness, group solidarity and the associated tendency to deny the full humanness of other peoples pose serious threats to the species. When we speak of "humans" it is important that we include not only ourselves and our immediate group but all four billion of those other bipeds, however strange their ways.

This is the primary reason for cross-cultural awareness. If we are to admit the humanness of those others, then the strangeness of their ways must become less strange. Must, in fact, become believable. Ideally, that means getting inside the head of those strangers and looking out at the world through their eyes. Then the strange becomes familiar and totally believable. As we have seen, that is a difficult trick to pull off. But there may be methods that will increase the probability of success. Further, there are lesser degrees of cross-cultural awareness than getting inside the head; these more modest degrees of awareness are not to be scorned.

LEVELS OF CROSS-CULTURAL AWARENESS

We might discriminate between four levels of cross-cultural awareness as follows:

Level	Information	Mode	Interpretation
I	Awareness of super-ficial or very visible cultural traits: stereotypes	Tourism, textbooks, National Geographic	Unbelievable, i.e., exotic, bizarre
II	Awareness of signifi-cant and subtle cultural traits that contrast markedly with one's own	Culture conflict situations	Unbelievable, i.e., frus-trating, irrational
III	Awareness of signifi-cant and subtle cultural traits that contrast markedly with one's own	Intellectual analysis	Believable, cognitively
IV	Awareness of how another culture feels from the standpoint of the insider	Cultural immersion: living the culture	Believable because of subjective familiarity

At level I, a person might know that Japanese were exaggerated in their politeness and gestures of deference. At level II are those who know, through either direct or secondhand experience, of cultural traits that significantly (and irritatingly) contrast with one's own practices. The French in their relations with some Indian tribes and the Peace Corps volunteers who failed to adjust might be at this level. So, too, might those who despair over the seeming inability of many developing countries to control population growth. At level III are those who might know, for example, that the really distinctive aspect of the Japanese social hierarchy has nothing to do with the forms of politeness but rather exists in the keen sense of mutual obligation between superior and inferior. The level III person accepts this cultural trait intellectually; it makes sense to him. Peace Corps volunteers might have had this kind of intellectual understanding before actual contact with host cultures. After that contact, some of them slipped to level II and some moved to level IV.

According to this scheme, "believability" is achieved only at levels III and IV. And I have argued that believability is necessary if one group of humans is to accept other members of the biological species as human. I have also noted the rigors of the climb to level IV. This seems to leave level III as the practical goal. But is level III enough?

My position is that level III is indeed more attainable than level IV, and it is a reasonably worthy goal. But not quite enough. We should try to attain at least some aspects of level IV awareness. We can. There are new methods to be explored. And there is a more general reason for encouragement. The evolutionary experience that seemed to freeze us into a small-group psychology, anxious and suspicious of those who were not "us," also made us the most adaptive creature alive. That flexibility, the power to make vast psychic shifts, is very much with us. One of its manifestations is the modern capacity for empathy.

BEYOND EMPATHY

Daniel Lerner in *The Passing of Traditional Society* writes:

> Empathy . . . is the capacity to see oneself in the other fellow's situation. This is an indispensable skill for people moving out of traditional settings. Ability to empathize may make all the difference, for example, when the newly mobile persons are villagers who grew up knowing all the extant individuals, roles and relationships in their environment. Outside his village or tribe, each must meet new individuals, recognize new roles, and learn new relationships involving himself. . . .
>
> High empathic capacity is the predominant personal style only in modern society, which is distinctively industrial, urban, literate and participant. Traditional society is nonparticipant—it deploys people by kinship into communities isolated from each other and from a center. . . .
>
> Whereas the isolate communities of traditional society functioned well on the basis of a highly constrictive personality, the interdependent sectors of modern society require widespread participation. This in turn requires an expansive and adaptive self-system, ready to incorporate new roles and to identify personal values with public issues. This is why modernization of any society has involved the great characterological transformation we call psychic mobility. . . . In modern society *more* individuals exhibit *higher* empathic capacity than in any previous society.[3]

If Lerner is correct, modern populations have a dramatically different outlook, a dramatically different readiness for change, than traditional populations. That difference must have been learned—and by millions of people. If the latent capacity for empathy can be learned or activated, then it may not be too much to work toward a psychic condition that reaches a step beyond empathy. Magoroh Maruyama, an anthropologist-philosopher, describes that next step as *transspection*.

> Transspection is an effort to put oneself in the head . . . of another person. One tries to believe what the other person believes, and assume what the other person assumes. . . . Transspection differs from analytical "understanding." Empathy is a projection of feelings between two persons with one epistemology. Transspection is a trans-epistemological process which tries to learn a foreign belief, a foreign assumption, a foreign perspective, feelings in a foreign context, and consequences of such feelings in a foreign context. In transspection a person temporarily believes whatever the other person believes. It is an understanding by practice.[4]

Empathy, then, means the capacity to imagine oneself in another role within the context of one's own culture. Transspection means the capacity to imagine pupils in a role within the context of a foreign culture. Putting Lerner and Maruyama together, we might chart the psychic development of humanity as follows:

Traditional peoples	Unable to imagine a viewpoint other than that associated with fixed roles in the context of a local culture.
Modern peoples	Able to imagine and learn a variety of roles in the context of a national culture.
Postmodern peoples	Able to imagine the viewpoint of roles in foreign cultures.

Or, we might show the sequence of development in a more graphic way, as involving a movement from the constrictions of local perspectives through the expanded psychological flexibility necessary for role learning in large, heterogeneous national societies, to the advanced versatility of "global psyches" that travel comfortably beyond the confines of the home culture. (The gray zone is home culture.)

The modern personality type did not develop because it was planned. It emerged in the context of changing social conditions. The postmodern personality type, similarly, is not likely to be produced by educational strategies. But if there is a broad social movement, an essentially unplanned intensification of human interaction on the world stage, then educators and other interested parties can play their minor but nonetheless useful roles in the unfolding drama. For educators, that will mean providing students with maximum experience in transspection. And maximum experience means more than time. It means a climate in which transspection is facilitated and expected—and in which the expectations are reinforced. Under such circumstances the schools might produce a slightly higher proportion of persons with the kind of psychic mobility displayed by D, the Peace Corps worker who could feel *with* others. That would be a gain.

If more and more individuals reach the vantage point of level IV awareness, there will be another kind of gain. Dispelling the strangeness of the foreign and admitting the humanness of all human creatures is vitally important. But looking at ourselves from outside our own culture is a possibility for those who can also see through the eyes of the foreigner—and that has significance for the *perspective consciousness* discussed earlier. Native social analysts can probe the deep layers of their own culture, but the outside eye has a special sharpness: if the native for even a moment can achieve the vision of the foreigner, he will be rewarded with a degree of self-knowledge not otherwise obtainable.

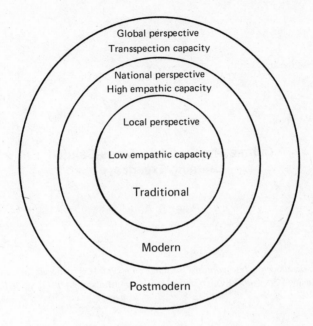

Global perspective
Transspection capacity

National perspective
High empathic capacity

Local perspective

Low empathic capacity

Traditional

Modern

Postmodern

NOTES

1. Lawrence H. Fuchs, "The Role and Communication Task of the Change Agent—Experiences of the Peace Corps in the Philippines," in Daniel Lerner and Wilbur Schramm (eds.), *Communication and Change in the Developing Countries,* pp. 242-245, East-West Center Press, Honolulu, 1967.

2. Wendell H. Oswalt, *Understanding Our Culture,* p. 19, Holt, Rinehart and Winston, Inc., 1970.

3. Daniel Lerner, *The Passing of Traditional Society,* pp. 50, 51, Free Press, 1958.

4. Magoroh Maruyama, "Toward a Cultural Futurology," Cultural Futurology Symposium, American Anthropology Association national meeting, Training Center for Community Programs, University of Minnesota, 1970.

Culture Shock and the Cross-Cultural Learning Experience

Peter S. Adler

Printed in *Readings in Intercultural Communication*, Vol. II (Pittsburgh: Intercultural Communication Network—RCIE, now at University of Pittsburgh, 1972), pp. 6–21.

Personally significant events take place for the individual who spends a good deal of time in a culture foreign to his own. A set of social and psychological mechanisms are activated by the experience of intensively living or working within a different cultural context. A gross reaction takes place within the individual in which the outward experiences of places, faces, and situations are internalized in a different way. We call such reactions culture shock, and we associate them primarily with individuals who have spent a good deal of time outside of their own national boundaries.

The idea of culture shock has received only passing attention. As a concept employed by agencies such as the Peace Corps, AID, and the Foreign Service Institute it has been used to explain away many of the initial frustrations encountered in the earliest part of the sojourner's stay abroad. As a concept, it comes under the domain of no particular discipline, though it has been studied by anthropologists, sociologists, and psychologists. In the academic underworld of carving up the existing turf, culture shock remains refreshingly undefined. No great studies have been undertaken, no collections of statistics appear to have been published, and no one seems to have yet dedicated an entire lifetime to its definition. Aside from Alvin Toffler's metamorphosis of the term into *Future Shock*, the term has not really been popularized.

It is the contention of this brief paper that culture shock can be viewed as a powerful learning tool in which the individual gains both experiential and cognitive learnings that facilitate a high degree of self-understanding and personal growth. Further, this paper is based on the idea that culture shock and the notion of a cross-cultural learning experience are essentially the same phenomenon, the difference being in the scope of focus or view.

THE FIRST VIEW:
CULTURE SHOCK AS THE PRELUDE TO ADJUSTMENT

Descriptions of culture shock by those who have experienced it reflect everything from mild irritability to psychological panic and crisis. The individual undergoing culture shock is thought to reflect feelings of estrangement, anger, hostility, indecision, frustration, unhappiness, sadness, and illness. We picture the person undergoing intense culture shock as being lonely, homesick, and neurotic. He views his new world out of paranoia and alternates between being angry at others for not understanding him and being filled with self-pity. We think of the person who is undergoing culture shock as having all his defense mechanisms triggered and ready to meet any situation. The person in culture shock may simply be bewildered and confused, as in the hypothetical example of Jones in Japan which Edward Hall wrote of:

> At first, things in the cities look pretty much alike. There are taxis, hotels, with hot and cold running water, theatres, neon lights, even tall buildings with elevators and a few people who can speak English. But pretty soon the American discovers that underneath the familiar exterior there are vast differences. When someone says "yes" it often doesn't mean yes at all, and when people smile it doesn't always mean they are pleased. When the American visitor makes a helpful gesture he may be rebuffed; when he tries to be friendly nothing happens. People tell him that they will do things and don't. The longer he stays, the more enigmatic the new country looks. . . .[1]

The case of Jones in Japan illustrates two crucial points about culture shock. First, the individual undergoing culture shock is comfortable in foreign surroundings as long as he can place himself in his new environment, or as long as he can see similarities. As long as he can perceptually screen his surroundings so that he internalizes only the things that are understandable to himself, he feels comfortable. Second, when the initial newness and excitement wear off, the individual becomes disoriented. He begins to see and feel differences.

Culture shock, then, is thought to be a form of anxiety that results from the loss of commonly perceived and understood signs and symbols of social intercourse.[2] The individual undergoing culture shock reflects his anxiety and nervousness with cultural differences through any number of defense mechanisms: repression, regression, isolation, and rejection. These defensive attitudes speak, in behavioral terms, of a basic underlying insecurity that may encompass loneliness, anger, frustration, and self-questioning of competence. With the familiar props, cues, and clues of cultural understanding removed, the individual becomes disoriented, afraid of, and alienated from the things that he knows and understands.

Dr. Kalervo Oberg, who seems to have coined the term culture shock, suggests that it manifests in a number of specific psychological and interpersonal symptoms:

> He is like a fish out of water. No matter how broadminded or full of good will he may be, a series of props have been knocked from under him. This is followed by a feeling of frustration and anxiety. People react to the frustration in much the same way. First they reject the environment which causes the discomfort: "the ways of the host country are bad because they make us feel bad." When Americans or other foreigners get together to grouse about the host country and its people you can be sure they are suffering from culture shock. Another phase of culture shock is regression. The home environment suddenly assumes a tremendous importance. To an American everything American becomes irrationally glorified.[3]

Oberg delineates a number of other manifestations of culture shock as well. Concerns with excessive cleanliness and dirtiness, for example, or fears of physical contact are both symptomatic of culture shock. Feelings of helplessness or irritations over delays suggest culture shock. Fears of being contaminated, cheated, injured, or simply disregarded all may be due to culture shock.

George M. Foster, an anthropologist with a good deal of cross-cultural experience, is more explicit. "Culture shock is a mental illness, and as true of much mental illness, the victim usually does not know he is afflicted. He finds that he is irritable, depressed and probably annoyed by the lack of attention shown him. . . .[4]

The development of the illness of culture shock takes place in stages according to Oberg and Foster. The *first* stage begins with the excitement and euphoria of foreign travel. The individual is captivated by sights and sounds, and he sees the new cultural surroundings through the eyes of the tourist. Involvement in local traditions, problems, and events is minimal and the victim's knowledge of the area is superficial and textbook. He is more excited by the discovery of cultural similarities than by differences, and is primarily concerned with securing his material well-being for the immediate future.

The *second* development of the culture shock disease takes place as personal, social, and cultural differences intrude more and more into the individual's image of self-security. The differences in daily routine, in tradition, in history and philosophy, and in life-style and outlook become more and more noticeable. In this second phase, the individual undergoing culture shock relies increasingly upon the support of his fellow countrymen, and his stay in the host country looks very much like personal exile. He takes solace in griping about the local customs and habits, and seeks respite and escape from the cultural differences he is now all too aware of.

The *third* phase of the model used by Oberg and Foster marks the victim's gradual recovery. He begins to learn more about the local traditions and customs, and his language skills increase. He begins to make friends with the local people, and his outlook and opinions begin to be tempered with more understanding and sensitivity. At this point, his sense of humor returns and he may begin to think of himself as somewhat of an experienced expert on the local scene.

The *fourth* or final stage of this view represents "near or full recovery."[5] In this last phase, the victim comes to a personal understanding of the local culture and is able to cope, in most instances, with the stresses that are placed upon him by cultural differences. He is able to derive pleasure from the relationships he has and is able to experience the culture in a relatively constructive and meaningful manner.

A simple explanation of culture shock is suggested by Conrad Arensberg and Arthur Niehoff, also anthropologists experienced in cross-cultural situations. Culture shock is simply a phase, "a temporary attitude that will pass as soon as he becomes familiar enough with local customs and manners."[6] From their point of view, the most salient aspect of culture shock is that it occurs during the earliest part of the sojourner's stay abroad. Culture shock, then, is simply a field problem in adaptation and adjustment.

Culture shock is most often related to the adjustment and readjustment crises that are experienced during the initial and concluding phases of the individual's experience abroad. Maurice Sill suggests four basic stages of adjustment or "transculturation." Dr. Sill, a former Peace Corps training officer, felt that volunteers first entered a period of *discovery* (0 to 4 months), then into a phase of *self-alignment* (4 to 8 months), later into a stage of intensive *participation* (8 to 20 months), and finally into a period of *devolution* (20 to 24 months). Writing of this process of adjustment, Sill states:

> When a Volunteer lands in the host country, his commitments to transcend the cultural barriers expose him to an assault on his personal way of seeing the world to which visitors rarely lay themselves open. The excitement and discovery cascade into frustration. A Volunteer resident in a new culture is living and working still on

American terms. By opening himself to experiencing the conditions of life and the view of the world of the host country, he has brought his own beliefs and values into question. He faces the necessity to realign his convictions to fit the experience into which he has plunged. A Volunteer may go through a deep depression at this time, "a dark night of the soul," and refuse to see the hope or significance of giving himself to the situation.[7]

In Sill's terms, culture shock is the phenomenon that occurs during the discovery and self-alignment phases of volunteer adjustment. The individual is given over to periods of depression and intense frustration that clearly change when successful adaptation has been completed.

Three interrelated viewpoints emerge from these different models of culture shock. *First*, culture shock is seen as a predominately negative experience attributable to the personal loss of what is culturally, socially, and psychologically familiar. *Second*, culture shock is viewed as a psychological illness or disease of those who venture out of their own culture. It is endemic to the sojourner much like amoebic dysentery. *Third*, culture shock is seen as the crisis in behavior and attitude that occurs prior to the successful adaptation and adjustment to the new surroundings.

The negative implication and connotation of the term culture shock derives from the use of the word "shock." To that extent, it may very well be a misnomer. Medically, shock is a condition that occurs to an organism when a violent disturbance of somatic equilibrium has taken place. It suggests the collision, impact, or disruption in a sudden or violent manner that results in excessive depression or stimulation of the body's resources. In the case of the victim of a severe car accident, the term shock and its symptomology are understandable; in the case of war-related situations, the term "shell shock" is also understandable. In shock, the victim's blood drains away from the head, he is in stupor, and he may be unresponsive to outside stimuli. But the term shock as applied to situations stemming from social, interpersonal, and cultural experiences may be an exaggerated use of the word, causing confusion and misplaced emphasis.

Oberg's and Foster's respective views on culture shock represent the dominant model. Culture shock is viewed as if it were a specific virus with specific symptoms and specific causation. Oberg, for example, calls it an "occupational disease of many people who have been suddenly transplanted abroad."[8] Toffler suggests that "a breakdown in communication, a misreading of reality, [and] an inability to cope"[9] are all caused by culture shock. The teleology implicit in the model is simple. Culture shock is caused by the encounter of an individual of one cultural heritage with the differences presented by another cultural system in which he is immersed. The shock is the shock of isolation and the loss of the familiar. The victim manifests a number of defensive attitudes and outlooks in order to protect the psyche from the uncertainty of dealing with the different. What is described, then, is not simply the encounter with a different culture, but a behavioral disorder.

The prevailing view of the culture shock experience is a picture of an unwitting and helpless victim. He has contracted an illness to which he must submit and for which the only known cures are relatively vague references to hard work, learning the language, and adapting to the local cultural ways. The initial experiences in the new culture are negative, and the individual, caught in transition, must constantly deal with personal crises, dilemmas, and paradoxes. He is the victim of stresses placed upon him by cultural understandings no longer appropriate in his new cultural surroundings. His recourse is to adjust, retreat into the safety of his own head, or terminate his stay in the country.

There is nothing implicitly wrong or invalid with the prevailing view of culture shock. As an attempt to describe and explain the difficulties of the first encounter with a foreign culture, this view delineates a number of important aspects of the cross-cultural experience. The prevailing view is limited, however, by the important questions that are not raised. What else, aside from crisis, adjustment, and adaptation, happens to the individual who lives or works in another culture? What types of learning and what positive personality changes take place as a result of the culture shock experience? The real issue of culture shock, finally, is not how it can be eliminated, but what are the consequences of it.

THE SECOND VIEW: CULTURE SHOCK AS A CROSS-CULTURAL LEARNING EXPERIENCE

Culture shock is an experience of personality in culture. It consists of the psychological events that occur to a person in the initial phases of his encounter with a different culture. As opposed to viewing culture shock only as the illness that occurs to a person during adjustment, culture shock can be thought of as a profound learning experience that leads to a high degree of self-awareness and personal growth. Rather than being only a disease for which adaptation is the cure, culture shock is likewise at the very heart of the cross-cultural learning experience. It is an experience in self-understanding and change.

Four basic questions come to mind. *First*, what is a cross-cultural learning experience and how can it be defined? *Second*, exactly what kind of learning actually takes place during this experience? *Third*, how is the individual significantly different as a result? *Finally*, what are the implications of this type of learning?

Many individuals who have had intensive experiences in different cultures have come away from their experiences feeling personally enhanced and enriched. Aside from the obvious broadening of horizons that takes place, individuals returning from a period of stay in another culture often state or imply that their experiences were something akin to a personal religious experience in profoundness, sublimeness, and personal significance. One former Peace Corps volunteer from Ethiopia, for example, wrote:

> I felt so alive over there I generally say that Asmara was my "renaissance" . . . my rebirth because in effect, it was a rebirth for me. I came away with a totally new concept of life and living, new values, stronger feelings, more experiences and far richer than I ever would have had in a lifetime in the states, and above all, a real understanding and empathy with other people and our place in the nature of things.[10]

A cross-cultural learning experience can be defined as a set of situations or circumstances involving intercultural communication in which the individual, as a result of the experiences, becomes aware of his own growth, learning, and change. As a result of the culture shock process, the individual has gained new perspective on himself and has come to understand his own identity in terms significant to himself. The cross-cultural learning experience, additionally, takes place when the individual encounters a different culture and as a result (1) examines the degree to which he is influenced by his own culture, and (2) understands the culturally derived values, attitudes, and outlooks of other people.

The culture shock process can be viewed as the core or essence, though not necessarily the totality, of the cross-cultural learning experience. In an extended stay abroad an individual is bound to have numerous types of experiences that contribute to his overall personal gratification. The culture shock process, however, is fundamental in that the individual must somehow confront the social, psychological, and philosophical discrepancies he finds in his new surroundings as compared with his own cultural props, self-image, and understandings. The cross-cultural learning experience, then, is in large part a function of the psychosocial impact of realizing how behavior, values, attitudes, and outlook are based on cultural dispositions.

The cross-cultural learning experience can be described with the following characteristics. The experience:

1. Involves change and movement from one cultural frame of reference to another. The individual is presented with changes in the cultural landscape.

2. Is unique and assumes unique importance and meaning to the individual. The individual undergoes a highly personal experience of special significance to himself.

3. Becomes provocative. The individual is forced into some form of introspection and self-examination.

4. Is extreme in its ups and downs. The individual undergoes various forms of frustration, anxiety, and personal pain.

5. Forces personal investigation of relationships. The individual must deal with the relationships and processes (as opposed to only the data and content) inherent in his situation as an outsider.

6. Forces behavioral experimentation. The individual must, of necessity, try out new attitudes and behaviors. This becomes a trial-and-error process until appropriate behavioral responses emerge.

7. Presents unlimited opportunity for contrast and comparison. The individual has at his disposal an unending source of diversity with which he can compare and contrast his own previous experiences.

The cross-cultural learning process, then, is a set of intensive and evocative situations in which the individual experiences himself and other people in a new way distinct from previous situations and is consequently forced into new levels of consciousness and understanding.

If consciousness and awareness can be viewed as instrumental in the learning process, then two types of learning seem to emerge from the cross-cultural experience. The first category of learnings can be described as increased *cultural awareness*, while the second category can be thought of as increased *self-awareness*. Though increased cultural and self-awareness are directly related to each other, it is useful to distinguish between them when viewing culture shock as a cross-cultural learning experience.

Cultural awareness can be thought of as attitudinally internalized insights about those common understandings held by groups that dictate the predominant values, attitudes, beliefs, and outlooks of the individual. Although there are numerous variations of the learnings involved in increased cultural awareness, two attitudes stand out. The individual learns that:

1. Every culture has its own internal coherence and logic. Each culture and its accompanying structures of norms, values, attitudes, and beliefs are an intertwined fabric and design that has an internal cohesion. No one culture, therefore, is inherently better or worse than another, since every culture is its own understandable system. Every culture is acceptable to itself on its own terms since it works.

The individual undergoing culture shock process, then, learns to legitimize different cultural systems and thus moves to a different level of cultural perception. When other cultural frameworks are legitimized, we no longer view them in judgmental and evaluative terms such as underdeveloped vs. developed, modern vs. primitive, or Christian vs. pagan. The individual also learns that:

2. All persons are, to some extent, products of the cultural frame of reference in which they have lived. Every culture provides the individual with some sense of his identity, with some regulation of his behavior, and some sense of his personal place in the scheme of things. Each culture is a frame of reference, orientation, and environment for the individual and, as such, influences the social-psychological cues, clues, props, and foundations necessary for functioning in life.

The individual caught up in the culture shock process further learns that he himself as much as the people of the local country are influenced and to some extent bound by their own culture. When we can recognize the degree to which we are all products of our own culture, the culturally influenced behaviors, attitudes, values, and beliefs of others are far more acceptable.

Increased cultural awareness, then, reflects personalized learnings about the ethnocentrism that shapes many of our attitudes in cross-cultural situations. Increased self-awareness, the second category of learnings that emerge in the cross-cultural learning experience, reflects the development of personal insights into egocentrism. Just as ethnocentrism influences behavior in cross-cultural situations, egocentrism can govern the dynamics of any interpersonal situation. Increased self-awareness can be thought of as behaviorally internalized insights about one's own identity, value structure, and communications patterns. Although the specific learnings that emerge are different in every person's experience, two general insights seem to occur. The individual learns that:

1. His own behavior is grounded in values, assumptions, and beliefs. He himself behaves out of a complex of motivations and intentions (many of which are culturally influenced) which, in turn, stem from different kinds of changing feelings. His own feelings change according to the situation he finds himself in. His own feelings, however, can greatly affect his effectiveness in communication and hence his personal relationships.

The individual undergoing culture shock learns that much of his own behavior is governed by feelings. When we can better understand the degree to which feelings based on values, beliefs, and assumptions affect the relationships we are engaged in, we can better accept our own behavior. In addition, the individual learns that:

2. His own behavior affects, to some degree, how others relate to him. His own feelings, cultural biases, and situational dispositions provide others with some basis for response and reaction. His own attitudes and behaviors provide others (for whom he is a stranger) with some evidence of personality and character, hence with justification for specific behaviors toward him.

The individual in the culture shock process learns that just as seemingly strange behavior of others affects him, so too does his behavior affect the degree and type of reciprocity in personal relationships and interpersonal communication. When we are open and warm, even to strangers, we tend to elicit open and warm responses in others.

In addition to learnings based on cultural and self-awareness, the individual undergoing the culture shock process develops a number of specific interpersonal skills to match the cross-cultural situation he is in. These skills can be thought of as behavioral and attitudinal learnings that are put into practical, day-to-day use. We can consider increased tolerance, for example, to be something more than an attitude. Tolerance for different life styles, value systems, and outlooks, when incorporated into behavior, is also a skill. We can likewise consider sensitivity and empathy to others as a corresponding skill. The learning of appropriate behavioral responses and reactions in a different cultural or social situation necessarily involves the development of skills in interpersonal competence and in communication. The individual learns how to interpret situations, how to deal with problems and conflicts, how to trust other people, and how to simply enjoy the diversity of people. When an individual undergoes a radical change in cultural environment, these skills become necessary for social survival.

Among those individuals who are able to complete a positive cross-cultural experience, these types of learning seem to prevail and, in turn, appear to be directly related to experiences in the culture shock process. Though culture shock can be a shattering experience, it can also be a source of reintegration of personality. Kazimierz Dabrowski has argued that frustration, discomfort, and anxiety are all instrumental to the process of self-understanding and personality development. In a book entitled *Positive Disintegration*, Dabrowski states:

> Disintegration is, a generally positive developmental process. Its only negative aspect is marginal, a small part of the total phenomenon and hence relatively unimportant in the evolutionary development of the personality. The disintegration process, through loosening and even fragmenting the internal psychic environment, through conflicts within the internal environment and with the

external environment, is the ground for birth and the development of a higher psychic structure. Disintegration is the basis for developmental thrusts upward, the creation of new evolutionary dynamics, and the movement of the personality to a higher level.[11]

Dabrowski argues that the very experiences that disrupt the personality and its relationships to the social environment also give rise to the reconstruction of personality at a significantly different level of awareness.

The cross-cultural learning experience is a very powerful and personal form of learning. In a sense, individuals who undertake such experiences, no matter what the conditions, are forced into realizations about themselves and others. The greater and deeper the realizations, the more personal and significant the learning is. Many different types of experiences take place in the culture shock process. The greatest *shock* in culture shock may be not in the encounter with a foreign culture, but in the confrontation of one's own culture and the ways in which the individual is culture-bound. Throughout the cross-cultural learning experience the individual is presented with differences, and when those differences cannot be ignored, they tend to be magnified. This magnification in itself gives rise to distortions that each individual must deal with himself. In dealing with them, learning takes place.

Similarly, the individual who lives and works in a different culture is forced to draw upon personal resources for both personal survival and self-renewal. In the normal routine of one's own culture, these resources are rarely needed. Thus, the cross-cultural learning experience is that rare set of situations which forces the individual into experimenting with new forms of attitude and behavior. The learning that emerges from such experimentation is facilitated because the individual must assume his own personal responsibility, because he is "doing" plus thinking, rather than only thinking, and because the individual must evolve his own strategies for making choices, decisions, and evaluations.

It is obvious that not every person who undergoes a cross-cultural situation experiences the development of the learnings and skills and the personal growth described here. For some individuals, the cross-cultural experience will always be more negative than positive. Not every person who lives or stays abroad has a successful, positive, productive, or even constructive experience. Still, for those individuals who have had successful experiences abroad, the culture shock process has served as a catalyst and a stimulant to deeply personal understandings about self and culture. Although the specific dynamics of the culture shock process are not completely understood, it is evident that for some individuals the process has many positive consequences.

Hopefully, as this process becomes understood, and as new models for training and simulation are developed, every individual contemplating working or living abroad will be able to undergo a successful cross-cultural learning experience.

NOTES

1. Edward T. Hall, *The Silent Language*, p. 43, Fawcett Publications, Inc., Greenwich, 1959.

2. Kalervo Oberg, "Culture Shock and the Problems of Adjustment to New Cultural Environments," an edited talk, Foreign Service Institute, Washington, 1958.

3. Oberg, "Culture Shock," p. 1.

4. George M. Foster, *Traditional Cultures*, p. 187, Harper & Row, New York, 1962.

5. Foster, *Traditional Cultures*, p. 190.

6. Conrad M. Arensberg and Arthur H. Niehoff, *Introducing Social Change*, p. 189, Aldine Publishing Company, Chicago, 1964.

7. Maurice Sill, "Transculturation in Four Not-So-Easy Stages," in *The Peace Corps Experience*, ed. Roy Hoopes, p. 246, Clarkson N. Porter, Inc., New York, 1968.

8. Oberg, "Culture Shock."

9. Alvin Toffler, *Future Shock*, p. 13, Random House, New York, 1970.

10. Sill, "Transculturation in Four Not-So-Easy Stages."

11. Kazimierz Dabrowski, *Positive Disintegration*, p. 5, Little, Brown and Company, Boston, 1964.

Guidelines for Cross-Cultural Communication Effectiveness

Brent D. Ruben

Among cross-cultural trainers and researchers, considerable attention has been focused on problems individuals encounter in adapting to new cultures or subcultures. For the many volunteers and professionals who live and work in a cross-cultural setting, the question of how to effectively transfer knowledge and skills to persons of different cultural backgrounds is an equally great concern.

INTRODUCTION

For many persons interested in cross-cultural relations, a continuing research and training concern has been the role of the sojourner or technical adviser in developing countries. In the literature, considerable attention has been devoted to the sojourner. Researchers and writers primarily have been interested in the problems of cross-cultural shock and the dynamics of psychological adjustment (Arensberg and Niehoff, 1971; Brislin and Pedersen, 1976; Gullahorn and Gullahorn, 1963; Hall, 1959; Oberg, 1960). In this paper, attention is devoted to the volunteer or professional sojourner, considered in terms of effectiveness in transferring skills and the relevance of particular interpersonal communication skills to this goal.

This paper provides a prototypical case study in which barriers to effective transfer of skills are indicated, suggests a framework for viewing the sojourner as teacher, and summarizes recent research on the role of particular communication behaviors in cross-cultural effectiveness.

GREAT BOOKS, GREAT SAVINGS!

When You Visit Our Website:

www.kensingtonbooks.com

You Can Save 30% Off The Retail Price
Of Any Book You Purchase!

- **All Your Favorite Kensington Authors**
- **New Releases & Timeless Classics**
- **Overnight Shipping Available**
- **All Major Credit Cards Accepted**

Visit Us Today To Start Saving!
www.kensingtonbooks.com

A CASE STUDY

Mr. S has accepted a position as an adviser in a Third World country. He will be working directly with Mr. Akwagara, a national. Together they will have administrative responsibility for their project.

Mr. S is eager to arrive at his post. With his work experience in the United States, he seems exceptionally well suited to the task he must accomplish in his post in the developing country, and his high level of motivation and record of consistently superior achievement reassure him—and those who selected him—that he will encounter little he cannot handle in his assignment.

After being on the job for several weeks, Mr. S experiences considerable frustration. To S, it appears that Akwagara and most of the subordinates lack both training and motivation. On a number of occasions, S has endeavored to point out tactfully to Akwagara that his practices are both inefficient and ineffective. Akwagara's responses seemed to S to indicate total indifference. On one occasion, S suggested that he and Akwagara get together one evening for a few drinks, thinking that in an informal setting he might be more successful in making Akwagara aware of some of these problems. The two went out together, but nearly every effort S made to bring up the work situation was followed by Akwagara changing the subject to unrelated chatter about family and friends.

The problem became increasingly severe in the weeks that followed. It seemed to S that the only way he could get the job done was to do most of it by himself. Gradually, he has assumed more and more of the responsibilities that had been previously performed by Akwagara. Although he feels some concern about this situation from time to time, these feelings are more than compensated for by the knowledge that he is getting the job done that he was sent to do.

Consider the question: Is S succeeding or failing? The answer, of course, depends largely on how one defines the role of volunteer or professional sojourner. If one takes the point of view that the task of the sojourner consists solely of getting the job done, one would probably conclude that S is functioning effectively. Viewed from another perspective, one cannot help but conclude that the adviser has failed sadly. The job is being done at the cost of successful transfer of skills. Probable consequences of his approach include the alienation of Akwagara, a loss of credibility for Akwagara among the subordinates he must supervise after S departs, and reinforcement of the view that Western advisers are insensitive, egocentric, and not sincerely interested in the welfare of the host country or nationals.

For S and the sponsoring agency and country, the consequence is a failure to share knowledge and skills meaningfully. The ultimate tragedy is that S, with the best of intentions and motives, may in fact spend two years of his life believing that he is functioning as the ideal adviser. All the while, he may actually contribute to forces that retard the process of growth, change, and development in his project and in the country as a whole. As this case and a number of others in the literature indicate, the ability to satisfactorily understand and relate to others in a cross-cultural setting is probably the single most critical ingredient necessary to an adviser's success—and essential if one is to translate his own skills and knowledge into the idiom of the culture. As Bunker and Adair (1959) note:

> The country folk can do without outside help—the farmer can still make a crop with his old plow, and the midwife can still deliver babies, and the village council can speak for the people (and the village elders can declare that vaccination is against the will of heaven). The question is what the brash innovator ... can do.

THE SOJOURNER AS TEACHER

In conceptualizing the role of the sojourner in terms of the effective transfer of skills, it seems useful to think of him or her broadly as a teacher. A teacher, after all, is a person who possesses particular knowledge and skills he or she wishes to impart to others. There are two distinct components of teaching—at least of effective teaching. First, the teacher must have an appropriate mastery of skills and knowledge in his or her field. Second, the teacher must be able to package and deliver this understanding to others in such a way that they will be able to accept, utilize, and integrate them. For the sojourner, these same components are crucial.

Most technical advisers selected for overseas postings satisfy the first requirement very well. Whether selected to assist with the installation of a computer or electronic communication system, the development of educational, governmental, agricultural, economic, or industrial policy, or any of a number of other less technical positions, job-related competencies are seldom a problem.

The second set of skills, however, is totally unrelated to the job. These skills have to do with communication, and research and reports from the field indicate that such capabilities are even more critical to the success of an adviser and a project than his or her job skills. As Schnapper (1965) noted:

> The history of international development efforts is strewn with the wreckage of many projects. One of the major conclusions that emerges from this history is the lack, not of technical skills but of interpersonal and intercultural adaptation skills. This history of international development failure is still being perpetuated today even though one of its causes has been identified in countless studies and reports.

For convenience, one can refer to this needed set of skills as *communication competence*.[2] If job or role competence is the ability to complete a task efficiently, communication competence is the ability to effectively relate to other persons in the process. Achieving an integration of the two is important in both the short and long run and from both idealistic and practical points of view.

The importance of communication to effective cross-cultural functioning is well illustrated by the case of Mr. S. As a member of a Western culture, it is likely that to Mr. S time and money are important criteria for success; he may well view wealth and power as essential to the solution of most problems, consider democratic or majority rule as the appropriate form of governance, revere technology, regard competition as good, and see winning as an important goal. He quite likely values material possessions, the scientific method, efficiency, organization, specialization, and a clear separation between work and leisure. In his communication style, he is likely to be reasonably aggressive, direct, impatient, and self-assured and to regard business as the topic of major importance in most of his interactions, attaching a lesser value to discussion of family and personal matters.

Depending upon Akwagara's cultural background, he is likely to have a quite different communication framework. For him speed and efficiency may be irrelevant or negative values. Material possessions, competition, and winning may be regarded with far less concern, and he may view extended family relationships as the primary source of power and status. The democratic model, technology, progress, and Western development may be viewed with cynicism and suspicion. Conditions of living may be regarded primarily as inevitable consequences of his manifest destiny, leaving little room for individual initiative or impact. Work and leisure may well be blended, and he may have little concern for systematic or efficient organization or specialization. In discussions, Akwagara may well be relatively passive, indirect, and patient, and he will very likely place a much higher priority on family and friends than upon business as a topic. He also may be accustomed to standing or sitting close to those he is talking to and to numerous gestures involving frequent physical contact.

In such an instance, the two individuals have a great many barriers to overcome if either is to understand with much accuracy the words and actions of the other.

A review of the cross-cultural literature and anecdotal writing in the area of cross-cultural effectiveness suggests that, for the sojourner, certain communication behaviors may be crucial to effective functioning in situations of this sort.

There has been considerable research concerned with identifying those communication behaviors that contribute to effectiveness within one's own culture. Wiemann (1975) identified three main schools of thought about face-to-face interaction. The first he characterized as the human relations or T-group approach, typified by the work of Argyris

(1965), Bochner and Kelley (1974), and Holland and Baird (1968). The second orientation, the social skill approach, is reflected especially in the work of Argyle and Kendon (1967), and the third is essentially a self-presentation approach suggested in the work of Goffman (1959, 1963, 1967), Rodnick and Wood (1973), and Weinstein (1966, 1969).

Efforts to consider how these approaches generalize to cross-cultural face-to-face interaction have been few (Ruben, 1976; Ruben et al., 1977). Case studies and anecdotal reports of behaviors that reportedly lead to failure and others that seem associated more often with success (Ruben et al., 1977) are available to help link the study of intracultural effectiveness to intercultural competency. Based on an integration of these sources with findings from studies of intracultural competence, seven dimensions of importance to intercultural competence can be identified (Ruben, 1976):

1. The capacity to be flexible
2. The capacity to be nonjudgmental
3. Tolerance for ambiguity
4. The capacity to communicate respect
5. The capacity to personalize one's knowledge and perceptions
6. The capacity to display empathy
7. The capacity for turn taking

Research was undertaken by Ruben and Kealey (1977)[3] to determine the order of importance of these communication behaviors for effectiveness. The findings suggest that an avoidance of extreme *task, self-centered,* and *judgmental* behavior—in that order—contribute most to effective transfer of skills. A *tolerance for ambiguity,* the *ability to display respect,* and a *personal orientation to knowledge* are next in importance in cross-cultural effectiveness, followed by *empathy* and *turn taking.* In the following section, each of these communication dimensions will be discussed and their relationship to effective transfer of skills will be explored.

TASK AND RELATIONAL BEHAVIOR

Individuals function in a variety of roles within group settings (Benne and Sheats, 1948). Behaviors that involve the initiation of ideas, requests for information, seeking of clarification, and evaluation of ideas are directly related to a group's task or problem-solving activities. Behaviors that involve harmonizing, mediation, gatekeeping, attempts to regulate the evenness of contribution of group members, and compromising are related to the relationship-building activities of a group.

Some situations call for an intense concern for "getting the job done." Others call for building group cohesiveness, encouraging participation, and making certain that no one feels excluded. Westerners seem to focus mostly on the former and are typically not very concerned about how involved people feel in the process, how much group or organizational solidarity develops, and how people value the products of their effort. But, as indicated previously, the transfer of skills requires not only getting a job done, but also the competence to get it done in such a way that people feel a part of the completed project and have learned something from the process. Research suggests that too much concern for getting the job done can lead to failure in terms of effectiveness at skill transfer (Ruben and Kealey, 1977). Again, the Akwagara case emphasizes the importance of being flexible and adapting one's behavior to the demands of the situation.

SELF-ORIENTED BEHAVIORS

Another category of role behaviors sometimes displayed by individuals in an interpersonal or group context is individualistic or self-centered behavior that functions in negative ways, from the group's perspective. Behaviors such as being highly resistant to the ideas of others, returning to issues and points of view previously acted on and/or dismissed by the group, attempting to call attention to oneself, seeking to project a highly positive personal image by noting achievements or professional qualifications, and attempting to manipulate the group by asserting authority are dysfunctional in intracultural as well as in intercultural contexts.

THE CAPACITY TO BE NONJUDGMENTAL

People like to feel that what they say is not being judged by someone else before they have had an opportunity to explain themselves fully. When people are interrupted before they have finished speaking or when they notice that someone is shaking his or her head in disagreement before they have finished presenting their thoughts, barriers to effective relating are set in place. The likelihood of teaching or transferring skills in such a situation is greatly diminished. Ideally, one should not pass judgments on what others have to say until one has enough information to be fairly certain that his or her evaluations will be based on a reasonably complete understanding of the other person's point of view. When people believe that they have been listened to fully and attentively, they are generally much more receptive to hearing reactions—whether positive or negative. In addition to improving the fidelity of transmission, nonevaluative postures seem likely to increase the receiver's regard for the source of nonevaluative messages and thereby improve the quality of the relationship.

TOLERANCE FOR AMBIGUITY

The ability to react to new and ambiguous situations with little visible discomfort is apparently an important asset when adapting to a new environment. Although most people probably do react with some degree of personal discomfort to new environments, some seem more able to adjust quickly to those around them. Excessive discomfort from being placed in a new or different environment—or from finding the familiar environment altered in some critical ways—can lead to confusion, frustration, or even hostility. This may well be dysfunctional to the development of effective interpersonal relations within and across cultural boundaries. Colleagues and would-be friends may easily become the unwitting and misplaced targets of verbal hostility during periods of adjustment, and although the frustrations are often short-lived, the feelings they may have initiated in a colleague might not be. Learning to manage the feeling of frustration associated with ambiguity thus can be critical to effective adaptation in a new environment.

THE DISPLAY OF RESPECT

The ability to express respect and positive regard for another person has been suggested as an important component in effective interpersonal relations (Carkhuff, 1969). The expression of respect can confer status on the recipient, contribute to self-esteem, and foster positive regard for the source of the communicated respect.

People like to feel that others respect them, their accomplishments, their beliefs, and what they have to say. If one is able, through gestures, eye contact, smiles, and words of encouragement, to indicate that he or she is sincerely interested in the other person, then that person is much more likely to respond positively. In the case study, by listening to Akwagara carefully, attentively, and encouragingly as he discussed family and friends and by reciprocating in kind, S would have communicated his respect and begun to establish a strong foundation for an effective relationship—one that would be productive and satisfying on a day-to-day basis and one that would facilitate the transfer of S's skills and knowledges, as he had intended.

PERSONALIZING KNOWLEDGE AND PERCEPTIONS

Different people explain themselves and the world around them in different terms. Some people tend to view their knowledge and perceptions as valid only for themselves; others tend to assume that their beliefs, values, and perceptions are valid for everyone. Presumably, the more a person recognizes the extent to which knowledge is individual in nature, the more easily he or she will be able to adjust to other people in other cultures, whose views of what is "true" or "right" are likely to be quite different.

People who recognize that their values, beliefs, attitudes, knowledges, and opinions are their own—and not necessarily shared by others—often find it easier to form productive relationships than do persons who believe they know *The Truth* and strive to sell their own perceptions, knowledges, skills, and values to others. If a person often begins sentences with "I think" or "I feel" or "In my own experience," he or she probably is more aware of the personal nature of knowledge and values than if he or she prefaces thoughts by saying "Africans tend to be" or "Americans are" or "Canadians believe." Among persons whose ideas of what is *True* and *Right* differ dramatically from that to which one has become accustomed, it is useful to keep in mind that one's beliefs, knowledges, and attitudes are products of one's own experiences. Remembering also that one's "truths" may have little in common with those of others gives one an important advantage as a teacher.

DISPLAYING EMPATHY

The capacity to "put oneself in another's shoes" or to behave as if one could often has been suggested as important to the development and maintenance of positive human relationships within and between cultures. Individuals differ in their ability to display empathy. Some people are able to project an interest in others and seem able to obtain and reflect a reasonably complete and accurate sense of another's thoughts, feelings, and/or experiences. Others may lack interest—or fail to display interest—and may be unable to project even superficial understanding of another's situation.

Many people are attracted to individuals who seem to be able to understand things from "my point of view." Certainly, because each individual has a unique set of past experiences, it is not possible to put oneself totally in someone else's shoes. Through careful listening and observing and with a sincere and diligent effort to understand the other person's communication framework, one can, however, achieve some degree of empathy, a critical ingredient for effective teaching. Had Mr. S devoted more effort to establishing this sort of understanding of Akwagara and had he been successful in reflecting the resulting awareness through his words and actions, many of the difficulties he encountered could have been avoided.

TAKING TURNS

People vary in the manner in which they "manage" (or fail to manage) interactions of which they are a part (Wiemann and Knapp, 1975). Some people are skillful at governing their own contributions to an interactive situation so that the needs and desires of others play a critical role in defining how the exchange will proceed. Effective management of interaction is displayed through taking turns in discussion and initiating and terminating interaction based on a reasonably accurate assessment of the needs and desires of others. Other individuals are less proficient and proceed with little or no regard for time sharing and initiation and termination preferences of others. It is almost too obvious to note that people enjoy having an opportunity to take turns in discussion. This fact strongly suggests the need to avoid monopolizing conversations and, conversely, to resist the temptation to refuse to share responsibility for even participation. This simple factor is important to how one is perceived in one's own culture, as well as in other cultures, in which reciprocity in discussion can serve to indicate interest in and concern for the other person. Additionally, taking turns has value for gathering information that can lead to an improved understanding of the other person's communicational framework.

SUMMARY

The central theme that emerged from research considering these dimensions is the importance of being alert and sensitive to the needs, orientations, values, and aspirations of other persons (Ruben and Kealey, 1977). One must learn to appropriately reflect insights gained in this fashion through words and actions. Although there is no foolproof formula to achieve this objective, it is critical to listen and observe attentively, sensitively, and nonjudgmentally and to be tolerant, accepting, and thoughtful. Of course, it will require a great deal of persistence, a willingness to be introspective, and an eagerness to examine and learn from failures as well as successes. Most critical is the necessary commitment to scrutinize and strive to improve one's capacity to be genuinely receptive to the communication frameworks of the other persons with whom one comes in contact.

In terms of effectiveness, the goal of the sojourner remains constant: to facilitate the transfer of skills, increase the likelihood of meaningful social interaction, and heighten the probability of achieving a sense of personal and professional accomplishment and growth.

NOTES

1. The author gratefully acknowledges the input of Daniel Kealy and Pri Notowidigdo of the Briefing Centre of the Canadian International Development Agency, and the support and enthusiasm of Pierre Lortie, director of the Centre.

2. Systematic efforts to conceptualize "effective," "successful," or "competent" communication behavior have been relatively few in number. The notion of communication competence—used interchangeably with communication effectiveness—is discussed in this paper as a dyadic concept. For a particular interaction to be termed effective, or a person to be termed competent, the performance must meet the needs and goals of both the message initiator and the recipient. The term communication competence, as used in this paper, is based on the work of John Wiemann, who credits E. A. Weinstein as the originator of the term; cf. Ruben (1972) and Wiemann (1975).

3. The results discussed here are based on a 2-year study conducted in Canada and Kenya (Ruben and Kealey, 1977).

REFERENCES

Arensberg, C. M., and A. H. Niehoff. *Introducing Social Change: A Manual for Community Development*, Aldine-Atherton, Chicago, 1971.

Argyle, M., and A. Kendon. "The Experimental Analysis of Social Performance," *Advances in Experimental Social Psychology*, 1967, *3*, 55–98.

Argyris, C. "Explorations in Interpersonal Competence—1," *Journal of Applied Behavioral Science*, 1965, pp. 58–63.

Benne, K., and P. Sheats. "Functional Roles of Group Members," *Journal of Social Research*, 1948, *4*.

Bochner, A. P., and C. W. Kelley. "Interpersonal Competence: Rationale, Philosophy, and Implementation of a Conceptual Framework," *Speech Teacher*, 1974, *23*, 279–301.

Brislin, R. B., and P. Pedersen. *Cross-Cultural Orientation Programs*, Gardner Press, New York, 1976.

Bunker, R., and J. Adair, *The First Look at Strangers*, Rutgers University Press, New Brunswick, N.J., 1959.

Carkhuff, R. R. *Helping and Human Relations*, Holt, Rinehart and Winston, New York, 1969.

Goffman, E. *The Presentation of Self in Everyday Life*, Doubleday, Garden City, N.Y., 1959.

Goffman, E. *Behavior in Public Places*, The Free Press, New York, 1963.

Goffman, E. *Interaction Ritual*, Anchor, Garden City, N.Y., 1967.

Gullahorn, J., and J. Gullahorn. "An Extension of the U-Curve Hypothesis," *Journal of Social Issues*, 1963, *19*(3), 33–47.

Hall, E. T. *The Silent Language*, Doubleday, New York, 1959.

Holland, J. L., and L. L. Baird. "An Interpersonal Competency Scale," *Educational and Psychological Measurement*, 1968, *28*, 508–510.

Rodnick, R., and B. Wood. "The Communication Strategies of Children," *Speech Teacher*, 1973, *22*, 114–124.

Ruben, B. D. "The Machine Gun and the Marshmallow: Some Thoughts on the Concept of Effective Communication." Paper presented at the annual meeting of the Western Speech-Communications Association, Honolulu, Hawaii, 1972.

Ruben, B. D. "Assessing Communication Competency for Intercultural Adaptation, *Group & Organization Studies*, September 1976, *1*(3), 334–354.

Ruben, B. D., L. R. Askling, and D. J. Kealey. "Cross-Cultural Effectiveness: An Overview." In D. S. Hoopes (ed.), *Intercultural Communication: State of the Art*, Society for Intercultural Education, Training, and Research, Pittsburgh, 1977.

Ruben, B. D., and D. J. Kealey. "Behavioral Assessment and the Prediction of Cross-Cultural Shock, Adjustment, and Effectiveness." Paper presented at the Third Annual Conference of the Society for Intercultural Education, Training, and Research, Chicago, February 1977.

Schnapper, M. Paper presented to the Society for International Development, Costa Rica, 1965.

Weinstein, E. A. "Toward a Theory of Interpersonal Tactics." In C. W. Backman and P. F. Secord (eds.), *Problems in Social Psychology*, McGraw-Hill, New York, 1966.

Weinstein, E. A. "The Development of Interpersonal Competence." In D. A. Goslin (ed.), *Handbook of Socialization Theory and Research*, Rand McNally, Chicago, 1969.

Wiemann, J. M. "An Exploration of Communication Competence in Initial Interactions: An Experimental Study." Unpublished doctoral dissertation, Purdue University, 1975.

STUDY QUESTIONS

1. Think about your own experiences with and knowledge of foreign cultures in terms of Hanvey's four levels of cultural awareness. What are the sources of your information or experience? What is your level of awareness with respect to each culture? What were some of the conflicts in level II? How were you able to move from level II to level III? From III to IV?

2. Do you think it is possible for people to achieve level IV awareness without actually living in the foreign culture? Without knowing the language?

3. Pick up an issue of *National Geographic* and read one of the features on a foreign culture. Are there customs that strike you as "exotic or bizarre"? Is there an attempt to portray the culture from the point of view of level III or level IV awareness?

4. Ruben says that some situations call for an intense concern for "getting the job done," but that in general Westerners have an excessive concern for this at the expense of interpersonal relationships. What kinds of situations might call for "getting the job done" and which might place a higher premium on better interpersonal/intercultural relationships? Is it possible to accomplish both goals in every case?

5. Think about small group activities you have been involved in within your own culture. Do the seven factors that Ruben cites as important in effective *inter*cultural communication strike you as any different from the factors involved in effective *intra*cultural communication? Would you rate their order of importance any differently from that found by Ruben and Kealey in their study?

6. Analyze your own values, assumptions, and beliefs in terms of those of your culture. Consider such things as attitudes toward cleanliness, orderliness, punctuality, physical contact, personal distance, privacy, and freedom. Which of your attitudes reflect those of your culture? Which are at variance with them?

7. Are there any universal values that one expects to find in any country and in any culture? Are there customs or values to which you feel you could not or even *should* not adapt?

8. What would you consider appropriate behavior if you were at a business meeting? At a dinner party in a home? At a religious service? What values are related to your sense of "appropriate behavior"?

VALUE ORIENTATIONS

Since our values are profoundly shaped by our cultures, what has shaped an American way of life may or may not shape the values and beliefs of other cultures. In fact, other sets of assumptions emerge from dissimilar cultural patterns. In Edward Stewart's article, *American Assumptions and Values: Orientation to Action*, he addresses the issue of American cultural identity and some of its underlying assumptions and values. When he sets concrete descriptions of American behavior beside contrasting cultural values from several parts of the world, the reader begins to focus on cross-cultural relations with a keener sense of who he is culturally and how this identity can affect cross-cultural interactions and understanding. In *Negotiators Abroad—Don't Shoot from the Hip*, Graham and Herberger examine the influence of traditional American values underlying the negotiating strategies of U.S. business in the international arena. In international trade negotiations, this style has often not been effective. After the authors analyze 11 different American traditional patterns of negotiation, they suggest ways to overcome the shortcomings. Such negotiation behaviors based on traditional American values can be readjusted to respect alternate cultural values. Training and education of business leaders in cross-communication skills becomes a requisite for Americans to compete successfully internationally. Cultural values that define masculinity and femininity have a profound effect on behavior patterns, according to Constance Sullivan in *Machismo and Its Cultural Dimension*. Recognizing that acceptable and unacceptable behavior for males is deeply ingrained in the cultural values of a country, Sullivan examines what occurs when the terms *macho* and *machismo* are borrowed from Hispanic culture and integrated into American culture. They are, in fact, redefined by the values of the U.S. culture. Lack of sensitivity to the original cultural context of such borrowed terminology can result in cross-cultural misunderstandings, especially for Latin American cultures and minority cultures within the United States.

(For further discussion on value orientations, see R. Reeves and S. Ramsey and J. Birk in the bibliography.)

American Assumptions and Values:
Orientation to Action

Edward C. Stewart

Action in the real world requires a source, since for the American, it does not simply occur. An agent or, in the more abstract sense, a cause is required. More often than not the American does not stop with the identification of the agent of action but continues to search for the background reasons which led the agent to decide to act. Furthermore, the agent exists for the purpose of getting things done. The orientation to action, or the phase preceding behavior, is frequently conceived as decision-making or problem-solving. Both of these concepts are vague in meaning and they are employed indiscriminately by Americans to refer to cultural norms of the society. Decision-making includes a loose constellation of both assumptions and values in American culture and hence provides a convenient entry into the subject.

In face-to-face situations the locus of both the action and the decision to act lies with the individual. Its foundation is established early in life. From the earliest age, the American child is encouraged to decide for himself—to make up his own mind; he is encouraged to believe he himself is the best judge of what he wants and what he should do. Even in those instances where the American cannot decide for himself, he still prizes the illusion that he is the locus of decision-making. Thus, when he needs to consult a banker, teacher, counselor, or expert of any kind, he perceives it as seeking information and advice that helps him to make up his own mind. The expert is treated as a resource person and not as a decision-maker. The American believes, ideally, that he should be his own source of information and opinions and, also, solve his own problems. Aesthetic judgments are frequently equated with personal preferences, since the American often resents accepting canons for judging the worth of a work of art. He prefers that value reside in the self; if the individual likes it, it is good. The result is an intense self-centeredness of the individual—so striking that an American psychologist has suggested this as a universal value (Rogers, 1964, 166).

Although American culture provides examples of situations in which another person decides for the individual who is chiefly affected by the decision, more striking instances of this kind of displacement of decision-making usually occur in non-Western countries. In many parts of the world parents choose a wife for their son. In this and in many other situations, the decision-maker is not the person most affected by the decision but the occupant of a traditional role in the social group—in the example above, the parents.

Another variety of decision-making prevalent both in the United States and in the non-Western world is that in which decision-making is localized in a group. More kinds of decisions are likely to be made by the group in a non-Western society than in the United States. Many matters that require action by family or community in the non-Western world will be settled by a private decision among Americans. Furthermore, the manner in which the individual participates in the group may differ considerably among societies. The American usually expects to be able to express his opinion and to exert a fair influence in the final decision. To fulfill his expectations, an American can be quite concerned with "matters of procedure," with "agenda" and voting procedures. These concerns are not ritualistic or ceremonial as they may be in some cultures, but are for the purpose of ensuring fairness to all and facilitating action. Even when bypassing formal procedures, the American is persuaded by the appeal to give everybody a chance to speak and an equal voice in the decision. When interacting with members of different cultures who do not hold the value of fairness and equality for all members of a group, or who do not discriminate between means and substantive questions, the American may be accused of subterfuge or evasiveness when he raises matters of procedure or agenda (see Glenn, 1954, 176).

The American value of majority rule is not universal. The Japanese reject the majority voice in decision-making, which becomes binding upon both the majority and minority alike. Rafael Steinberg writes:

One Western concept that has never really functioned in Japan, although written into constitution and law, is the idea of majority rule. The Confucian ethic, which still governs Japan, demands unanimity, and in order to respect the "rights of the minority" the majority will compromise on almost every issue until a consensus of some kind is reached.

This principle applies not only to government, but to business board rooms, union halls, association meetings and family councils. No one must ever be completely defeated, because if he is, he cannot "hold up his face."[1]

In American society the participation of many members of a group in a decision ideally is based on the assumption that all those, insofar as possible, who will be affected by a decision are capable of helping to make it. Overseas, the group's function in decision-making may be quite different from American expectations. A group meeting, ostensibly held to reach a decision, may represent only public confirmation of a decision previously made in privacy by critical members of the group. In addition, the deliberations of the group may be neither substantive nor rational according to American concepts.

In certain areas of American life, decisions are reached by a process significantly different from those described above. The first point of difference is the locus of decision-making: in the examples mentioned the individual took part in the decision as a person, as a vote, or as the occupant of a role. The American doctor, however, reaches a decision about his patient's symptoms in a different manner. The patient's report and the doctor's observations are matched against categories of diseases. The doctor's diagnosis and prescription follow automatically from the particular category in which the constellation of symptoms fall. When the fit is not close between symptoms and categories defining disease, the doctor may call certain symptoms "benign," a label indicating the lack of correspondence between symptoms and disease categories. The process by which the doctor makes his diagnosis and prescription is pertinent because it conforms with the manner in which people in the non-Western world habitually reach decisions. The individual merely applies preestablished principles to classify an issue; his actions follow from the result of the classification. Normally, Americans reach decisions on the basis of anticipated consequences for the individual.

These points can be illustrated in the following example taken from an interview with an AID technician in Cambodia charged with training the police:

When we first tried to get a program of first aid for accident victims going, we did have some trouble because people said if somebody was struck by a car, it was fate, and man had no business in interfering because the victim was being properly punished for past sins. We tried to explain to them that auto accidents are different. They were not due to supernatural intervention, but rather to causes, to violations of laws. Now we do get policemen to give first aid.

It will be noticed that the technician did not attempt to change the ways of the Cambodians along American lines by emphasizing the personal consequences of suffering and the danger to the auto victims or by appealing to the personal humanitarianism and sense of duty of the Cambodian policeman. Instead, he modified the scheme of classification by which the Cambodians evaluated an automobile accident and decided that a victim was not their concern. The accident was reclassified into the human sphere, where its effects could be ameliorated by human efforts.

The American locus of decision-making in the individual is paralleled by the insistence that motivation should also arise with him. Responsibility for decision and action devolve on the individual. The idea of individual responsibility is reflected in the typical questions of "Who did this?" and "Who is responsible?" Overseas, where the locus of decision-making is not the individual, the question of responsibility is relatively meaningless. Responsibility is likely to be delocalized in cultures where the people have strong ties to their immediate family or community and reach decisions by consensus.

In Japan, the typical formal or semiformal group decision is reached by a system that provides for a feeling around—a groping for a voice, preferably the chairman, who will express the group's consensus.

> The code calls for the group to reach decisions together—almost by a sort of empathy. The function of a chairman is, therefore, not to help people express themselves freely but to divine the will of the group, to express its will and state the decision reached—presumably on the basis of divine will. This ability of the chairman is called *haragei* (belly art) (Kerlinger, 1951, 38).

The Japanese consider it brash for an individual to make definite decisions regarding himself or others. It is offensive for an individual to urge the acceptance of his opinion as a course of action. He must use circumlocution and maintain a rather strict reserve (Kerlinger, 1951, 38). These features of Japanese decision-making contrast sharply with the American pattern where responsibility for the decision is normally attached to the individual decision-maker. Among Americans, the individual is ideally the locus both of decision-making and of responsibility for it. The relationship is usually symmetrical, although instances occur in which one individual makes a decision while another shoulders responsibility. In government circles, for instance, it is not unusual for an administrator to call in an individual who is asked to make a decision on a given issue. Once the decision is reached, the decision-maker departs, leaving the issue and decision in the hands of the administrator.

Among the Japanese, the relationship between loci of decision-making and responsibility is asymmetrical. The individual Japanese is subjugated to the group, and when faced with a decision leading to action, he

> shrinks and may go to what seem fantastic lengths to avoid making a decision. Even if he should commit himself verbally to a course of action, he will frequently end by doing nothing. He lacks a sense of personal responsibility; he feels only a sense of group responsibility. If at all possible, he will try to throw the onus of decision responsibility on a group or, at least, on some other person (Kerlinger, 1951, 37-38).

The Japanese pattern of decision-making is to some degree characteristic of all peoples whose self-reference is the group or for whom decisions should be unanimous—the Samoans, for example (Goodenough, 1963, 511-515).

The American's concept of the world is rational in the sense that he believes the events of the world can be explained and the reasons for particular occurrences can be determined. It follows, then, that certain kinds of training and education can prepare the individual for working in the real world. Experience itself is not the only source of effective performance. Training and education and the kind of knowledge the American values must be practical and applicable. Overseas, the American adviser is prone to act on his rationalism and knowledge, believing that in dealing with non-Westerners it is sufficient to tell them what they should do and how to do it. The assumptions and values of the non-Westerner are often ignored.

The stuff of rationalism turns out to have a typical American flavor, eventually derived from the assumption that the world is mechanistic and the things worthy of effort are material. It is saturated with facts, figures, and techniques, since the American's tendency is to be means-oriented toward the world. He is not a philosopher or logician. He is impatient with theory; instead, he conceives of the technological goal of the material world in terms of problems which a rational problem-solver can solve.[2]

Since it is a popular and pervasive cultural norm, the conceptualization of the world in terms of problems is difficult to evaluate. Perhaps only the foreigner who has failed to exploit its terms can effectively analyze it and then oppose it. His resentment would stem from the realization that his country, himself, and his work, all differently, may be problems for his American counterpart. It is this focus that arouses resentment in the counterpart when he recognizes he is a problem—an obstacle in the American's smooth path. This conceptualization of the world in terms ripe for action is likely to give rise to a feeling of depersonalization and a lack of proper regard for others and their ascriptions. The distinguishing aspect of a "problem" is that it includes anything and everything which impinges upon it.

In decision-making the individual focuses on the preliminary step to action, whereas conceptualizing the world in terms of "problems" shifts the focus to the action itself.

Usually, the American does not conceive of only one possible course of action for a given problem. Instead, he tends to conceive of alternative courses of action and chooses one. His attitude is comparative; a particular course of action is best for a given purpose rather than the only one. The notion of absolute rightness is repugnant to Americans in the world of action; a purpose for judging the action is present if only implicitly (see Glen, 1954).

The concept of a plan for action leads us to the idea that action (and, indeed, the world itself) is conceived of as a chain of events. The term "course of action" already suggests this. In the ideal form, the world is seen as a unilateral connection of causes and effects projecting into the future. Since the American focuses on the future rather than the present or the past, the isolation of the critical cause becomes paramount. If events in the world are conceived in terms of a multiplicity of causes or even, more radically, in terms of multiple contingencies, as with the Chinese, planning and the control of events and actions become more difficult. The action orientation of the American, therefore, is conducive to a concept of a simple cause for events conceived as a lineal chain of cause and effect.

The final aspect of the American's orientation toward action is his emphasis on choice. After anticipating the future and, specifically, the consequences or effects of his actions, he then chooses that course which will produce the preferred consequences. His conception of desirable consequences is arrived at through a practical empiricism. The effects desired are preferably visible, measurable, and materialistic. While the material or empirical effects are more or less objective, what is practical is not. What is practical for one person may not be practical for another. Practicality refers to the adjustment to immediate situations without consideration for long-term effects or theoretical matters. The means-orientation of operationism of the American from the point of view of the non-Westerner often appears to sacrifice the end for the means.

VARIATIONS OF FORM OF ACTIVITY

The foreign visitor in the United States quickly gains an impression of life lived at a fast pace and of people incessantly active. This image reflects that *doing* is the dominant activity for Americans. The implicit

assumption that "getting things done" is worthwhile is seldom questioned (Kluckhohn and Strodtbeck, 1960, 17).[3] The ramifications of the
doing assumption impinge upon other values and assumptions of the
culture and pervade the language of Americans, as in the colloquial
exchanges of greeting: "How're you doing?" "I'm doing fine—how are
you coming along?" All aspects of American life are affected by the
predominance of *doing*.

> Its most distinctive feature is a demand for the kind of *activity* which results
> in accomplishments that are measurable by standards conceived to be
> external to the acting individual. That aspect of self-judgment or judgment
> of others, which relates to the nature of *activity*, is based mainly upon a
> measurable accomplishment achieved by acting upon persons, things or
> situations. What does the individual do? What can he or will he accomplish?
> These are almost always the primary questions in the American's scale of
> appraisal of persons (F. Kluckhohn, 1963, 17).

Kluckhohn's definition of *doing* is compatible with other characteristics of Americans such as the importance of achievement, emphasis on
visible accomplishments, and the stress on measurement. *Doing*, however,
is not to be interpreted as a member of an active-passive dichotomy,
since people who are not distinguished by this form of activity can be
very active (F. Kluckhohn and Strodtbeck, 1961, 16). The converse can
also hold—some persons who are oriented toward *doing* can be relatively
inactive. In American culture, however, along with the assumption of
doing, there is a dominant value of "keeping busy." "Idle hands are the
devil's workshop." Approximate synonyms to "keeping busy" approach
the status of accolades, as when someone is described as "active" or
"energetic." Being active may also refer to career-related activity. When a
man is characterized as no longer "active" what is frequently meant is
that he has retired. Both the assumption of *doing* and the value of being
active are dominant patterns in American life.

In the non-Western world, the two remaining forms of activity, *being*
and *being in becoming*, are dominant (Kluckhohn and Strodtbeck, 1961,
15-17). Quite often it is the contemplative man, the intellectual, who is
prized, rather than the cultural hero of the American—the man who
performs visible deeds. Differences in values and assumptions regarding
what are the qualities of a leader sometimes confuse Americans overseas
who expect the influential persons in a community to be men
distinguished by doing. Quite often, however, it turns out to be the
intellectual or the man who contemplates and meditates who is
respected, honored, and listened to.

> In the being form of activity, there is a preference . . . for the kind of
> *activity* which is a spontaneous expression of what is conceived to be
> "given" in the human personality. As compared with either the *being in*

becoming or the *doing* orientation, it is a nondevelopmental conception of *activity*. It might even be phrased as a spontaneous expression in *activity* of impulses and desires; yet care must be taken not to make this interpretation a too literal one (Kluckhohn and Strodtbeck, 1961, 16).

Concrete behavior usually reflects several assumptions and values simultaneously. Pure impulse gratification of the *being* form of activity is restrained by the demands of other assumptions and values (Kluckhohn and Strodtbeck, 1961, 16).

The notion of being is very similar to, if not identical with, self-actualization—"the motivational and cognitive life of fully evolved people" (Maslow, 1968, 72). Maslow's description of the experiences of self-actualizing people—or the rare, peak experiences of most people—can be interpreted as the ideal manifestations of the *being* variation of activity. Maslow cites several features of the peak experience which are frequently described as characteristics of non-American cultures. During peak experiences objects tend to be seen as intrinsic wholes, without comparisons; perception can be relatively ego-transcending, appearing unmotivated; the peak experience is intrinsically valued and does not need to be validated by the reaching of goals or the reduction of needs; during the peak experience the person is fused with the experience which occurs outside the usual coordinates of time and space (Maslow, 1968, 74-76). These characteristics of experience are similar to descriptions given by persons who come from societies where *being* is assumed to be the proper form of activity.

A focus on the person is found with the *being in becoming* form of activity. This is in contrast with *doing*, as we have seen, which emphasizes visible and measurable actions. *Being in becoming* introduces the idea of development of the person, which is absent in the other two forms. It emphasizes:

> that kind of activity which has as its goal the development of all aspects of the self as an integrated whole (Kluckhohn and Strodtbeck, 1961).

All aspects of the personality receive due attention. The intellect, emotions, and motives are seen as synthesized into a developing self.

WORK AND PLAY

One of the most important distinctions in the forms of activity in American life is the separation of work from play; application of this twofold judgment yields an unbalanced dichotomy. Work is pursued for a living. It is what a man must do and he is not necessarily supposed to enjoy it. Play, on the other hand, is relief from the drudgery and regularity of work and is enjoyable in its own right, although many

Americans engage in recreation with the same *seriousness* of purpose expended on work. The American overseas often finds this distinction between work and play absent in the men with whom he associates. His counterpart may appear to take work very casually. Non-Westerners do not usually allow work to interfere with the amenities of living and are also likely to expect the foreign adviser to integrate his own personal life and work. In Latin America the American who calls upon a businessman encounters difficulties in expeditiously concluding his agenda. The Latin makes the meeting into a social event and hence does not feel compelled to be brief and businesslike in his conversation (Hall and Whyte, 1960). Essentially, the Latin does not make the American discrimination between work and play (or business and play). In each case, the view regarding activity matches the definition of the person provided by Latin and by North American cultures.

TEMPORAL ORIENTATION

The American's concepts of work and action are attached to his orientation toward the future. The unpleasantness which may be connected with work and the stress of doing result in the cultural values of change and progress. These values, however, are not part of societies which look either to the present (as in Latin America) or the past (China, for example) and hence tend to focus on immediate conditions or on traditions rather than the intermediate steps required for change and progress toward the future. These differences in temporal orientation are distinguishing marks of cultures and are very important since time is a major component in any constellation of values. For Americans, as an illustration, the orientation toward the future and the high value placed on action yield the principle that one can improve upon the present. Action and hard work will bring about what the individual wants; hence Americans are described as having the attribute of effort-optimism (C. Kluckhohn and F. Kluckhohn, 1947). Through one's effort or hard work one will achieve one's ambitions. No goal is too remote, no obstacle is too difficult, for the individual who has the will and the determination and who expends the effort. Hard work is rewarded by success. The converse also holds—failure means the individual did not try hard enough, is lazy, or is worthless. These harsh evaluations may be moderated, since one can have bad luck. Nevertheless, they remain as vital American values which shed light on the frustrations of many American advisers in trying to initiate action and attain achievements with a people who are oriented to the past or present, who assume a fatalistic outlook toward the future, and whose individualism is upset by the American drive and energy.

Effort-optimism, with its underlying orientation toward the future, gives rise to one of the most frequent and pervasive problems for overseas advisers who often complain about the delays and dilatoriness involved in trying to accomplish anything. The American finds it difficult to adapt to the frustrations that accompany giving advice to people of different cultural backgrounds, with the consequence that the morale of the adviser is impaired and his optimism is dampened. His failure to achieve strikes at the heart of his value system. Think, too, of the foreign student adviser who fails to get results. The foreign student may be placing greater importance on his relationship with the adviser or others with whom he is associated than on *doing* what is suggested.

Some advisers interpret their experiences overseas in terms of the long-range effects their work will have. Others point out that their mere presence and personal example were beneficial. A third way of avoiding the consequences of failure is to interpret the mission overseas as a learning situation. The next mission will be more successful, since the adviser has profited from the frustrations and experiences of the last one. This reaction makes use of the American values of training and education as well as the orientation toward the future—in this case, the next mission.

MOTIVATION

Doing describes what a person does to express himself in action of some kind. As we have seen, however, Americans insist on identifying an agent who can take purposeful and sequential action. The concepts of *motive* and *motivation* provide the link between action on the one hand and the agent (and his purposes) on the other. Motives are attributes of the individual which arouse him to action. The concept of motivation reveals the connection and direction in a sequence of actions and, in everyday life, provides a convenient explanation for performance. It is appropriate to say someone succeeds or excels because he is well motivated. The observation is usually a tautology, since the inference about motivation is commonly derived from the performance and not independent knowledge of the individual. As commonly used, however, it is not questioned.

The importance of motivation in American society may well be associated with the phenomenon that the self-images of Americans tend to be general and vague. Motivation helps to fill this void, since it is a dynamic concept that associates the self with action and leads to the belief that the self is what the self does. The fulfillment of the individual, isolated in a mechanistic world, is attained in achievement—the motiva-tion that propels the American and gives the culture its quality of "driveness" (Henry, 1963, 25-26). Restless and uncertain, he has recurrent need to prove himself and thereby attain an identity and success through his achievements. Hence his accomplishments must be personal, visible, and measurable, since the culture does not provide a means of evaluating the knowing the self except through externals of performance and attainment. It is this kind of motive which has been called *achievement.*

The achievement motive has been intensively studied in the United States and other societies. The results of the research reported by David McClelland (McClelland, 1961) portray the individual with high achieve-ment motive as a person who enjoys taking the initiative in making decisions. He prefers to participate in activities that challenge his skills and abilities. He is usually confident of success, but tends to be too optimistic when the conditions for a successful performance are unknown. When he possesses information which permits an objective appraisal of success, he is inclined to use it for a rational assessment of the situation, his abilities and skills, and for guiding his performance. Persons with high achievement, often identified with the business or economic entrepreneur, have been described as risk-takers. This attribute emerges from the research studies as a complex quality subject to many contingencies. McClelland concludes that those who have high achieve-ment motivation appear to prefer situations involving risk "only when they have some chance of influencing the outcome through their own skills and abilities" (McClelland, 1961, 214). In this conclusion, the focus returns to the individual.

Although achievement is the dominant motive for Americans, ascription exists as a variation. It is marked by an emphasis on *being*; the individual may be defined as the member of a family, for instance, as is sometimes found in New England and the more traditional-oriented parts of the South, or the individual is defined according to his status or profession, as in the military. It is this kind of motivation, rather than achievement, which is shared by many cultures throughout the world as the dominant motivation. Many of the actions of people in non-Western cultures can be understood as directed toward preserving and enhancing their particular position within the social structure, whereas considera-tions about tangible progress and improvement are secondary in importance, if present at all.

Individuals with an ascriptive motivation are usually enmeshed in reciprocal relations with members of their family, community, or trade and profession. These social links are much more binding than in the case of Americans. In Vietnam, for instance, an operator of a printing shop reports supporting his employees to the limits of his ability for six months after he was put out of business by government action. An American would probably not expect the same responsibility from his employer. When an American joins an organization or a business he does so as a free agent and usually preserves the right to move out whenever his purposes are no longer served by being a member. On the other hand, he usually accepts the fortunes of the organization, and if it fails, then it is up to the individual to find another position. The organization is not expected to maintain its employees on the payroll.

The patron system prevalent in much of Latin America also presents an intricate set of social relations between the individual and the patron. The latter may be the godfather of members of his estate and may extend, as a matter of obligation, personal services and considerations which would be foreign to the American overseer. As with the Vietnamese businessman, the obligations incurred are expected to transcend adventitious events of failure, poverty, or change of plans.

Ascriptive motivation introduces assumptions about the sources of action and purposes of behavior which differ from the view implied in the achievement motive. The individual is perceived to belong to a social group and to behave according to the obligations, duties, and privileges inherent in his social and professional position. To understand and manage behavior, the American must contend with the psychological predisposition of the person, since motivation is a quality of the individual. In ascriptive societies, however, the sources of motivation are more likely to be in the group or society. In the words of a Ghanaian, an employee of the government, "We do not concern ourselves with motivation, as Americans do. We know what our job is and we do it."

American assumptions regarding the dynamics of behavior are so thoroughly dependent on some motivational concept that it is nearly inconceivable that other people in the world find it more natural to refer behavior to role or social order. Yet, in one work enterprise with Dutch medical missionaries in Africa it was necessary to analyze their work and the problems of their hospital from the perspective of their duties, responsibilities, and privileges as doctors, nurses, technicians, and administrators of the hospital. An analysis of human relations problems based on conflicting motives of hospital personnel and the consequences for the work and management of the hospital was unconvincing to the Dutch personnel. In American language, it did not communicate. American members of the same medical society, operating a hospital in East Pakistan, perceived their hospital problems in terms of conflicting motives of individuals. Issues of human relations within the hospital were readily perceived as conflict among personal, religious, professional, and social motives of the medical personnel. The Americans then naturally accepted a description of human relations according to a loose analysis of motives. The Dutch rejected the same terms of analysis, since motivation in the American sense was not a significant concept in their thinking.

MEASURABLE ACHIEVEMENT

In American culture, achievement is given a material meaning or, at least, a visible and measurable interpretation. This attitude leads to the American emphasis on technology and, secondly, on publicity—rendering visible unrecognized accomplishments. Acting on these assumptions, technicians and advisers in the field define progress in terms of technological change, more often than not reported in statistical data. Social progress too often comes to mean the number of schools erected, while there is no mention of the training of teachers. The concern with visible achievement often leads the American to lose sight of main issues; he may settle for a sensation, a personal triumph over a counterpart of a specific accomplishment which has visibility and therefore can be reported as an achievement. One military adviser is described as becoming personally involved in the choice of headgear for a particular unit, which he finally succeeded in changing. This was his achievement and he was described as determined to have it before his tour of duty was over. Another frequent visible achievement in the military is the building of latrines. This cannot be dismissed as lightly as the incident of the new caps. The persistence of Americans all over the world, however, in building latrines for people who refuse to use them suggests that their appeal as projects may reside in part in their concrete visibility rather than in their potential role in controlling disease.

Since achievement has to be visible and measurable, Americans become very sensitive to praise or blame—more so than perhaps any other people except the Japanese. They do not develop the Englishman's self-assurance and confidence in his own judgment or the self-sufficiency of the French. They depend on feedback from associates and particularly on the visibility of their achievements. Both of these factors are missing in the overseas situation: achievements are usually few and the reactions of one's associates are likely to be both delayed and diffuse (the same is true in many situations for a foreign student adviser). The American adviser is quite often uncertain about the effects, if any, of his advising. His work is incompatible with an achievement orientation, since he should only be a catalyst to his counterpart with the primary function of providing information, skills, and judgment rather than concrete achievements. The counterpart is likely to have an ascriptive orientation and hence to be somewhat unconcerned with achievements. Deprived of his own visible success and frequently not seeing it in his counterpart, the adviser considers himself a failure; Americans find this kind of situation very difficult to handle. They tend to shift their sights to another future achievement or disregard the present situation as the fault of another person. Finally, Americans may face failure with the "let's get the hell out of here" attitude (see C. Kluckhohn, 1954, 120), which may be interpreted as a disguised admission that their actions have been on the wrong track. This suggests one way of removing the stain of failure—that is, by considering it as part of the learning process.

COMPETITION AND AFFILIATION

Competition is the primary method among Americans of motivating members of a group, and some have seen it as a basic emphasis in American culture (Potter, 1954, 59-60). Americans, with their individualism and ideas on achieving, respond well to this technique but, where the same approach is applied to members of another culture who do not hold the same values, the effort is ineffective at best and may produce undesirable consequences. People for whom saving face is important or for whom dependency on others is desirable will not accept competition among members of the group with the same enthusiasm as Americans. Thus attempts to instill a competitive spirit in social, economic, or military activities in many non-Western countries, such as Laos and Vietnam, have not been very successful, as the American advisers should have been able to foresee from observing the intense attachment of the people to their family and village. The communal feeling toward each other excludes the incentive to excel over others either as a member of a group or individually. An adviser shows his bewilderment at the Lao's lack of competition in the following words:

> Watching them play a game—volleyball. To us, it's a game. I know when our teams compete, whether it's baseball or basketball—anything, we'd be serious, playing it because we like to win. With them, they wouldn't be; they would team up and have teams going, but they just didn't give a hoot whether they won or not.

The non-Westerner, with an aversion to competition, is likely to show more strongly developed *affiliation*,[4] as we have seen, for his own family and community. He knows, and knows of, fewer people than the typical American. Both his direct interaction with others through travel, work, and social life and his indirect contact through the mass media are likely to be much more circumscribed than for an American. He will be less self-conscious (see Bell, 1965, 209-212) and less analytical of himself as an individual than the American. Beyond the confines of his immediate world and interest lies a world largely unknown to him. It is often endowed with danger to the unwary who travels beyond the limits of his own territory. An American adviser in Laos, training the Meo tribesmen for military service, points out that they were effective soldiers only within their own environment. Their knowledge of the outside world was meager and overridden with superstitions which made the soldiers fearful and ineffective in operations outside their own geographical area. Within their own domain, however, their willing acceptance of military discipline and complete dedication to training made them excellent trainees.

The example of the Meo tribesmen is perhaps extreme, but the lack of feeling for being a member of a political entity, a nation, is generally prevalent. This fact is often obscured by the reports in the mass media of instances of intense nationalism on the part of individuals and groups in the non-West. These certainly exist but are not typical of the great majority of the people throughout the world. It is misleading to consider peoples such as the Lao and the Vietnamese to be self-conscious members of their respective countries in the sense that most Americans consider themselves to be citizens of the United States.

Although Americans have been described as primarily motivated by achievement, it does not mean that they do not show some affiliative tendencies. These tendencies, however, are diluted in contrast to the strong social and territorial adhesion found in affiliations in the non-Western world. Margaret Mead describes the American's nostalgia for his home town as symbolic of the question: "Are you the same kind of person I am? Good—how about a coke?" (Mead, 1965, 29). But the preoccupation with the home town is not an establishment of the influence of family and community with defined status and prescribed norms of behavior, as in ascriptive societies. It is instead a way of establishing an affiliation among people who have little in the way of "common origins and common expectations" (Mead, 1965, 30).

It has been mentioned that the values of American culture are changing, that Americans are becoming more group-oriented and less autonomous in their behavior. It is well to point out that in the case of the American military we find a well-documented thesis that the primary motivational force for the American soldier during World War II was affiliation. It was not achievement, since military service usually represented an interruption in the typical American's career and life. Nor was it ascription, since the military usually did not provide a needed or desired identity to be preserved and nurtured. The force to fight for the typical American soldier was derived from a sense of loyalty to the other men in the immediate group (Stouffer et al., 1949). The spread of loyalty was primarily horizontal and based on equality rather than vertical and based on authority. There can be no doubt that affiliation is a motive in other areas of American life, and it may be ascendant as American individualism becomes subservient to organization and the goals of groups and institutions.

THE LIMITS OF ACHIEVEMENT: THE INDIVIDUAL

Externalized achievement is the dominant motivation for the typical American. The pursuit thereof has produced in the United States an unparalleled economic abundance (Potter, 1954, 78-90). It has been argued that the achievement motive provides a key psychological factor in economic development (McClelland, 1961; 61, 105, 157). But hand-in-hand with this motivation there has been in the United States a willingness to exploit and control the physical environment (Potter, 1954, 164-165). These two characteristics of Americans, found as both individual and collective qualities, have been key factors in producing economic abundance.

During their history, Americans have exploited their physical environment as if it were unlimited. The vastness of the land and the opulence of its resources no doubt strengthened the preexisting belief that the limits to achievement are measured within the individual. The limitations on success are not ascribed to resources, to the actions of others, to the agency of government, or to fate. For, as the Protestant ethic prescribed, if one has the desire and works hard enough, his labors will be rewarded with success. "Where there's a will, there's a way."

Furthermore, the achievements of the individual are not gained at the expense of others since there are enough rewards—material wealth, prestige, popularity—for everyone who aspires and tries. Doctrines such as Marxism which promulgate inevitable conflict among classes because the limited goods of the world are acquired by a few who exploit the masses have rarely achieved great favor among Americans. Traditionally, Americans have seen failure as a lack of will and of effort on the part of the individual. Successful accumulation of worldly wealth was a sign that the individual belonged to the select group who enjoyed the grace of God. The same idea is still present in a newer version: a rich man cannot be completely bad—or else he would not be rich.

This expansive view of achievement and of a world of economic abundance contrasts sharply with the perception of limited wealth prevalent throughout much of the rest of the world. This latter outlook is more than just a view appropriate to an economy of scarcity in which the individual's aspirations and potential achievements are necessarily limited. It is central to an ascriptive view of society which tends to maintain the status quo in relationships among people. To explain the norms of behavior of such societies, especially those which are traditional and peasant, we turn to George Foster's idea of the Image of the Limited Good. The individual or family that acquires more than its share of a "good," and particularly an economic "good," is viewed with suspicion (Foster, 1965, 302). Likewise, the individual who accepts a role of leadership will find his motives suspected and

> he will be subject to the criticism of his neighbors. By seeking or even accepting an authority position, the ideal man ceases to be ideal. A "good" man therefore usually shuns community responsibilities (other than of a ritual nature); by so doing he protects his reputation (Foster, 1965, 303).

People do not compete for authority by seeking leadership roles, nor do they compete in material symbols such as dress, housing, or food which might make the individual stand out from the rest of the members of the village. The people in peasant villages show a strong desire to look and act like everyone else. By means of uniformity they attempt to be inconspicuous in position and behavior (Foster, 1965, 303).

Despite the stress on conformity in traditional peasant villages, there is a place for individuality. Once a person fulfills the obligation of family, community, and tradition, he may be allowed considerable freedom to express his own individuality. Both conformity and individuality can be found in non-Western societies where the individual is perceived in terms of ascriptive qualities. It is necessary, however, to ascertain for each society those areas in which individuality or uniformity holds.

The motive of achievement, along with its stress on effort, work, and the taking of rational risks is not widely evident outside the West. The individual works to survive, but not to amass wealth, which, like land, is perceived as inherent in nature (see Foster, 1965, 298).

> It can be divided up and passed around in various ways, but, within the framework of the villagers' traditional world, it does not grow. Time and tradition have determined the shares each family and individual hold; these shares are not static, since obviously they do shift. But the reason for the relative position of each villager is known at any given time, and any significant change calls for explanation (Foster, 1965, 298).

It follows from the above discussion that innovation or new techniques of working are also not perceived as related to wealth or, in our terms, to achievement. Instead, achievement is a matter of fate, an intervention by an outside agent that does not disrupt the relationships among the members of a community. One such agent is the lottery. By winning, the individual can improve his position without endangering the community (see Foster, 1965, 308-309).

People who have a "lottery" motivation, or a belief in an outside and adventitious intervention in their behalf, are difficult to convince of the virtues of hard work, effort, frugality, and initiative. Even if this attitude does not exist, or if it has been penetrated, the individual may still not accept the necessity of improving his position, for it will extend his obligations. Thus a young Peruvian fisherman refused aid to modernize his fishing technique for the reason that if he had more money he would have more relatives to take care of. He doubted that he would be better off because of his increased responsibilities (Foster, 1962, 92).

An absence of achievement motivation is not necessarily connected to the social and economic conditions of the peasant society. Apparently a belief in "fate" or "luck" can be found in parts of the non-Western world where density of population and limited land holdings are not a problem. In the interior of Brazil there exists a frontier environment. Land holdings are not limited, population is not dense, and to the west there is new land offering economic opportunities. Yet the people still subscribe to the "luck" motivation, being more concerned with buying tickets for the local game of "bicho" than with developing their local resources or moving west.[5] It might be argued that the psychological horizon is limited and that they do not recognize that land and economic opportunities are available. Nevertheless, in the same area there is the precedent for squatters' rights. Individuals and families take possession of land, work it, and eventually acquire a right to it. This tradition does not indicate that the possession of land is seen as traditionally limited; there are ways of acquiring it even if the individual is not aware of new land to the west.[6] This particular case of Brazil suggests that the absence of achievement motivation is not necessarily associated with closed communities of dense population and limited land holdings. Indifference to personal achievement, associated with a belief in "luck," can also be found among people for whom the attitude has little relation to the economic conditions in which they live. It reflects their perception of the self and of the world as well as their concepts of motivation and of fate.

THE LIMITS OF ASCRIPTION: TOTAL POWER

In a society in which motivation rests on an ascriptive base rather than on achievement, cultural norms will be different. Status and inequality will characterize the value system. Each person will have his own fixed position in a vertical, hierarchical tier. In some cases, though not all, as we have seen, ascriptive motivation is associated with an image of a world of restricted resources—in contrast to the American perception of a world of abundance. Some of the permissiveness and competitiveness of American society can no doubt be traced to the belief that there are enough material goods for everyone. David Potter argues that the majority of the world, even Europe, assumes an economy of scarcity, so that the volume of wealth is assumed to be fixed (Potter, 1954, 118). If there is not enough for everyone, if a generous volume of the goods of the society are restricted to only the select few, it is unlikely that the society will countenance perpetual (and probably internecine) competition for the economic and social spoils. It is more sound to assign arbitrarily to each person a status which is transmitted by heredity and rigidly maintained by authority, with both the favored few and the unfavored bulk of the people maintained in their respective statuses from generation to generation.

> The status-bound individual often gained a sense of contentment with his lot and even of dignity within his narrow sphere, and all that he sacrificed for his new psychological advantage was a statistically negligible chance for advancement (Potter, 1954, 115).

Within its limits the ascriptive way of life, flourishing in an economy of scarcity, will most often develop a relatively rigid culture pattern with authority providing a primary focus. Authority rather than the self or the individual will become a center for motivation. In contrast, authority in American culture is seen as a social rather than as a motivational question, since the dominant pattern in American culture limits the role of authority to providing services, protecting the rights of the individual, inducing cooperation, and adjudicating differences. Although many variations on the dominant value exist in American society—the military for example—or in individuals who prefer strong, clear authority, these deviant patterns provide little help in understanding the complete display of authority traditionally found in governments in many of the countries of Asia, the Middle East, and elsewhere. In these states total power may be vested in the members of the government. The centralized organization of political and social power permeates the society, profoundly affecting the way of life of individuals. Considerations of status, loyalty, and ascription replace the American stress on individual competition and achievement.

Delineating a few of the characteristics of a society organized according to what Karl Wittfogel calls "total power" should be helpful in putting into perspective American attitudes toward authority as they are contrasted with those of many non-Westerners. Rather than pick a country which has these characteristics and contrast it with American patterns, we shall follow Wittfogel's analysis of total power in its political, social, and psychological characteristics. Wittfogel draws his materials from historical and contemporary examples and develops a theme regarding total power which, while not fitting any one society precisely, characterizes in a general way many societies around the world.

In societies with more or less absolutist governments, political power is not checked by nongovernmental forces found in most Western countries. Historically the power of the central governments in the West has been limited by constitutions, large individual landholdings, and political, cultural, and organizational subdivisions. In absolute governments, these checks are generally not present or not effective. Religious and military power are normally both identified with the state and do not place a check on the government (Wittfogel, 1957, 49-100). There is no nongovernmental center of power (Wittfogel, 1957, 101-103). Intragovernmental balances such as those found in the American system also do not exist (Wittfogel, 1957, 101-103). Therefore, "there develops what may be called a *cumulative tendency of unchecked power*" (Wittfogel, 1957, 106). The exercise of unchecked authority easily becomes arbitrary and results in intimidation, secrecy, unpredictability—and in the extreme, terror and brutality (Wittfogel, 1957, 137, 141). The psychological climate thus created engenders mutual mistrust and suspicion among officials of the government. The key factor for the official is his relation to the authority figures (Wittfogel, 1957, 345). Promotions may relate to aptitude but more often depend on the loyalty and subservience of the individual. The prized quality for promotion is "total and ingenious servility" (Wittfogel, 1957, 364).

Parts of the society may lie outside the power system of the absolute state. To varying degrees families and villages, for example, may enjoy autonomy to run their own affairs. There are official requests, impositions from the central government, constables, and often a tax collector, but beyond this, outside control usually ends (Wittfogel, 1957, 122-124). The central government does not intrude into those areas where its authority and revenue are not jeopardized.

The people usually have little love for the government and its representatives. The society is clearly demarcated into the ruled versus the rulers, with the people demonstrating a fear of involvement with the government (Wittfogel, 1957, 156). The aloofness of the people from the government and from others with whom specific social relations are not established may approach pathological proportions from the point of view of the American. Thus assistance to the victim of an accident or a drowning may be withheld for fear that the rescuer will be saddled with the responsibility for the occurrence. The reason for this fear of involvement is certainly not entirely traceable to the nature of authority and of the government, but these are contributing factors. This very brief and simplified description of a state of "total power" is not intended to describe any particular country at any particular point in time. It nevertheless shows us some of the characteristics of states with highly centralized governmental structures and helps us understand certain aspects of the value systems which develop therein. In such countries motivation is rooted in efforts to maintain status and in the personalized ways in which both official and social relations are conducted. There is little incentive for achievement or change. Significant relations are vertical; hence the impetus for successful action, or for change, usually comes from above. There is little precedent for initiative, information, or opinion to originate spontaneously with the people and move upward to the leaders. There are no serious competing interests to the government officials who see the people tied to them by obligations. They do not assume responsibility toward the people in the manner characteristic in more decentralized governments. Government traditionally, as in Burma, for instance, is not concerned with problem-solving or with improving society, but in maintaining loyalty and status (Pye, 1962, 78). Thus authority becomes a source of both social control and motivation.

It is clear from the above examples that the nature of motivation may be quite different in the non-Western countries with centralized governments from what it usually is in the United States. Especially significant is the fact that the definite acceptance of a personal bond between subordinate and superior makes the authority figure an acceptable source of motivation. Direct orders, explicit instructions, and demands for personal conformity may be much more acceptable, and even desired, in the non-Western world than in the United States. American preference for persuasion may be seen as weakness, and self-determination may become egotism and a threat to others.

NOTES

1. In the *Washington Post,* June 7, 1964.

2. A means orientation, like the concept of *problem,* carries a meaning similar to that of the term *operationism.*

3. The component of form of activity is a rewording of Kluckhohn's value-orientation—activity. The three variations also come from her as well as the important distinction between *doing* and *action.*

4. *Affiliation* refers to the social need for the company of others, for companionship; whereas ascription refers to the qualities of being a person, a member of a family, a profession, etc.

5. Foster, 1965, pp. 308-310, argues that the "brakes on change are less psychological than social." Foster might disagree with the example above. On the other hand, the case of Brazil might be considered outside the scope of peasant societies. Foster stresses limited land holdings and density of population.

6. Communication from Charles T. Stewart, Jr.

REFERENCES

Bell, Daniel, "The Disjunction of Culture and Social Structure: Some Notes on the Meaning of Social Reality," *Daedalus,* 94, 1 (Winter, 1965), 208-222.

Foster, George M., *Traditional Cultures and the Impact of Technological Change,* Harper & Row, New York, 1962.

Foster, George M., "Peasant Society and the Image of Limited Good," *American Anthropologist,* 62, 2 (April, 1965), 293-315.

Glenn, Edmund S., "Semantic Difficulties in International Communication," *ETC.,* 11, 3 (1954), 163-180.

Goodenough, Ward H., *Cooperation in Change,* Russell Sage Foundation, New York, 1963.

Hall, Edward T. and William F. Whyte, "Intercultural Communication: A Guide to Men of Action," *Human Organization,* 19, 1 (Spring, 1960), 5-12.

Henry, Jules, *Culture Against Man,* Random House, New York, 1963.

Kerlinger, Fred N., "Decision-Making in Japan," *Social Forces,* 30 (October, 1951), 36-41.

Kluckhohn, Clyde, "Some Aspects of American National Character," in *Human Factors in Military Operations,* Richard H. Williams (ed.), Technical Memorandum ORO-T-259, Operations Research Office, The Johns Hopkins University, Maryland, 1954, pp. 118-121.

Kluckhohn, Clyde and Florence Kluckhohn, "American Culture: Generalized Orientations and Class Patterns," in *Conflicts of Power in Modern Culture: Seventh Symposium,* Lyman Bryson (ed.), Harper and Bros., New York, 1947.

Kluckhohn, Florence R., "Some Reflections on the Nature of Cultural Integration and Change," in *Sociological Theory, Values and Sociocultural Change: Essays in Honor of P. A. Sorokin,* E. A. Tiryakian (ed.), Free Press, New York, 1963, pp. 217-247.

Kluckhohn, Florence R. and Fred L. Strodtbeck, *Variations in Value Orientations,* Row, Peterson, New York, 1961.

McClelland, David C., *The Achieving Society,* D. Van Nostrand, Princeton, 1961.

Maslow, Abraham, H., *Toward a Psychology of Being,* D. Van Nostrand, Princeton, 1968.

Mead, Margaret, *And Keep Your Powder Dry,* William Morrow, New York, 1965.

Potter, David M., *People of Plenty: Economic Abundance and the American Character,* The University of Chicago Press, Chicago, 1954.

Pye, Lucian W., *Politics, Personality, and Nation Building: Burma's Search for Identity,* Yale University Press, New Haven, 1962.

Rogers, Carl H., "Toward a Modern Approach to Values," *Journal of Abnormal and Social Psychology,* 68, 2 (1964), 160-167.

Stouffer, Samuel A., *et al., The American Soldier,* Princeton University Press, Princeton, 1949.

Wittfogel, Karl A., *Oriental Despotism: A Comparative Study of Total Power,* Yale University Press, New Haven, 1957.

Negotiators Abroad —
Don't Shoot from the Hip

John L. Graham and Roy A. Herberger, Jr.

When it comes to bargaining overseas, the Old West style usually won't work.

Influenced by their frontier past, many American business people come to the negotiating table with a do-or-die attitude that often defeats their purpose. They tend to "shoot first; ask questions later." But with the growing role of the United States in international trade, this naive attitude may cause them, instead of their adversaries, to bite the dust. By recognizing their own shortcomings and by learning more about other cultures and negotiating styles, Americans can improve their image and enhance their chances for success.

Picture if you will the closing scenes of John Wayne's Academy Award-winning performance in *True Grit*, Sheriff Rooster Cogburn sitting astride his chestnut mare, a Colt .45 in one hand, a Winchester .73 in the other, whiskey on his breath, reins in his teeth, stampeding across the Arkansas prairie straight into the sights and range of the villains' guns. A face-to-face shootout with four very bad men erupts. How often has this scene been played before our eyes? And, sure enough, the John Wayne character comes through again.

Great entertainment, yes! We *know* it's all fantasy and that in real life Sheriff Rooster Cogburn would have ended up face down in the blood and dust, alongside his dead horse. But it's more fun to see it the other way.

There's just one problem. Such scenes from movies, television, and books influence our everyday behavior—in subtle but powerful ways. Many of us model our behavior after such John Wayne figures. And when everyone else plays the same game, often the bluff and bravado work. We need only look to Washington, D.C., to see examples.

A problem arises when we sit face to face across the negotiating table with business executives from other lands. Our minds play out the same Western scene again. Here, instead of six-guns and bowie knives, our weapons are words, questions, threats and promises, laughter and confrontation. And we anticipate the taste of victory, despite the odds— four against one is no problem. But, unfortunately, this time it's real life. At stake are the profits of our companies, not to mention our own compensation and reputation. But, like the "real life" Rooster, we lose.

Such scenes repeat themselves with increasing frequency as U.S. enterprise becomes more global. The John Wayne bargaining style that may have served us well in conference rooms across the country does us a great disservice in conference rooms across the sea. That this style may be hurting us is not a new idea. Back in the 1930s Will Rogers quipped, "America has never lost a war, and never won a conference." Twenty-three years ago anthropologist Edward T. Hall warned: "When the American executive travels abroad to do business, he is frequently shocked to discover to what extent the many variables of foreign behavior and custom complicate his efforts."

More recently, the former chairman of the Senate Foreign Relations Committee, J. William Fulbright, said, "Our linguistic and cultural myopia is losing us friends, business, and respect in the world." The notion that our negotiating style doesn't work well overseas may not be new, but it needs new emphasis in light of our growing interdependence with foreign trading partners.

"SHOOT FIRST; ASK QUESTIONS LATER"

Probably no single statement better summarizes the American negoti-ating style than "shoot first; ask questions later." Though the approach is right out of a Saturday afternoon Western, the roots go much deeper. Some basic aspects of our cultural background, in particular our immigrant heritage, our frontier history, and finally much of the training in our business and law schools, all contribute to the American negotiating style.

Throughout its history, the United States has been, and still is today, influenced by its immigrants. Certainly this continuous mixing of ideas and perspectives has enriched all our experiences. And every newcomer has had to work hard to succeed—thus the powerful work ethic of America. Another quality of our immigrant forefathers was a fierce independence—a characteristic necessary for survival in the wide open spaces. This latter quality is a disadvantage, however, at the negotiating table. Negotiation is by definition a situation of *inter*dependence, a situation Americans have never handled well.

Our frontier history has encouraged this immigration-for-independence mentality. "Don't try to work things out—move out West where you don't have to see your neighbors so often, where there's elbow room." So runs one strain of the conventional wisdom of the first 150 years of our nation's existence. For Americans there was always somewhere else to go if conflicts couldn't be resolved.

And the long distances between people allowed a social system to develop not only with fewer negotiations but also with shorter negotiations. A day-long horseback ride to the general store or stockyard didn't favor long-drawn-out bargaining. "Tell me yes, or tell me no—but give me a straight answer." Candor, "laying your cards on the table," was highly valued and expected in the Old West. It still is today in our boardrooms and classrooms.

What goes on in the classrooms in our business and law schools strongly influences our negotiating style. Throughout the American educational system, we are taught to compete—both academically and in sports. Adversary relationships and winning are essential themes of the American male's socialization process. But nowhere in the U.S. educational system are competition and winning more important than in a case discussion in our law and business school classrooms. The student who makes the best arguments, marshals the best evidence, or demolishes the opponents' arguments wins the respect of classmates and receives high marks. Such skills will be important at the negotiating table.

But neither business nor law schools emphasize the most important bargaining skills. We don't teach our students how to ask questions, how to get information, how to listen, or how to use questioning as a powerful persuasive tactic. Yet these latter skills are critical at the international negotiation table. Few of us realize that, in most places in the world, the one who asks the questions controls the process of negotiation and thereby accomplishes more in bargaining situations.

Thus it becomes clear that by nature and training Americans will have difficulty at the international bargaining table. We are inherently competitive, argumentative, and impatient—a bad combination indeed when the negotiation game is being played in a boardroom in Rio or in a Ginza night club, and when the other side is playing the game by Brazilian or Japanese rules.

Before we discuss specific aspects of the negotiating style that get us into trouble in international business negotiations, we must make a disclaimer. So far, we hope it is obvious that we are talking about the average or dominant behavior of American negotiators; we recognize that not every American executive is impatient or a poor listener. Nor is every American manager argumentative. Most of us do have trouble, however, in international negotiations when compared with business people from other countries.

THE JOHN WAYNE STYLE

A combination of attitudes, expectations, and habitual behavior comprises our negotiating style. We call it the John Wayne style for short, but it reflects the influences of immigrants and educational philosophies. Though we discuss each characteristic separately, each factor interacts with others to form the complex foundation for a series of negotiation strategies and tactics that are typically American.

I Can Go It Alone   Most U.S. executives are convinced they can handle any negotiating situation by themselves. "Four Japanese versus one American is no problem. I don't need any help. I can think and talk fast enough to get what I want and what the company needs." So goes the rationalization. And there's an economic justification, "Why take more people than I need?" as well as a more subtle reason, "How can I get the credit if I've brought along a gang of others to help? They'll just confuse things." So most often the American side is outnumbered when it begins.

Being outnumbered or, worse, being alone is a terrible disadvantage in most negotiating situations. Several activities go on at once—talking, listening, thinking up arguments and making explanations, and formulating questions, as well as seeking an agreement. Greater numbers help in obvious ways with most of these. Indeed, on a Japanese negotiation team one member often has the sole duty of listening. Consider how carefully you might listen to a speaker if you didn't have to think up a response.

But perhaps the most important reason for having greater, or at least equal, numbers on your side is the subtle yet powerful influence of nodding heads and positive facial expressions. Negotiation is very much a social activity, and the approval and agreement of others (friend *and* foe) can determine the outcome. Also, numbers can be an indicator of the seriousness and the commitment of both parties to a successful outcome.

Just Call Me John   Americans, more than any other national group, value informality and equality in human relations. The emphasis on first names is only the beginning. We go out of our way to make our clients feel comfortable by playing down status distinctions such as titles and by eliminating "unnecessary" formalities such as lengthy introductions. All too often, however, we succeed only in making ourselves feel comfortable while our clients become uneasy or even annoyed.

For example, in Japanese society interpersonal relationships are vertical; in almost all two-person relationships a difference in status exists. The basis for this distinction may be any one of several factors: age, sex, university attended, position in an organization, and even one's particular firm or company. For example, the president of the "number 1" company in an industry holds a higher status position than the president of the "number 2" company in the same industry.

Each Japanese is very much aware of his or her position relative to others with whom he or she deals. There are good reasons behind these distinctions. In Japan, knowledge of one's status dictates how one will act in interpersonal relations. Thus, it is easy to understand the importance of exchanging business cards—such a ritual clearly establishes the status relationships and lets each person know which role to play.

The roles of the higher-status position and the lower-status position are quite different, even to the extent that the Japanese use different words to express the same idea depending on which person makes the statement. For example, a buyer would say *otaku* (your company), while a seller would say *on sha* (your great company). Status relations dictate not only *what* is said but also *how* it is said. Americans have a great deal of difficulty in understanding such conventions. In the United States we can perhaps get by with our informal, egalitarian style when we are dealing with foreigners. However, U.S. executives only make things difficult for themselves and their companies by saying to executives in Tokyo, Paris, or London, "Just call me John [or Mary]."

Pardon My French   Americans aren't much good at speaking foreign languages, and often we don't even apologize about it. We correctly argue that English is the international language, particularly when it comes to technology and science, and anywhere we go we expect to find someone who speaks English. But sometimes we don't, and we find ourselves at the mercy of third-party translators or middlemen.

Even when the other side (our clients or suppliers) does speak English, we are at a big disadvantage at the negotiating table, for three reasons. First, the use of interpreters gives the other side some great advantages. For example, we have observed the following pattern of interaction between U.S. managers and business people from several other countries. Often high-level foreign executives use interpreters even when they have a good understanding of English. In one case a Chinese executive asked questions in Mandarin. An interpreter then translated the questions for the American executive.

While the interpreter spoke, the American turned his attention to the interpreter. The Chinese executive, however, gazed at the American so he could unobtrusively observe the American's nonverbal responses (facial expressions, etc.). When the American spoke, the Chinese executive had twice the response time. Because he understood English, he could formulate his response during the translation process.

Bargaining in English puts a second, powerful negotiating tool in the hands of our opponents. On the surface, bargaining in our first language appears to be an advantage—we can more quickly formulate and articulate powerful arguments. But even the best argument fizzles when the other side responds, "Sorry, I'm not sure I understand. Can you repeat that, please?" Bargainers listening to a second language can use the tactic of selective understanding. It also works when they speak. Previous commitments are more easily dissolved with the excuse, "Well, that isn't exactly what I meant."

A third disadvantage has to do with our assumptions about those who speak English well. When facing a group of foreign executives we naturally assume that the one who speaks English best is also the smartest and most influential person in the group, and therefore we direct our persuasive efforts to that member. But this is seldom the case in foreign business negotiations; so our argument suffers.

Check With the Home Office   American bargainers get very upset when halfway through a negotiation the other side says, "I'll have to check with the home office"—that is, the decision makers are not even at the bargaining table. The Americans feel they have wasted time or have even been misled.

Limited authority among negotiators is common overseas, however, and can be a very useful bargaining tactic. In reality the foreign executive is saying, "To get me to compromise you not only have to convince me; you've also got to convince my boss, who is 5,000 miles away." Your arguments must be most persuasive indeed. Additionally, this tactic lets the home office make the final decision.

This tactic goes against the grain of the American bargaining style. Indeed, Americans pride themselves on having full authority to make a deal. John Wayne never had to check with the home office.

Get to the Point   As we mentioned earlier, Americans don't like to beat around the bush; they want to get to the heart of the matter quickly.

Unfortunately, what is considered the heart of the matter in a business negotiation varies across cultures. In every country we have found that business negotiations proceed in the following four stages: (1) non-task sounding, (2) task-related exchange of information, (3) persuasion, and (4) concessions and agreement.

The first stage, non-task sounding, includes all the activities that establish rapport, but it does not include information related to the "business" of the meeting. The information exchange in the second stage of business negotiations concerns the parties' needs and preferences. The third stage, persuasion, involves negotiators' attempts to modify one another's views through various persuasive tactics. The final stage involves the consummation of an agreement that often is the result of a series of concessions or smaller agreements.

From the American point of view, the "heart of the matter" is the third stage—persuasion. We have a natural tendency to go through the first two stages quickly. We may talk about golf or the weather or family, but we spend little time on these subjects relative to other cultures. We do say what our needs and preferences are, what we want and don't want; and we're quick about that too. We tend to be more interested in logical arguments than the people we're negotiating with.

But in many other countries the heart of the matter, the point of the negotiation, is not so much information and persuasion as it is to get to know the people involved. In Brazil much time is spent in developing a strong relationship of trust before business can begin. Brazilians cannot depend on a legal system to iron out conflicts; so they depend on personal relationships. Americans new to the Brazilian way of doing business are particularly susceptible to the "wristwatch syndrome." In the United States looking at your watch almost always gets things moving along. However, in Brazil, impatience causes apprehension, thus necessitating even longer periods of non-task sounding.

American impatience causes problems in the second stage of negotiations also. Like no other cultural group, Americans tend to start bargaining at a price pretty close to what they want and expect to achieve—what they consider a fair price. Almost everywhere else in the world bargainers leave themselves room to maneuver. A Chinese or Brazilian bargainer expects to spend time negotiating and expects to make concessions. Americans do not have the same expectations and are often surprised and upset by the other side's "unreasonable" demands. But the demands are unreasonable only from the perspective of the American's slam-bang, "Old West" bargaining style. To the Oriental or Latin American it makes perfect sense to ask for a lot initially.

Lay Your Cards on the Table   Americans expect honest information at the bargaining table. When we don't get it, negotiations often end abruptly. We also understand that like dollars, information must be traded. "You tell me what you want, and I'll tell you what I want." Sounds logical, doesn't it?

The problem is that in other countries people have different attitudes and values about "honest" information. For example, in Brazil, being tricky is a less serious transgression of negotiation ethics. It's even expected if a strong personal relationship between negotiators does not exist. Brazilian executives explain that such attitudes and values are changing, but the tradition is strong.

In Japan, it can be difficult to get a straight answer for two reasons: first, the Japanese team often has not decided what it wants out of the deal; so a representative cannot give a definite yes or no. His group must be consulted, and he cannot yet speak for the group. If the answer is no, the Japanese side is unlikely to use that specific word. Even if the American demands, "Tell me yes or tell me no," the Japanese will sidestep, beat around the bush, or even remain silent. It is the Japanese style to avoid conflict and embarrassment and to save face at all costs.

We misread and often feel misled by the subtle negative responses characteristic of the Japanese bargaining style. Japanese executives, particularly the younger ones (educated after World War II) with international experience, say they are learning to value directness, but here too the tradition is long-standing and has a powerful influence on behavior at the negotiation table.

Don't Just Sit There, Speak Up   Americans don't deal well with silence during negotiations. It seems a minor point, but often we have seen Americans getting themselves into trouble (particularly in Japan) by filling silent periods with words.

The Japanese style of conversation includes occasional long periods of silence—particularly in response to an impasse. The American style consists of few long silent periods (that is, of ten seconds or more). We have found that American negotiators react to Japanese silence in one of two ways: either they make some kind of a concession or they fill the space in the conversation with a persuasive appeal. The latter tactic has counterproductive results—the American does most of the talking, and he learns little about the Japanese point of view.

It should be noted that while handling silent periods is a problem for American negotiators, for Brazilians it is even worse. American conversational style is orderly and efficient—that is, each speaker takes his or her turn, with few silent periods. In Brazilian conversational style, particularly during the persuasion stages of negotiations, bargainers often speak simultaneously, fighting for the floor. To the American eye Brazilians appear to be poor listeners and rather rude. Seldom indeed would an American bargaining with a Brazilian executive have to say: "Don't just sit there, speak up."

Don't Take No for an Answer   Persistence is highly valued by Americans and is part of the deeply ingrained competitive spirit that manifests itself in every aspect of American life, particularly every aspect of the American male's life. We are taught from the earliest age never to give up. On the playing field, in the classroom, or in the boardroom, we learn to be aggressive, to win; thus, we view a negotiating session as something you *win*. Like a game, the negotiation should have a definite conclusion—a signed contract. We are dissatisfied and distressed if negotiations do not end with the biggest piece of pie going to our side. But even worse than losing a negotiation is not concluding it. We can take a loss ("We'll do better next time"), but not the ambiguity of no decision.

Our foreign clients and vendors do not necessarily share this competitive, adversarial, persistence-pays view of negotiation. Many countries see negotiations as a means of establishing long-term commercial relations that have no definite conclusion. They see negotiations more as a cooperative effort where interdependence is manifest, where each side tries to add to the pie.

When these two views (cooperative and competitive) meet across the table, difficulties naturally crop up. Americans tend to use tactics such as threats and warnings—pushing too far even when the other side is clearly signaling no. One can imagine what happens when a Japanese client, for instance, gives a subtle negative response. The Americans do not back off. They expect minds to be changed at the negotiation table, when in many situations attitudes and positions can change only with time. In some circumstances Americans might do better to take no for an answer while preserving the all-important relationships among people and companies.

One Thing at a Time   Americans usually attack a complex negotiation task sequentially—that is, they separate the issues and settle them one at a time. For example, we have heard U.S. bargainers say, "Let's settle the quantity first and then discuss price." Thus, in an American negotiation, the final agreement is a sum of the several concessions made on individual issues, and progress can be measured easily: "We're halfway done when we're through half the issues." In other countries, particularly Far Eastern cultures, however, concessions may come only at the end of a negotiation. All issues are discussed with a holistic approach—settling nothing until the end.

Because the other side never seems to commit itself to anything, U.S. executives invariably think that they are making little progress during cross-cultural negotiations. Agreements may come as a surprise, and they often follow unnecessary concessions by impatient American bargainers.

A Deal is a Deal   When Americans make an agreement and give their word, they expect to honor the agreement no matter what the circumstances. But agreements are viewed differently in different parts of the world. W. H. Newman describes this problem:

> In some parts of the world it is impolite to refuse openly to do something that has been requested by another person. What a Westerner takes as a commitment may be little more than a friendly conversation. In some societies, it is understood that today's commitment may be superseded by a conflicting request received tomorrow, especially if that request comes from a highly influential person. In still other situations, agreements merely signify intention and have little relation to capacity to perform; as long as the person tries to perform he feels no pangs of conscience, and he makes no special effort, if he is unable to fulfill the agreement. Obviously, such circumstances make business dealings much more uncertain, especially for new undertakings.

I Am What I Am   Few Americans take pride in changing their minds, even in difficult circumstances. Certainly John Wayne's character and behavior were constant and predictable. He treated everyone and every situation with his action-oriented, forthright style. He could never be accused of being a chameleon.

Many American bargainers take the same attitude with them to the negotiation table, but during international business negotiations, inflexibility can be a fatal flaw. There simply is no single strategy or tactic that always works; different countries and different personalities require different approaches.

HOW TO NEGOTIATE IN OTHER COUNTRIES

Now let us map out an action strategy to deal with such problems. Americans must adjust their negotiation behaviors to fit the style of the host country executives. The following prescriptions correspond to each element of the bargaining style we have discussed.

I Can Go It Alone   Use team assistance wisely. Don't hesitate to include extra members on your team such as financial or technical experts. The extra expense may be an excellent investment. Also, observation of negotiations can be a valuable training experience for younger members of the organization. Even if they add little to the discussion, their presence may make a difference.

Just Call Me John   The way to make foreign clients more comfortable is to follow *their* traditions and customs. American informality and egalitarian views are simply out of place in most countries in the world. Status relations and business procedures must be carefully considered with the aid and advice of your local representatives.

Pardon My French   Ideally, U.S. negotiators should speak the local language, although in practice this is seldom possible. Americans usually travel overseas for short trips, and the investment in executive time for extensive language training appears unwarranted. However, American representatives should recognize the conversational disadvantages when foreign executives use an interpreter even though they understand English. Even a rudimentary knowledge of key foreign terms or numbers may aid the American.

Check With the Home Office   An important part of the preparations for any negotiation is the determination of authority limits—both theirs and yours. Americans should weigh the disadvantages of having full authority against the expenses of communication with the home office. Not having the final say may be a useful strategy for maintaining the proper interpersonal relationship and harmony, particularly in international negotiations.

Get to the Point   We Americans depend on tightly written contracts and corporate lawyers for protection against the unscrupulous. Since in many places in the world legal systems are not as dependable, foreign executives invest much time in establishing personal relationships. Americans bargaining in foreign countries must be patient and plan to spend more time in non-task sounding. Let the other side bring up business and put your wristwatch in your coat pocket.

Moreover, remarks such as "We will need to get our legal staff to review this proposal" can quickly sour international deals. Other countries see us as a nation of lawyers in a world where law is used to handle business agreements that are in trouble, not at the beginning of the discussions. Be careful of open references to "legal review." For the foreigner, it may be a signal that the business relationship will be short-lived.

Lay Your Cards on the Table   Foreign executives seldom lay their cards on the table. They are more likely to hold an ace or two in reserve. Often, initial demands will be irritatingly high from the American point of view. Most foreign executives expect to spend more time negotiating and expect to make concessions. You should adjust your initial offer accordingly and anticipate having to ask the same question in several ways to get what we would call straight answers.

Don't Just Sit There, Speak Up   Recognize that silence can be a much more powerful negotiating tool than good arguments. Consider its uses, but in particular be aware of its use against you. Look at your notes, fiddle with your pen, anything, but let *them* break the silence.

Don't Take No for an Answer   Take the situation in Japan as a good example. The correct strategy for Americans negotiating with Japanese or other foreign clients is a Japanese strategy: ask questions. When you think you understand, ask more questions. Carefully feel for pressure points. If an impasse is reached, don't pressure. Suggest a recess or another meeting. Large concessions by the Japanese side at the negotiation table are unlikely. They see negotiations as a ritual where harmony is foremost. In Japan, minds are changed behind the scenes.

One Thing at a Time   Avoid making concessions on any issue until the group has fully discussed all issues. This is good advice for bargaining with American clients too. Also, do not measure progress by the number of issues that have been settled. In other countries different signals may be much more important.

A Deal is a Deal   Recognize differences in what an agreement means across cultures. A signed contract does not mean the same thing in Tokyo, Rio, or Riyadh as it means in New York.

I Am What I Am   Flexibility is critical in cross-cultural negotiations. Americans must adapt to the circumstances of world economic interdependence. Our power at the international negotiation table will continue to erode as our trading partners develop industrially. We must change our negotiating style accordingly.

TRAINING IMPLICATIONS

The American negotiating style is part of a larger problem—our entire approach to export trade. With the dramatic growth in international business activity during the last ten years, U.S. industry has slowly adjusted business approaches to foreign markets. Early on, U.S. companies sent their executives to live overseas and deal directly with foreign clients. The point of contact for the two cultures was often between an American sales representative and foreign client personnel. Thus, Americans had to operate in a new environment and had to promote communication and understanding not only between cultures but also between organizations—a demanding task. This strategy has proved successful.

In response to these difficulties and others (such as unfavorable tax laws) American corporations are increasingly hiring foreign nationals to represent their interests overseas. This moves the point of cross-cultural contact into the company where it can be more effectively managed. Consequently, the trend is for American executives (managers and technical experts) to take only short trips to other countries.

Such a strategy for marketing our products and services overseas neatly avoids the serious problem of training executives to live in other cultures, but we must now focus our attention on teaching executives how to negotiate with people from other countries.

Such training is not easy—for two reasons. First, knowledge and experience in another culture do not necessarily help in understanding still others. Various writers have tried to generalize about doing business in "similar" cultures, but their contributions are limited.[4] Second, executives' time has practical limitations. Often management or technical people must participate in sales negotiations in other countries on short notice. The focus is on commercial and technical issues, not on how to communicate effectively with foreigners.

Given these two contraints—the need for knowledge of several cultures and time limitations—what can be done to better prepare our representatives? Both short- and long-term actions can help American companies solve such problems.

Our lack of knowledge about other cultures is losing us business overseas. Ideally, a prerequisite for work in international operations would be participation in an experimental training program involving cross-cultural interactions in a low-risk environment. Feedback from foreign participants and videotaped sessions would aid in building awareness of one's own negotiation behavior and values, as well as those of foreigners.

If experiential training is not practical, videotape as a training medium is the next best thing. Most large companies with international clients have a few people with knowledge and experience in individual cultures who have learned to overcome the natural tendencies of the American negotiating style. The cost of sitting these people down in front of a videotape camera, with an expert in cross-cultural communication to lead a discussion on important aspects of negotiation (language, nonverbal behavior, values, and decision processes), say, in Saudi Arabia, is minimal. Larger companies might develop a library of such training tapes for management and technical people embarking on short-notice and short-term foreign assignments.

The long-run solutions to the cultural myopia of our business community are more challenging. If we are to take advantage of our technology, creativity, and other natural resources, we must invest in the education and training of our potential business leaders. This training must start early, for true understanding of another culture comes from total immersion in it. Ideally, training for U.S. multinational executives of the future would begin in high school.

During their freshman and sophomore years they would learn a foreign language (of one of our major trading partners). They would spend their junior year living with a family in a foreign country where the language they have studied is spoken, as part of the exchange programs now available. Students would continue their language training in college and again spend one year in a university in the country of focus. Finally, initial assignments in the multinational corporation would include a tour of duty in the foreign country. Through such a program, American executives of the future would gain an understanding of our foreign trading partners and their environment, a bicultural competence that would open the many doors that foreigners frequently shut in our faces.

Such a long-term plan sounds idealistic; however, the leaders of our large corporations are beginning to recognize our weaknesses in the world marketplace. These same executives must make the commitment to invest in high school and college foreign exchange programs and language training programs that look forward to the growth of international trade rather than back to a part of our own cultural heritage.

THOUGHTS ON NEGOTIATION

Keep strong, if possible. In any case, keep cool. Have unlimited patience. Never corner an opponent, and always assist him to save his face. Put yourself in his shoes—so as to see things through his eyes. Avoid self-righteousness like the devil—nothing so self-blinding.

Basil Henry Liddell Hart, "Advice to Statesmen," *Deterrent or Defense*, 1960.

America cannot be an ostrich with its head in the sand.

Woodrow Wilson, speech given in Des Moines, Iowa, Feb. 1, 1916.

Americans are people who prefer the Continent to their own country, but refuse to learn its languages.

Edward Verrall Lucas, "The Continental Dictionary," *Wanderings and Diversions*, 1926.

I have with me two gods, Persuasion and Compulsion.

Themistocles, from Plutarch, *Lives*, Sections 21 and 29.

The speech of man is like embroidered tapestries, since like them this too has to be extended in order to display its patterns, but when it is rolled up it conceals and distorts them.

In America, getting on in the world means getting out of the world we have known before.

Ellery Sedgwick, *The Happy Profession*, Chapter 1, 1946.

Men are never so likely to settle a question rightly as when they discuss it freely.

Thomas Babington, Lord Macaulay, *Southey's Colloquies*, 1830.

Let us not be blind to our differences—but let us also direct attention to our common interests and the means by which those differences can be resolved.

John Fitzgerald Kennedy, address given at American University, Washington, D.C., June 10, 1963.

NOTES

1. Edward T. Hall, "The Silent Language in Overseas Business," *Harvard Business Review*, May-June 1960, p. 87.

2. "We're Tongue-Tied," *Newsweek*, July 30, 1979, p. 15.

3. James L. Massie, Jan Luytjons, and N. William Hazen (eds.), "Cultural Assumptions Underlying Management Concepts," in *Management in International Context*, p. 75, Harper & Row, New York, 1972.

4. Edward T. Hall and others suggested classifying cultures into two categories—high context and low context. Such a concept is useful but does not hold for negotiation style. For more detail see Warren J. Keegan, *Multinational Marketing Management*, p. 86, Prentice-Hall, Englewood Cliffs, N.J., 1980.

Machismo and Its Cultural Dimension

Constance A. Sullivan

In the United States in the late 1970s and early 1980s it became very difficult to listen to the radio, watch television, see a movie, or read a newspaper, magazine, or book without frequent encounters with the words "macho" and "machismo." One of the hits of disco music in 1979 was "Macho Man" by a New York-based group called the Village People, and during the 1980 Presidential campaign then President Carter attacked his opponent's foreign policy stance as warmongering and jingoistic, saying that it would "push everybody around and show them the macho of the United States." Obviously the incumbent presidential candidate believed that his audience would recognize the term and would share his view that to be macho is unacceptable behavior. Macho and its companion term, machismo, are so current in today's English that they are rarely italicized in print to indicate that they belong to another language. They have been adopted into English as valid and expressive terms, and most speakers and writers who use them appear not to connect them with Hispanic culture but to regard them as descriptive of patterns in their own culture.

The adoption of these two words from the Spanish language into English raises three questions: (1) How and when did they come into English? (2) How do American English speakers use them? (3) Do macho and machismo mean something different in the Hispanic cultures of Spain and Latin America?

Two major factors explain how macho and machismo came into American English. One is the increasing presence in the United States of Hispanic people, from Puerto Rico, Cuba, Mexico, and other Latin American countries. In the 1970s Hispanics came close to representing the largest minority group in the United States and gained high visibility not merely because of their numbers but from the effects of civil rights and ethnic pride movements (particularly of Chicanos), increased pressure for bilingualism in schools and governmental matters, and large concentrations of Hispanics in the communities of the Southwest and in large Eastern cities. Thus, one possible origin of the English adoption of macho and machismo may lie in that Hispanic cultural presence and Anglo-American contact with it. But a second and more essential factor is the simultaneous burgeoning of feminism in those years. Feminist consciousness and popularization of the idea of gender role stereotyping and of how people are socialized into those stereotypical roles provided the basis for taking these two words from Spanish and using them as new English words. With Anglo-American society newly sensitive to the existence of the "male chauvinist pig" and the ideology of sexism, macho and machismo seemed perfect labels for the individual male figure and the systematic male dominance that serves as a structuring principle in society.

Macho and machismo began to appear in elite North American publications like *The New Yorker* magazine and *Time*, and national newspapers like the *New York Times*, the *Washington Post*, and the *Los Angeles Times* in the 1950s and 1960s. The words referred exclusively to Latin American countries and conveyed a sense of cultural superiority over Latin American societies where patterns of exaggerated male dominance prevailed. The tone was disapproving and the words were used to criticize. At that time, they were "exotic" and foreign words, and the connection between the Hispanic world and two Spanish-language terms was never in doubt. This situation changed rapidly in the late 1960s and early 1970s, when macho and machismo were used much more widely in English. Dictionaries began to list the words, first in publications like the *Dictionary of American Slang* that pick up transitional stages of adoption. No standard dictionary of American English included either word in 1973, but by 1975 they all did, complete with current meanings of the words and all variant pronunciations in English.

In these years there was a great deal of confusion among speakers of American English about how to use the new terms. The 1976 Supplement to *Webster's Third International Dictionary* contained these pronunciations for machismo: "mä chēz(,) mō, mə-, -'kē-, -ki-, -'chi- -s(,) mō." Mispronunciations like "ma-ko" and "ma-kis-mo" existed into the late seventies, indicating that many people were activating terms that they had read, not heard. Syntactical use of macho in English is different from the Spanish in some ways. Macho in both languages can serve as an adjective ("Get a macho shave") and as a noun ("He's a macho"). Speakers of American English also nominalize the adjective in a way that would be extremely awkward in Spanish, as in "He has macho" and "his macho." This usage can be interpreted, like the un-Spanish pronunciations, as ignorance of the Spanish language as well as a possible reluctance to allude to any relationship beyond the physical and behavioral characteristics of the individualized macho figure. North Americans have also attempted to invent an equivalent for macho that expresses exaggerated female pride, coming up with curiosities like "facho," "fachismo," and "machisma"—among others—while avoiding the Spanish word *macha*.

Speakers of American English use the word macho much more than they do machismo. There is ambiguity whether macho is a positive or a negative term: in contexts where individual male pride, beauty, or sexuality are the issue, it conveys a compliment, but in intellectual circles and elite publications (and, of course, feminist publications) the word carries negative connotations. With the latter group, the predominant use is critical or sardonic, if not always disparaging, and alludes to strutting, overbearing male insistence on his sexuality, his bodily attractiveness and strength, his domination of others by violence or brutality, or his capacity to show that he performs well under stress. Emphasis is on male posturing, excessiveness in bravado, daring, and courage, the will to power, and dominating by means of force or intimidation; the context is usually one of high competitiveness. Basically, the main negative feature in this way of using macho is the *exaggeration* of maleness. The typical Anglo-American attitude is captured in phrases that contrast the acceptable with the too intensified, like "He's very male without being macho" or "it is a masculine society, but not a macho one."

On the other hand, contexts where open or direct male eroticism or attractiveness are valued, as in sexual relationships, will call forth an affirming and admiring use of macho. One example is a highly successful television advertisement for Super Schick razors and blades, first aired in pregame programming before the January 1981 Super Bowl football game, which recommended that men "get macho close" with "a macho shave." The visual images accompanying this entreaty were of an attractive, business-suited male surrounded by sexually alluring and admiring females. Of course, in this instance the viewing context was also one of competitive sports which, like other highly competitive realms—big business, the military, hazardous or physically demanding jobs—is an area that bestows a positive valuation on being macho.

Contrary to this occasional admiration for the positive features of the macho as an individual figure or stereotype, the word machismo in English generally expresses strongly negative values. This almost exclusive negative use can perhaps best be explained by the fact that this "-ism" is seen as a systematic ideology of domination or oppression, an interlocking structure of values, attitudes, and patterns of behavior that ultimately have destructive effects for males as well as females. Machismo appears often in analytical writings and discussions where the speaker/author seems aware of feminist perspectives or of current research into sex role stereotyping. For sociologists, psychologists, and health care professionals the term describes negative patterns. In the recent flurry of publications that deal with the topics of masculinity and male roles in American society, machismo has been equated with systematic exaggerated male aggressiveness, competitiveness, power, risk taking, and dominance. Some cultural phenomena like the violent team sport of football, excessively militaristic foreign policy, and a number of other male-bonding associations or activities have been called the "machismo syndrome." To suggest with that label that a whole set of accepted male values in society forms a profile of illness is to call them into question; the expression definitely indicates an awareness of an organized structure of agreed-upon patterns of behaviors and expectations.

Hispanics living in the United States have protested against the negative connotation in English of the words macho and machismo. Their protest indicates clearly that there are some major differences between North American and Latin American cultures in the values associated with the individual macho figure and the culture of machismo. If, for example, Chicano activists claim—as they have— that anyone who criticizes machismo is attacking Hispanic culture as a whole, they are implying that Latin American societies consist of interrelated spheres of cultural activities in all of which male pride, authority, and dominance are basic, unquestionable cultural values.

Latin American machismo has been defined as the cult of virility, or the supervaluation of masculinity in all areas of human activity. Its basis lies in the strict differentiation with Latin American societies of the attributes of masculinity from the attributes of femininity, in other words, in the establishment of rigid and separate gender role prescriptions for men and women. The stereotypical ideal model for men is the macho; women are expected to pattern their behaviors and attitudes on the female ideal, the Virgin Mary. But because maleness constitutes a primary value, marianism, the cult of the Virgin Mary that provides a so-called opposing power to machismo in seeing women as the moral center of the home and family is an essential part of machismo rather than a separate force. Any culture that prescribes certain ways of being as appropriate only to men, as machismo does, is determining at the same time what is proper for female lives. Describing the features of one gender role therefore implies all their opposites as features of the other role.

In the culture of machismo being born biologically male carries with it not only assumptions about activities or behavior that are permitted to men, but clear concepts of male responsibilities. In the areas of sexuality, those privileges and responsibilities can be problematic for men. The expectations for males include the idea that they will be sexually active and have many sexual partners, while women must remain sexually pure (virginal before marriage and chaste within it). All women except those in a man's own family are fair game for the sexually aggressive male, but he must protect his female relatives—mother, wife, sisters, daughters—not merely from the reality of sexual misconduct with other men but from insult or innuendoes about their sexual purity. A man risks his own personal honor if he fails in that protective duty. The inherent contradiction between the society's acceptance of male sexual activity and the individual macho's need to keep his female relatives from being its object leads to highly conflictive and often violent situations. Such male authority over female sexual behavior has been reflected in custom and law, which traditionally have forgiven even murder by an aggrieved male who avenged his dishonor by killing the offending seducer or adulteress.

Within the family unit the father figure is the person with the authority to make all essential decisions. He does not usually take part in the routine day-to-day raising of children, for that bearing and rearing of children is considered to be the woman's unique function in life, and her proper place the home. A man's self-esteem as a macho is also a function of the number of children he has and supports; if he wishes to be highly regarded in his community, he must be known to provide for the material needs of his wife and children.

In machismo the public sphere and not the private space of the home is the arena appropriate to male activities. Those activities are seldom religious in nature, and men are not fervent attenders of church functions. Women are permitted and encouraged to seek the spiritual support and direction of the church, while the concept of male autonomy and independence tends to inhibit his public display of contrition or faith. Ecclesiastical hierarchy entails levels of authority, and the individual male parishioner is subject to direction by a male priest to whom he must humble himself. Therefore, he avoids it as much as possible.

Such male-to-male competitiveness exists in the areas of friendship, work, economics, sports, and the hierarchies of the military, politics, and the class structure. The compelling principle for the macho is to be considered equal to, or better than, the next man, and one's status as a superior male needs constant reaffirmation. If a man has enough power either personally or through his military, political, or socioeconomic position to exert control over other men, he shows his dominance by using that power. A man of the lower economic strata has fewer opportunities to assert male pride and superiority by controlling other men in the fierce competition of business or politics. Rather, he has the options of using direct physical dominance as his way of showing his authority, or of allying himself with an admired stronger man whose influence and aura he shares. Man-to-man loyalties of this type are a basic aspect of the personalism that characterizes much of Latin American political activity where it is the personality of a particular male leader that inspires his followers. Some analysts have linked this phenomenon, called *caciquismo*, to the historical prevalence of dictatorships, especially of military dictatorships, in Latin America.

The requirements necessary to status as a macho in Hispanic societies include the readiness to show courage, bravado, or willingness to take risks, to be a man of initiative and enterprise who can carry projects or tasks to completion, and to have the will to dominate—or at least not to be dominated by any other person. A macho's integrity, his word, his sense of personal honor are of extreme importance. He must show confidence in the truth and logic of his opinions, and attempt to build enough of an emotional shell around himself that he becomes invulnerable to being hurt or betrayed by anyone. Thus, Hispanic men are said to be very reluctant to show their real emotions, even when the emotion is love, because the mere fact that he loved someone and let them know it would make him open to the possibility that that person could either manipulate him or cause him hurt.

All these characteristics and approved behaviors have their opposite counterparts in what machismo prescribes as the female role. However, women are much more readily labeled as good or bad than men are; the female role is a dichotomy where even a small deviation from the ideal will mean failure to live up to the requirements. The good woman, based on the marianist ideal, should be nonsexual, or at least never appear to enjoy sexuality and never take sexual initiatives. Machismo regards women as naturally passive and as fulfilling her primary function when she becomes a mother, nurturing her children and her husband in silence, with forbearance, forgiveness, and total self-sacrifice. Hispanic machismo regards women as highly emotional, dependent beings who cannot be trusted to think logically or abstractly, to undertake any public activity, or to be outside the control of male authority if their goodness is to be maintained. For it is easy for a woman to "fall" into the second category provided for females in the culture: that of the bad woman. The figure of Eve is counterpoised to the ideal woman that the Virgin Mary embodies: Eve is the principle of female evil, betrayal, and wantonness that is conveyed also by the witch and the whore. If a woman is sexually active, aggressive, opinionated, independent, dominating, or self-assertive she is thought to have failed to live up to the preferred female role.

Latin Americans realize, of course, that these are stereotypes on which men and woman are to base their activities, and that no individual always can live up to the role models' demands. They also know that the culture of machismo that delineates such distinctly different gender roles for the two sexes gives preference, a higher status, to the essence, values, attitudes, and activities associated with being male. Machismo's hierarchical lines of male power and respect, in the family with its authoritative father and beyond the family into the fabric of society, are the lines of traditional patriarchy. Perhaps the main distinction between Latin American patriarchal culture and other patriarchies is the fact that the Spanish language has named the system of male dominance machismo, based on the word for the biological male of any animal species (not just humans), the macho. Machismo has been a consciously articulated ideology in Latin America, and for any person—an outsider or a marginalized insider—to use the word machismo negatively immediately places that ideology in question. Because the connotative values associated with the words macho and machismo are still predominantly positive in Latin America, such implicit questioning of traditional cultural patterns can give rise to significant tensions and animosities.

STUDY QUESTIONS

1. What are some areas in which you make your decisions privately, without consulting others? Do you consider these major or minor decisions? In what areas do you seek advice? From whom? Can you think of group decisions in which you have participated? Are these typical?

2. What is meant by a "peak experience"? Have you ever had one? What kinds of opportunities for "peak experiences" does American society provide?

3. Do you agree that "Americans are becoming more group-oriented and less autonomous in their behavior"? Do you feel a sense of pride in and loyalty toward your hometown? Your school? Your family? Toward other groups with which you are affiliated?

4. A popular song of a few years ago exhorts us to "stop and smell the roses." To what American value is this advice a reaction? What other cultural value does the song itself illustrate? Can you think of another song that shows American values at work? What values?

5. In a small group, assign one person the role of the representative of an American steel mill visiting Japan, and the others that of Japanese businessmen who are interested in buying steel from this particular mill. The American should use the "John Wayne style" of negotiating, and the Japanese should employ the techniques outlined by Graham and Herberger. Then shift the roles so that there are equal numbers of Americans and Japanese and have the Americans follow the guidelines of "How to negotiate in other countries." Compare the outcomes.

6. Look for uses of the words "macho" and "machismo" in articles about Hispanic people and cultures. Be alert for uses of the term on television and in conversation as well. Notice how often and by whom the terms are used pejoratively and when they are used objectively. What conclusions can you draw? What observations can you make with regard to cultural patterns and values? Are the values and patterns similar to those noted by Sullivan?

7. Notice how Latin American women are portrayed in print. Does their image conform to the stereotype of the "cult of marianism" which Sullivan describes?

8. What observations can you make about the "machismo" and the feminist movement in this country? Why does the word "machismo" appear frequently in feminist rhetoric? Can you find examples in articles by or about feminists?

9. Do you agree with Stewart's position regarding the American's manner of relating to the environment? What are other options? Can you relate a personal experience or one reported in the media that demonstrates any of these options?

NONVERBAL COMMUNICATION

In the first of the two articles in this section, *Out of House and Home,*
John Condon and Fathi Yousef explore the cultural significance of
space. The use and arrangement of space (proxemics) as a nonverbal
communication mode affects significantly the nature of social interaction and determines communication behavior within a culture.
Specifically, Condon and Yousef explore the use of home space and
styles. Through examples drawn from the eastern and western world,
they show how houses both reflect and shape communication patterns
in different cultures. We discover, for example, a correlation between
such values as privacy or community and the type of spatial
differentiation within the home. In this sense, the house is more than an
extension of personal space. Condon and Yousef state that because of
the cultural assumptions the home discloses, the home could well be
considered a microcosm of society as a whole. Understanding use and
arrangement of space in the home across cultures is a valuable tool for
understanding nonverbal communication cross-culturally. In Morain's
article, *Kinesics and Cross-Cultural Understanding,* she begins by
reviewing three nonverbal aspects of communication: body language,
object language, and environmental language. However, her main
emphasis in the article is on body language—the discipline of kinesics.
The awareness of different cross-cultural meanings for different body
positions and movements is as critical, if not more critical, to effective
cross-cultural communication as verbal communication. These movements are culturally determined in terms of the meaning they reflect.

(For further discussion on nonverbal communication, see G. D.
Spindler, J. Boucher, D. Druckman in the bibliography.)

Out of House and Home

John C. Condon and Fathi Yousef

From *An Introduction to Intercultural Communication* by John C. Condon and Fathi S. Yousef, © 1975 by the Bobbs-Merrill Company, Inc., reprinted by permission of the publisher.

Although we designate food, clothing, and shelter as life's "necessities," across cultures we find extraordinary variety in each of these categories. So much variety, in fact, that what makes the mouth water in one culture turns the stomach in another; the variation in dress, even within what might be considered a single culture over a relatively short period of time, hardly needs to be mentioned. Housing, too, offers considerable variety even within a single culture, and it may be that people fantasize about their "dream home" even more than they do about food or clothing. The number of popular and folk songs which recall or idealize home is extensive. What should be obvious is that the symbolic values of these three far outweigh their survival functions for most persons. What is less obvious and more intriguing is the extent to which such "necessities" reflect and influence cultural patterns of communication.

In some societies dietary customs have been credited with reflecting and promoting more basic values: spokesmen for vegetarian societies, for example, have often contrasted their values with those of the aggressive, predatory meat-eating peoples.[1] The influence of clothing on lifestyle and outlook is also a frequent source of conscious cultural distinction; Charles Reich's paean to bell-bottom trousers in *The Greening of America* is one of the more recent, as he claims it is impossible to take yourself too seriously while wearing that fashion.[2] (He overlooks the long tradition of bell-bottom trousers in the Navy.) In this chapter we will concentrate on the possible influence on patterns of communication of house structure and its use by a family.

"First we shape our buildings and then they shape us," Churchill observed, and it is in this spirit that we approach the subject. Our parents and those who lived before we were born helped shape the home into which we were born, and to some extent that home has influenced us. The same can be said for the language we are "born into" or for any aspect of our culture, of course. But homes are both more personal (each home being notably different, to members of the same culture) and more subtly influential.

Before beginning our brief discussion of house and home styles in several different societies, we must acknowledge the fact that these are described in general terms and without any effort to be comprehensive about any one of them. It is also true that homes in some societies are easier to generalize about than those in others, simply because of greater cultural homogeneity and a relative lack of economic, social, or regional variations. We have tried to limit our observations on house and home styles to a few characteristics that seem to be especially revealing of cultural values and related patterns of communication.

We are indebted to Dr. Ben Goodwin, and Professor Leland Roloff for developing the first of these themes in the American context.[3] Over a period of many years, Goodwin, a psychiatrist in Dallas, Texas, found patterns of behavior in his patients which seemed to be consistent with home styles; the source of such data and the need to generalize into some kind of composite house/home styles should caution us, but the concept of the approach seems valid.

TWO STYLES OF HOMES IN THE UNITED STATES

The authority-centered home   In this home there is some "authority" which serves as a standard by which most or many important matters are judged. The authority may be a person, father or grandfather, or it may be a religion or a religious book, such as the Bible. It may be education or some symbol of that, such as a weighty set of *The Great Books*. It might be the family business or the family name. But there is a sense of a fixed authority, a core, around which communication is centered. (Note that this need not be an *authoritarian* home.) While this home is described as one type of American home, arising from Goodwin's observations, it shares much in common with many European homes. Comparisons with a German home will be described later.

In this home there is often a clear distinction between family areas of the home and guest areas; typically there is a livingroom or parlor where guests are received and entertained, and this room is ordinarily not used by family members. In this room are displayed the treasures of the home: antiques, heirlooms, a portrait, perhaps, and the most sacred and salient symbols of the family.

Ideally in this home the family dines together. Children are expected to be present for dinner, and it is at dinner that the children are socialized into the family and its values. Conversation proceeds typically in a question and answer form, the parents asking the questions, the children supplying the answers: "What did you learn at school today? You came home at 4:30, but school is out at 3:15; where did you go after school! Have you started on your homework yet? Did you do the chores?" The children give the answers. Goodwin notes that among his patients who come from such a background there is often tension associated with eating.

There are to be no secrets in this family; anything and everything of importance is to be discussed within the home. Mother or father feel free to check on the children's reading materials, and to open and read letters received by the children, and to approve or censor what is found. That which takes place outside of the home, away from the eyes and ears of the parents, is suspect. The house has doors and the doors have locks, but one must not go into a room and lock the door: "What are you doing in there? Why did you close the door? You don't have to close the door; if we're making too much noise for you to study we will be quiet. Open the door."

For these reasons, the bathroom becomes an important room for intrapersonal communication—for being alone and "thinking" or even talking out loud. The bathroom (and toilet) is the only place where one can be alone without arousing suspicion, and the bathroom provides the added advantage of a mirror for "mirror talk" while shaving or putting on makeup.

The kitchen is often a setting for "negotiation" between children and their mother, particularly when it is necessary to talk father into something. As many questions and problems and requests by children are likely to be answered by, "ask your father" or "ask your mother," and as mother is more accessible physically and psychologically than father, mother's area in the kitchen is extremely important. (It is interesting that in a study of word values conducted independently, the word "kitchen" was found to rank among the most highly valued words by Americans.)

The parents' bedroom is a setting for *little intimate communication.* Largely off-limits to the children and often symbolically divided between mother's and father's areas (separate closets or wardrobes, often with mother's "little shrine of perfumes," as Roloff describes it, and father's tie rack, comb and brush set), even the sides of the bed (or twin beds) also limit communication between the parents. (In the bathroom, "His" and "Hers" towels may reflect the division.)

Outside of the home, the best place for the children to be—from the parents' point of view—is the school. There the parents assume that control is maintained, and, moreover, competitive values are sharpened. Competition is regarded as essential to the development of character and appears to influence even patterns of speech.

There is more to be said about this kind of home, but this may be sufficient to contrast this authority-centered home with another style, the social-centered home.

The Social-centered Home   The social-centered home is embued with an air of social activity, and the entire home is prepared for sociality. In contrast to the authority-centered home, where the parents have clear authority over their children, in the social-centered home the parents often act as assistants to their children's social interests: "Would you like to have a party this week? I will help you plan some games, and Dad can bring the other children here in the car if you like."

There is a great informality about the home, so that there are no clearly marked divisions between "family" and "company" areas. A guest is as likely to be invited to the kitchen as to the livingroom. Movement within the house is free and casual, so that almost no room is likely to be more of a center for communication than any other. In sharp contrast to the authority-centered home, the family is not likely to take meals together: The very social activities may prevent everybody from being home at the same time. The kitchen sometimes resembles a central information exchange, with messages substituting for conversation: "Johnny—sorry, but I have to go to a meeting—there are leftovers in the refrigerator, fix yourself something for supper. Dad has bowling tonight. Mom." "Mom: Peter came home with me and we made sandwiches. We have play rehearsal tonight. See you about 9:30. Johnny. P.S. Betty called and said she will be home late."

Along with such activities as Scouts, community projects, sports, and music lessons, party-going and dating is urged upon the children at an early age. And one of the significant results of all this socializing is that serious conversations are more likely to take place away from home than within the home. Thus, Goodwin notes, when persons from such home backgrounds marry, they often find it difficult to talk to each other at home! They are so accustomed to going out to parties, dances, and dinners where they are with other people, that the two alone in a home are not prepared for significant conversations. And so they may continue the pattern of socialization very soon after marriage, inviting friends over and going out to parties. A wife may receive some important information secondhand, overhearing her husband saying something to a friend before she herself is told: "Mat, I heard you telling Mrs. Bensen that you thought we might go to Mexico this summer. You didn't tell me that before." "Didn't I? Oh, I guess I didn't—well, what do you think of the idea?"

Although both of these *models,* oversimplified and stated very briefly, might characterize American homes, there are clearly different values reflected in each: The authority-centered home seems more traditional and may be associated with older, established families. The social-centered home seems much more typical of the dominant suburban middle class. (Those who have read Reich's *Greening of America* may identify the former with his "Consciousness I," the latter with the values of his "Consciousness II.") The social-centered home is particularly characteristic of those values most associated with American culture: informality, openness, constant busyness, "other-directed," and what some critics might call "superficiality" or fragmentation.

It is no accident that the social-centered home flourishes in a consumer society such as the United States, with billions of dollars spent on home furnishings and leisure activities (including what is surely the largest producer of "games" of all kinds). The social-centered home is likely to be in a constant state of rearrangement, and every change becomes the subject of display for visitors. For this reason, too, the kitchen (which is likely to be the most expensive room in the house, with all the gadgets and luxury utensils) is a more interesting and information-filled room than any other.

Many visitors to the United States are invited to homes as part of any number of "people-to-people" programs, and the kind of homes they are most likely to visit are those of the social-centered type (since inviting foreign visitors is yet one more social activity and an excellent expression of this concept of a home). For many visitors such a home is in startling contrast to their own homes. For many of these guests, the visit is likely to be startling, discomfitting. American norms of informality and blurring of host-guest relationships are unique in the world: "Make yourself at home," Americans say, and as this is a most peculiar home, it may be very difficult for a guest to feel at home. To be invited to the kitchen, even to be invited to help prepare a meal or to fix a drink, even to answer the door and invite others inside ("tell whoever it is to come in, and introduce yourself—I'll be out in a few minutes").

Similarly, the American abroad is likely to be surprised—sometimes delighted, sometimes disappointed—when he finds that this house and home values and behavior are not appropriate. He may never be invited to a home in the first place, and this he may interpret as unfriendliness. Or if invited, he may be treated so much as a guest that he feels uncomfortable about all the special attention he is getting. He is afraid that he is causing his hosts too much trouble for he would never go to such trouble for his guests. He is likely to be curious about the house, particularly if he is a first-time visitor in the country, and he may ask if he can see the kitchen and sleeping rooms. But in some countries this is like a visitor arriving at an American home and asking if he could inspect the toilet.

Probably the ideal home for most Americans is one which is occupied by only one nuclear family and one in which each member of the family has his own private room. (Recently there has been a reaction against this norm by some younger members of the society in the so-called "counterculture" who value community living, but even within most of these communes, the members join voluntarily and tend to be of about the same age and with very similar outlooks toward life. Few communes will contain three or even two generations, and in this sense even the counterculture is still an extension of many of the dominant American values.)

In many societies, however, the concept of a family is not restricted to parents and children; grandparents, in-laws, uncles, and aunts all may be considered when one thinks of a family. And the home may include many such relations. In Africa it is a common problem for young people who have come from the countryside to find work in the city to soon be visited by other members of their family, who simply move in on them. House complexes, if not a single house, are very likely to accommodate a large number of family members. And within a home, the divisions and organization of space are likely to be very different.

THE SWAHILI HOME

A common style of home in the coastal cities of Tanzania is what is sometimes called the Swahili house. To the outsider, the house looks like a small single-family dwelling, rectangular in shape, with a single door in the middle of the front of the house. When one enters the door, however, he looks down a long hallway often with three doors opening on each side of that corridor. In each of these six rooms, usually, there is a family; as many as six families, often from fifteen to twenty-five people, living in this single house. At the rear of the home is a common area for cooking, and another area for a toilet and possibly a place for bathing as well.

The six families may or may not be related, may or may not even be from the same tribe, and thus within the house there may be several different languages spoken. Obviously the values of privacy, community, and many other related values are very different for persons growing up in a Swahili house than for those growing up in a suburban American home. We might assume that this Swahili home is a product of a low standard of living, a point in the socioeconomic process leading to single-family homes. But such an interpretation is clearly biased by values of individuality, privacy, contractual friendships, and the like. The Swahili home bears resemblance to many living patterns in the country where all aspects of life are shared among neighbors and members of the extended family.

The socialist program of President Julius Nyerere (*"Ujamaa"*—literally "familyness") is built upon these values which are reflected and reinforced in such living styles. In this case it is possible to extend the influence of home style even to political systems for an entire nation. Nyerere sometimes quotes the Swahili proverb, *Mgeni siku mbili; siku ya tatu mpe jembe,* which means you should treat a guest as a guest for two days, but on the third day, give him a hoe, so he can work like one of the family. Sharing a home, sharing work and problems, and sharing in celebrations and in the simple pleasures of life are all related. Mother rarely prepares her meal alone; she is almost always cooking with the other mothers. The men, who keep away from the women's territory, may sit outside of the home and talk and watch the people pass by the house. Social organizations, community dances, and other such functions are similarly communal and divided among ages and sexes but not usually among individual family units.

Neighboring houses, too, are extensions of the principle. If there is a thief or a fire or a wedding or a baby born, everybody in the neighborhood feels obliged to assist in any way possible. And if a visitor comes, the host is sure to take the visitor around the neighborhood to meet the neighbors just as he would introduce members of his own family. To fail to do so would be impolite. Or worse, if a family remained unto themselves they might not receive the help from the community when problems arose.

Much of this description from East Africa is quite similar to what would be described in traditional communities in most of the world. There are unique patterns to each society, but the spirit of community, of sharing, of a lack of private property and privacy appear throughout the world as the rule rather than as the exception.

THE JAPANESE HOME

With the exception of some apartments and very small living quarters, most "Western homes" clearly distinguish between a living room, a dining room, and a bedroom. Each is characterized by its own furniture. In the traditional Japanese home, however, a single room can serve all three of these functions, and thus it is sometimes difficult to speak of the bedroom or the dining room, for it may depend more on the hour of the day than the areas themselves. One reason this is possible is that traditionally very little furniture is used in the home; there are no beds as such, for example, but instead *futon* (thick sleeping mats with a comforter-like top) are spread out when it is time to sleep, and folded up and put into special closets when not being used; cushions rather than chairs are used for sitting, and these, too, are easily moved or removed as required. Where Western homes may have several tables (a coffee table, a dining table, study table) a single low table may serve several of these purposes and may also be put out of the way when it is time for the *futon* to be spread. The lightness and airiness, and the sense of space characteristic of Japanese aesthetics is thus expressed in the practical day-to-day living. Moreover, the doors which separate most rooms are also lightweight sliding doors which thus can be removed entirely when necessary, unlike the fixed, hinged Western doors; and therefore a room may be made to seem larger or smaller as needed by closing or removing these doors.

These sliding doors (both the thicker, elegant *fusuma* and the translucent, thin *shoji*) have no locks. One cannot go into his own room and lock the door. The sliding glass doors and windows which open out onto the garden or street do have locks and there is also an additional set of wooden doors (*amado* or "rain doors"), which completely block out all vision. These, too, are always closed and locked at night.

Although we cannot prove any cause or even significant correlations between home structure and cultural patterns of communication, we would expect less individualism within the Japanese home, and a stronger separation of the home from the outside than would be true in the West. And, of course, this is exactly what is usually said about Japanese culture.

This aspect of home structure seems very consistent with contrasting values of Japanese and Western peoples. That is, the family as a whole, rather than the individual, is highly valued in Japan. As the action of any one member of the family reflects on the entire family, individual choices and decisions must be made with great care and after considerable discussion within the family. Moreover, several scholars have noted that there is no word for privacy in Japan, at least not in the sense that we can speak of a *private room* or a *private car*. And while Americans are likely to speak of "*my* house," Tanzanians (and many others with similar related values) will always say "*our* house"; in Japanese it is the word for house itself ("*uchi*") which serves as the pronoun for possession: *uchi no kuruma,* for example, meaning "our car" (or "my car") literally translates as "the house's car."

Although it is impossible to treat all the characteristics of homes in any culture in so short a discussion as this, it might be worth considering a few other characteristics of the traditional Japanese home style, for in many ways it provides a striking contrast with Western homes.

Bath and Toilet   In Japan, the bathing area and the toilet are always in separate rooms (except in some Western-style hotels or apartments); the American euphemism "bathroom," meaning toilet, is thus very confusing to Japanese who take care to distinguish the two as the clean place and the dirty place. In the past, and to a great extent today even in Tokyo there is no large hot-water tank to provide hot running water. Thus in the evening when it is time for a bath, the *ofuro* or Japanese bathtub is filled with cold water, and a small stove is lit which heats the water. Preparing for a bath at home thus requires as much as an hour just heating the water.

Unlike Western bathing, the Japanese style is to do all the soaping and scrubbing and rinsing outside of the tub; the tub itself is for soaking and relaxing. In this way the same bath water can serve the entire family. (Perhaps the Western counterpart is taking a shower before entering a public swimming pool.) We mention these details not because bathing customs are interesting in themselves, but because even in the bath the individualistic versus family orientation is clearly reflected. An entire family may bathe together, and it is very common for mothers to bathe with their children or for older children to bathe together.

When family members bathe in sequence in Japan, the traditional order of bathing also reflects and reinforces the authority structure of the home. The most important person, father, bathes first. The water is of course hottest and cleanest for the first person who bathes, and thus the order of the bath also reflects cultural values. In Japan the traditional pattern was quite simple: father bathed first because he was the most important person; then the older sons bathed, with the children and wife being the last.

Values are further reinforced by that shared hot water. If one should be the first to bathe and find the water too hot, it is improper to add cold water to lower the temperature, for this makes the water still colder for the next person who may prefer it even hotter. The bathing pattern thus also reinforces in such a subtle way values of group-consciousness, conformity, acceptance of what is provided. No claim is made that cultural values arise from such routines as bathing, but neither are they separable. To some extent for the child growing up, cultural values are introduced in such ways.

While bathing is generally regarded as relaxing and refreshing in the West, there are also those children who avoid taking baths whenever possible ("Do I have to? I took a bath last night."). This attitude is not found in Japan where the bath is consistently associated with relaxation and family ties, rather than the "hurry up I'm waiting to take a bath" attitude sometimes felt in Western families. (The English musical review of several years ago, *At the Drop of a Hat,* by Michael Flanders and Donald Swann, contained a delightful song called "In the Bath." The song extolled the pleasures of bathing and concluded by encouraging all of the political leaders in the world to get together in a bathtub, for this was surely the best of all places to be friendly—and agreeable. Something of that attitude is characteristic of Japan, not so much within a home as at the thousands of bathing spas throughout the country which are favorite meeting places for friends and social groups.) One American girl recently married to a Japanese man confided: "Whenever my husband and I get into a fight, we always find it easiest to make up in the bath. It is impossible to be angry in the bath."

At Home and Away   It is very unusual to telephone a Japanese home and receive no answer. Somebody is always at home it seems; it is still very rare for a wife to work. (*"Okusan,"* the polite word used when referring to any mature woman except one related to the speaker, means literally "deep in the middle of the home," the traditionally valued place for a woman.) And when the wife must go shopping or take a child to school, her mother-in-law, who is likely to live in the home, will answer the telephone. And if there is no mother-in-law in the home, then things may be arranged so that the house is occupied by somebody else.

So Near, So Far   The Japanese language contains many expressions for organizations of houses. One has obligations toward the neighbors which date back centuries. During the Second World War, this pattern was applied by the military government to make a whole neighborhood of ten houses culpable for the criminal act of any member of any of the homes. The positive virtues of neighborliness remain (except in the tall, grim apartment buildings of large cities) in forms such as offering service on special occasions (such as weddings) or giving gifts to families returning from a vacation. The traditional patterns of obligations extend to neighbors on either side of the house plus the neighbor across the street.

This relationship is similar to the East African pattern in its sense of obligations to neighbors. It differs sharply, however, in the individual's view of his own home, which is far more private in Japan than in any of the other homes described here. For a visitor, even a neighbor, to be invited into a Japanese home brings with it even more obligations: serving tea, food, the obligation of a return visit, and probably gift exchanges as well. Therefore, the inside of one's house is regarded as very different from the outside. Again the language reveals the importance of this distinction: *uchi no* (literally means "the house's," but it is used to mean "our") affairs, business, problems, is contrasted with *soto* (literally, "outside," but covering everything else that is not *ours*). Nearly everything in Japan, it seems, from problems to friends, is distinguished in this way.

All of these observations may help to explain the puzzlement felt by foreign visitors in Japan when they find they are treated with generosity and kindness but almost never are allowed to feel "at home." Emotionally and quite literally they must always be *yoso no hito,* "people outside our house."

THE MIDDLE EASTERN HOME

The nature of social interaction in the Middle East is reflected in the structure of the average home in the area. In urban or rural settings, a room is usually set aside for receiving and entertaining guests. That room is the pride of the family. Valued heirlooms, pictures of the dear, living or dead, and cherished souvenirs are displayed in the *salon,* an Arabicized word from the French. By the same token, the room's furnishing reflects the family's degree of education, affluence, and modernity. The taste, the quality of furnishings, and the degree of Westernization that the room reflects are a mirror of the family's status and the light in which it likes to be viewed. For example, the family that seats its guests on rugs and hassocks reflects a different structure of internal relationships from the family that seats its guests on sofas and armchairs. The message reflects an advertised measure of identification with the Western, the modern. Although the *"salon"* is a very important room in the home, it is not the most frequently used. It is, paradoxically, both focal and peripheral. It is the center of the family's formal social interaction with visitors, while it is physically located on the periphery of the home.

In the Middle Eastern home, a door usually opens into a family room with a hallway and a number of rooms that are open either on the family room or on the hallways. In the back, close to the kitchen, are the bathroom facilities.

In most homes all rooms look alike. The use and function of every room is decided upon by the family. However, the *salon* is usually the room farthest away from all others and the closest to the door leading to the outside. Actually, in older buildings, the *"majlis"* or the salon or the guest room (which is a literal translation in certain Arabic dialects), a door leading to the outside opens directly into this room on one end and another door opens to the inside of the home. In such a layout the guest knocks at the door and is either led into the *salon* through the home or asked to please wait until the other door leading immediately to the salon is opened for him. The behavior reflects two of the primary cultural values of the area. The first is the preoccupation with the concept of face, facades, and appearances. The guest is exposed only to the most shining, formal, and stylized part of the home and gets to meet only the members whom the family intends for him to meet. On the other hand, relationships in the Middle East reflect contextual varieties of guest-host interactions with territorial expectations of welcome and hospitality on the part of the guest and situational obligations of maintaining the traditional image of an open house on the part of the host. Thus, in receiving the guest in the most distinguished part of the home and in having him meet only the members of the family dressed for the occasion, the guest is honored and the family status is reflected.

With close association and the development of friendship, a guest comes to be accepted by the family and received in the family room or what is commonly referred to in the Middle East as the *sitting room.* However, between the time a guest is received in the salon and the time he is accepted as "one of us," a translation from the Arabic expression, certain social processes take place in terms of the guest's relationship to the family. The pace at which the guest meets the members of the opposite sex in the host family, and the length of the interaction reflect the internal sociocultural norms of the family. For example, it is not unusual in the Middle East for two men to have known each other for a number of years without either of them having met the female members of the other's family, even though they may know a lot about each other's life. This is in contrast to a modern, Westernized family in which a guest may meet most of the members during his first visit.

Until a guest is accepted and received informally in the family room his movement is usually restricted to the salon. Unlike the custom, in the

United States, for example, where a guest wanting to use the toilet just gets up and heads toward the bathroom perhaps mumbling an "excuse me" or perhaps not, in the Middle East, the guest asks for permission to go to the bathroom and for guidance to it. The request allows the host to go out first and check to make sure that the way to the bathroom is clear. That is, he makes sure that there are no family members that the host doesn't want to introduce to the guest, that those around are decent, and that the place is tidy and in agreement with the image that the host would like to create. Consequently, because of all these little inconveniences, it is uncommon for a salon-only guest to go to the bathroom in a host's house. The situation is of course different in the case of a guest who is invited to a meal.

In one sense, the most exclusive place in the Middle Eastern home is the kitchen. Its territory is the domain of the household members and mainly the females in the family. To that extent it is the most intimate place in the Middle Eastern home. A guest, whether male or female, has to have achieved the highest degree of familiarity with a family to be admitted to their kitchen.

Depending upon the socioeconomic level of the family, the home may have a sitting room and a family room with one of them the equivalent of a North American den. The use and functions, however, are different. In the Middle East, it is not too frequent that all members of the family gather together in the sitting room. In fact, when the older members are in the sitting room, the young may stay away in the "den" or in their bedrooms out of deference, unless there is something specific that they want to discuss with their parents or aunts or uncles. In behavioral terms, deference is reflected in subduing physical noise or keeping it away from the ears of the elders in the family. Hence the different connotations of silence in certain contexts, for example, for the Middle Easterner and the North American.

In the Middle East, however, the men usually congregate together in the early evening and night hours in indoor or outdoor cafés. Meanwhile, the women visit together, and the young have uninhibited access to all parts of the home, since it is usually the presence of the father or the elder male members in the family that regulates movement and noise in the home. However, with the introduction of television, and the appeal of contemporary programs, family togetherness has begun to center around the television set. Even popular cafés in the Mideast have had to acquire television sets to help maintain their appeal.

The allocation and use of private space in the Middle Eastern home reflect the value system and lines of authority within the family. In some homes, for example, only the elder male members of the family may have access to the whole home. That is, only they are allowed to disturb or invade the privacy of any member of the family who might be alone in his room working, sulking, or visiting with a friend. Also, it is not unusual to find that only the mother has access to the father if he is alone in his room behind a closed door.

The Middle Eastern home, like others, reveals the authority system within the home, the roles and norms of behavior for each sex, and a culture's outlook toward friends and neighbors. The home is a miniature replica of its society and a propagator of many of its values and patterns of communication.

THE GERMAN HOME

Doors, hedges, fences: these physical features of a German home reflect an emphasis on privacy which is pervasive throughout German life.[4] Add to privacy formal and regimented behavior, tempered by a love of the outdoors, and you have much that is at the heart of the German home and basic to many characteristically German patterns of communication. Two centuries of industrialization, plus the devastation and forced migration wrought by the war, have not lessened the ideal of a *Heimat,* a place of one's own, a family home, even if the ideal must sometimes be accommodated to the realities of small apartment living in the larger cities.

In contrast to the kind of neighborhood fostered by the American social-centered home, one which is likely to stress good schools, good companions for the children, and friendly neighbors on the block, in Germany a "good neighbor" is likely to be one who is quiet, knows his place, doesn't object when children make noise, and keeps his own sidewalk clean. Good fences make good neighbors. There is no place here for the welcome wagon, and relatively little "dropping by" for a chat. Even leases are likely to enforce some of these qualities. A lease will often specify who may use the garden or the yard in the back of the house, if there is one, and at which hours. It will probably require the tenant to sweep and wash the stairwell outside of the apartment, and quite possibly the front steps and the sidewalk, too. Time periods for making noise may be prescribed: no running water after 10 P.M.

Even in smaller towns in Germany, formality and social distance are notable in home style and house construction. The door to the average home is made up of two parts, and usually only the top part, about waist height, is opened to receive goods or for conversing with neighbors. When housewives gather for the *Kaffeeklatch,* which is really a gossip session, they usually refer to each other—and to those about whom they are speaking—as Frau or Fräulein so-and-so, not by first names. Thus here, too, the formality of a proper social distance is maintained.

People in small towns and in large cities throughout Germany share a great love for the outdoors; the outside is a central part of the concept of an ideal home. However, the outdoors is a private nature and not at all like the expansive front lawns and floor-to-ceiling picture windows glorified in so many American home magazines. Yards are in the back and well shielded from neighbors by shrubbery. Even in city apartments, balconies are very common and well planted. Since city apartments often lack a dining room or a dining-kitchen, the balcony serves to stretch the available space and helps to give the illusion of being in contact with nature. Yards are used for gardening as well as for dining.

Germans eat meals or snacks outdoors at all hours of the day. Garden restaurants, such as the familiar Biergarten, are among the most frequent settings for communication. Indeed, except for family and very close friends, homes are not used for entertaining guests. Restaurants usually have a special table marked by the sign, *"Stammtisch"* (regular's table) for patrons who come every evening to talk, dine, and drink.

For the woman who stays at home, the morning is probably spent in doing housework and shopping and preparing for the midday meal, *Mittagessen,* the main hot meal usually served around 1 P.M. As in most countries outside the United States, both the limitations of space as well as cultural values require shopping daily. When the meal is served, the whole family should be present. School has ended by this time, many shops close, and father has at least an hour free from work. (Increasing problems of traffic threaten this pattern in Germany as elsewhere, however.) Only a serious problem justifies the absence of any member of the family. There is little tolerance for a child's declining to join the family because he says he is not hungry or has promised to eat elsewhere.

After the meal, although school is over, schooling is not. German schools are demanding, and thus mother and child (or children) will spend the afternoon bound together in school work. The parent is a taskmaster (or mistress). Home offers no respite for the child. Headaches, tension, even nervous breakdowns are cause of concern in Germany, but much of the child's day at home is spent under such pressure. And everything may be reviewed again in the evening when father returns. (Except for the hours involved, this description of schooling in the German home is nearly identical to that of contemporary Japan, we might note.)

As we have indicated in our comments on house and home styles in other cultures, the physical plan of the German home also seems to reflect and help maintain many basic cultural values which recur in communication patterns. The ideal German home has foyer or entryway that leads visitors into the house without exposing them to specific rooms and a resultant loss of privacy for the family members. The living room, or *Wohnsimmer,* is the most formal room in the house, and it shares much in common with such rooms in the other homes described (except for the case of the social-centered home in the United States). Whatever the family considers an heirloom is there: a wall scroll showing the family tree, an antique statue, a piano, a Bible, or a wall full of books. Here guests are entertained. If there are children in the family who are old enough to be quiet, they may be expected to appear immediately, greet the guests, and stay quietly for the length of the visit. They speak when spoken to; they are to be seen but not heard. Thus their behavior in the living room is usually quite different from that of many American children who can drop in and say "Hi" and then leave in order to pursue their own interests.

As we have already indicated, a balcony or a back yard may also be a center of social activity, each well hidden from public view and as overflowing with flowers as is possible. Similar guarantees of privacy are provided by heavy drapes on the windows, or with the drapes opened but lighter white sheer curtains drawn. (We recall that Freud's colleague and a noted psychoanalyst himself, Theodore Reich, has also written about the importance of curtains. Reich noted that curtains or drapes were the first things a woman wanted in a house, and he interpreted this in terms of female sexuality and modesty. A better guess might be in terms of German values of privacy.)

The typical bedroom closely resembles that described for the authority-centered home in the United States. The rooms tend to be smaller than those in the American model, but twin beds are far more common than double beds. In fact, double beds are sometimes referred to as *"Französische Betten"* (French beds), and many Germans find the idea of such a bed tantalizing if not quite erotic.

Closed doors and massive furniture are themes already explored by Edward Hall in *The Hidden Dimension.* He sees the double doors often used in offices and hotels as evidence of the German search for privacy via soundproofing as well as physical barriers. In this respect the German sense of privacy within a home or office is completely different from that found in Japanese homes, where walls and doors must be among the thinnest in the world. However, in regard to privacy and mutual obligations in regard to neighbors, the German and Japanese patterns show some remarkable similarities. Hall has also observed that the heavy German furniture seems to fill a need for stability and at the same time ensure that social relationships will remain at an acceptable distance.

Finally, we might mention one element of contemporary life we have not considered in the previous descriptions: the use of the telephone. Professor Mary Badami has noted that where homes in Germany have telephones, the use of the phone seems to conform to the general pattern described here.[5] Older Germans are especially prone to follow an elaborate but informal etiquette of phone usage: the morning is a good time to call a private house; calls should not be made around noon (since meals would be interrupted), calls should not be made through the early afternoon (people might be napping); late afternoon is acceptable, but not the evening meal time; a brief after-supper time segment is acceptable, if not too late—calls should not intrude on the bedtime hours.

CONCLUDING COMMENTS

Apparent in several of these descriptions of homes is a parallel between a strong central authority in the home and a set of norms which seem to help shape and regulate family life. Formality, a sharp distinction between guest and family member, and a related concern for properly impressing the guest; role behavior according to sex and age, and the corresponding use of particular rooms of the home; and throughout a sharply defined hierarchy within the home: These aspects seem so consistent in the previous descriptions of home that it is clearly the American "social-centered home" that stands out in sharp contrast. Such comparisons, for whatever they are worth, should not be twisted into preferential distinctions between "traditional" and "modern," or "stable" and "dissolving" kinds of family structures, however. In any case, our descriptions are intentionally brief and incomplete, for purposes of illustration and comparison.

Perhaps what is of greatest value has not been the description of any one composite home or even the more obvious similarities and differences when comparing these; rather it may have been the approach itself—seeing the home as a microcosm of society, the place where each person first learns how to communicate within the norms of his culture. We should each think back to our own homes and recall as best we can where, when, how, and with whom we first learned to communicate. Increasingly now, and not only in the United States, an individual's memories are of more than a single home. And that is significant, too.

NOTES

1. A recent expression of this appeared in a letter to *Time* (Sept. 24, 1973), from Shigeo Tahara of Osaka, Japan. He wrote that there was a marked difference between Americans and Japanese in the face of rising meat prices in each country. "Americans are protecting cows and shops with firearms and are experiencing violence and burglary. Here in Japan, prices are skyrocketing faster than in the U.S., but people are still quiet. Meat-eating people seem to get hot more easily than vegetarians. Meat seems to give people an irresistible urge for action."

2. Charles Reich, *The Greening of America,* pp. 235-239, Random House, New York, 1970.

3. Leland Roloff, personal correspondence; we express appreciation to Dr. Goodwin for this concept, though interpretations and application here are original.

4. These observations were provided by Mary Badami and Caroline Yousef.

5. Personal correspondence.

Kinesics and Cross-Cultural Understanding

Genelle G. Morain

I grew up in Iowa and I knew what to do with butter: you put it on roastin' ears, pancakes, and popcorn. Then I went to France and saw a Frenchman put butter on radishes. I waited for the Cosmic Revenge—for the Eiffel Tower to topple, the Seine to sizzle, or the grape to wither on the vine. But that Frenchman put butter on his radishes, and the Gallic universe continued unperturbed. I realized then something I hadn't learned in five years of language study: not only was *speaking* in French different from speaking in English, but *buttering* in French was different from buttering in English. And that was the beginning of real cross-cultural understanding.[1]

Those who interact with members of a different culture know that a knowledge of the sounds, the grammar, and the vocabulary of the foreign tongue is indispensable when it comes to sharing information. But being able to read and speak another language does not guarantee that *understanding* will take place. Words in themselves are too limited a dimension. The critical factor in understanding has to do with cultural aspects that exist beyond the lexical—aspects that include the many dimensions of nonverbal communication.

Students of human nature have always been aware of messages sent by movement. Wily old Benjamin Franklin packed his new bifocals into his valise when he left for Paris and confided later to his diary how much they facilitated cross-cultural communication:

I wear my spectacles constantly.... When one's ears are not well accustomed to the sounds of the language, a sight of the movements in the features of him that speaks helps to explain: so that I understand better by the help of my spectacles.[2]

Today, 200 years later, Americans are becoming increasingly interested in nonverbal communication. The current spurt of books on movement and gesture finds an audience eager to speak "body language" and to "read a person like a book." To the student of communication, however, there is something disquieting about this popular approach to a sober subject. A book jacket whispers, "Read *body language* so that you can penetrate the personal secrets, both of intimates and total strangers"—and one imagines a sort of kinesic peeping Tom, eyeball to the keyhole, able to use his awful knowledge of blinks, crossed legs, and puckers to some sinister end. In reality, the need for gestural understanding goes far beyond power games or parlor games. There is a critical need on the part of anyone who works with people to be sensitive to the nonverbal aspects of human interaction.

Dean Barnlund has developed a formula for measuring communicative success in person-to-person interaction. His "interpersonal equation" holds that understanding between people is dependent upon the degree of similarity of their belief systems, their perceptual orientations, and their communicative styles.[3] With regard to belief systems, Barnlund contends that people are likely to understand and enjoy each other more when their beliefs coincide than when their beliefs clash. Experience confirms that shared attitudes toward fashion, sex, politics, and religion make for an agreeable luncheon or golf game.

The second factor described by Barnlund—perceptual orientation— refers to the way people approach reality. There are those who look at the world through a wide-angle lens—savoring new experiences, new ideas, new friends. Because they have a high tolerance for ambiguity, they can suspend judgment when confronted with a new situation and postpone evaluation until further information is acquired. There are others who look at the world through a narrower lens. They prefer familiar paths, predictable people, ideas arranged in comfortable designs. Because the unknown unnerves them, they do not go adventuring. They resolve ambiguities as quickly as possible, using categories ("hippies," "Orientals," "good old boys") to protect themselves from the pain of exploration. Those who perceive the world through the same lens—be it wide-angle or narrow—feel more comfortable with others who share the same perceptual orientation.

The third element of Barnlund's formula—similarity of communicative styles—presents the likelihood that congenial communicants enjoy talking about the same topics, tune easily into the same factual or emotional levels of meaning, share a preference for form (argument, banter, self-disclosure, exposition), operate intelligibly on the verbal band, and—most critical to the present discussion— understand each other at the nonverbal level.

Barnlund's formula underscores what Allport pointed out two decades ago in *The Nature of Prejudice*:[4] human beings are drawn to other human beings who share their own beliefs, customs, and values;

they are repelled by those who disagree, who behave unpredictably, who speak—at every level of communication—an alien tongue. It follows that if language teachers are to help bridge gulfs in understanding between cultures, they must teach more than verbal language. They must help students develop a tolerance for belief systems at odds with their own and a sensitivity to differences in modes of perception and expression.

THE NONVERBAL CHANNEL OF EXPRESSION

Teachers in our highly literate society are oriented toward the verbal channel of expression. They tend to see the word as the central carrier of meaning. At an intuitive level they recognize the importance of prosodic elements (pitch, loudness, rhythm, stress, resonance, and pauses), because these add emotional dimension to the spoken word. They are less inclined, however, to accord importance to what Edward Hall terms "the silent language." Enmeshed in the warp and the woof of words, teachers find it hard to believe that the average American speaks for only 10 to 11 minutes a day and that more than 65 percent of the social meaning of a typical two-person exchange is carried by nonverbal cues.[5]

For simplicity, the nonverbal aspects of communication may be divided into three classes:

1. *Body language,* comprising movement, gesture, posture, facial expression, gaze, touch, and distancing
2. *Object language,* including the use of signs, designs, realia, artifacts, clothing, and personal adornment to communicate with others
3. *Environmental language,* made up of those aspects of color, lighting, architecture, space, direction, and natural surroundings which speak to man about his nature.

Although it is critical that students of other cultures be perceptive when it comes to understanding both object and environmental language,[6] the focus of this monograph is on body language. Ray L. Birdwhistell gave the name "kinesics" to the discipline concerned with the study of all bodily motions that are communicative.[7] An understanding of kinesics across cultures necessitates a close look at posture, movement, facial expression, eye management, gestures, and proxemics (distancing).

Posture and Movement   Because human bodies are jointed and hinged in the same fashion, we tend to think of all people around the globe as sitting, standing, and lying in virtually identical postures.

Actually, scholars have found at least 1000 significantly different body attitudes capable of being maintained steadily. The popularity of one posture over another and the emotion conveyed by a given posture seem to be largely determined by culture.[8] Among those postures used to signal humility, for example, Krout cites the following:

Sumatrans:	Bowing while putting joined hands between those of other person and lifting them to one's forehead.
Chinese:	Joining hands over head and bowing (signifying: "I submit with tired hands").
Turks and Persians:	Bowing, extending right arm, moving arm down from horizontal position, raising it to the level of one's head, and lowering it again (meaning: "I lift the earth off the ground and place it on my head as a sign of submission to you").
Congo natives:	Stretching hands toward person and striking them together.
New Caledonians:	Crouching.
Dahomeans (now Benins):	Crawling and shuffling forward; walking on all fours.
Batokas:	Throwing oneself on the back, rolling from side to side, slapping outside of thighs (meaning: "You need not subdue me; I am subdued already").

No matter how poetic the meaning, this gymnastic parade of posture would either embarrass or disgust most Americans, who are not readily inclined to show humility in any guise. A slight downward tilt of the head and lowering of the eyes are as much kinesic signaling as they would be willing to accord that emotion. In fact, Americans are conditioned to accept a relatively narrow band of postures. A few parental admonitions continue to ring in the ear long after childhood and find their way to adult lips: "Stand tall!" "Sit up straight!" "Keep your hands in your lap!" But because the postural vocabulary of Americans is limited, they have difficulty accepting the wider range of postures found in other cultures. For example, the fact that one-fourth of the world's population prefers to squat rather than to sit in a chair leaves Americans uneasy. To most Americans, squatting is something savages do around campfires. They find it inconceivable that refined adults might sit on their heels in movie theater seats, as they sometimes do in Japan.[10]

The need to be aware of postural differences became dramatically clear to an American student who was visited by a friend who had come home from a long stay in the Ivory Coast. She brought her little son along, and the student was enchanted when the child toddled over to him and climbed into his lap. Instead of cuddling there, however, the child squirmed under the student's arm, around his side, and crawled onto his back. The startled young man, suddenly ill at ease, expected the mother to instruct her son to get down. Instead, she explained that mothers in the Ivory Coast carry their infants on their backs. As a result, when a child seeks a warm and loving spot, it is not in a lap, but on a back. Unfortunately for cross-cultural understanding, Americans are conditioned to regard this position as onerous, an attitude reflected linguistically every time a harassed individual snarls, "Get off my back!"

Cross-cultural studies of posture and movement indicate that macrokinesic systems may be determined by cultural norms. Sociologist Laurence Wylie, studying mime in Paris with students from 25 countries, found that national differences seemed to be accentuated by nonverbal techniques.[11] For example, when improvising trees, French students are "espaliered pear trees, and the Americans, unpruned apple trees." Differences in walking styles are so marked, Wylie maintains, that "in Paris one can recognize Americans two hundred yards away simply by the way they walk." To the French eye, the American walk is uncivilized. "You bounce when you walk" is their negative assessment. Wylie concludes that French child-rearing practices, which stress conformity to a disciplined social code, produce adults who reflect the tension and rigidity of French society. "They stand," he observes, "erect and square-shouldered, moving their arms when they walk as if the space around them were severely limited." Americans, on the other hand, seem to have a loose and easy gait. They walk with free-swinging arms, relaxed shoulders and pelvis, as though "moving through a broad space scarcely limited by human or physical obstacles."[12] Interestingly, this perception of American gait conflicts with the findings of an unpublished study reported by Hall, in which Spanish Americans perceive Anglo Americans as having an uptight, authoritarian walk whenever they aren't deliberately ambling; the Anglo, conversely, perceives the Spanish American male walk as more of a swagger than a purposeful walk.

The degree to which kinesic activity is culture-bound becomes obvious when one watches a foreign movie where English has been dubbed in by the process of "lip synching." The audience watches the foreign actors but hears a specially taped version of the script read in English by native speakers. Although the English words are timed and even shaped to fit the lip movements, they do not accord with the total body gloss as represented by facial expression, gestures, and posture. French actors, for example, are seen gesturing in the tight, restricted French manner while seeming to say English words that require broad, loose gestures. Observers may feel amused or irritated, but the sense of imbalance is so subtle that they rarely pinpoint the source.[14]

Speeches given by New York's colorful mayor, Fiorello LaGuardia, who spoke fluent Italian, Yiddish, and American English, illustrate how closely kinesic activity is linked to culture. An observer familiar with the three cultures could watch LaGuardia on a newsreel film without a sound track and tell readily which of the three languages he was speaking. There seems to be a subtle shift of kinesic gears when a fluent speaker slips from one language to another.

Alan Lomax and associates analyzed folk dance styles with a recording system called "choreometrics."[15] They found that the patterns of movement used by members of a culture in their work or recreation were reflected in the movements of their dances. Eskimo hunters, for example, assume a stocky, straddled stance and bring their weapon arm diagonally down across their body when harpooning a seal or spearing a salmon. When they dance, they assume the same stance, holding a drum in the left hand and bringing the drumstick held in the right hand diagonally down across the body.

Lomax's choreometric analysis revealed that people seem to fall into two distinct groups: those who move the trunk as if it were a solid, one-unit block, and those who move the trunk as if it were two or more units—bending and swaying the upper and lower sections independently of each other. One-unit cultures—including aboriginal Australians, American Indians, and most Eurasians—use rigid, energetic movements that contrast sharply with the undulating, sinuous motions of the multiunit cultures (Polynesian, African, and Indian). The choreometric contrast becomes clear when one pictures the fluid grace of the hula juxtaposed with the angular tension of an American Indian dance.

Recent studies of rhythm as it relates to body movement have revealed astonishing new insights into human interaction.[16] William Condon found that when individuals talk, their body keeps time to the rhythm of their own speech. We are aware of this synchrony when someone sings; the sight of people swinging and swaying (or tapping and twitching) to the beat of the song they sing is so familiar that we take it for granted. The same thing happens at a much subtler level when a person speaks. Movements of the fingers, eyelids and brows, head, and other body parts occur as a sort of rhythmic punctuation to the rise and fall of the voice and the flow of syllables. The whole body moves "in sync" with the words.

Not only are people in sync with themselves, but as they converse with each other, their body movements gradually fall into rhythmic harmony with those of their conversation partner. Sometimes this interactional synchrony is on a microlevel and is not easy to observe. At other times, two people in synchrony will assume the same postural configurations, almost as if they were mirror images of one another. Condon found that when two people in conversation were wired to electroencephalographs, "the recording pens moved together as though driven by a single brain." When a third person entered the picture and called one of the speakers away, the recording pens no longer moved in unison. When synchrony does not occur between speakers, it is usually a signal that an unconscious tension is inhibiting the microdance.

It is probably unrealistic for foreign language students to expect their textbooks to provide a model for behavior in this area ("Sync or Swim in Spanish"?). Nevertheless, as research uncovers significant information about differences in rhythms across cultures, it should be transmitted to language students to enhance their kinesic awareness.

Facial Expression   Poets and philosophers have always been aware of the role played by the face in communication. "The features of our face are hardly more than gestures which have become permanent," wrote Marcel Proust in *Remembrance of Things Past*. And, according to Emerson, "A man finds room in the few square inches of his face for the traits of all his ancestors; for the expression of all his history, and his wants."[17] It takes a kinesicist like Birdwhistell, however, to analyze how man uses those few square inches of his face. According to his research, middle-class Americans display about 33 "kinemes" (single communicative movements) in the face area:[18]

Three head nod kinemes (single, double, and triple nod)
Two lateral head sweep kinemes (the single and double sweep)
One head cock kineme
One head tilt kineme
Three connective, whole head motion kinemes (head raise and hold, head lower
    and hold, and current head position hold)
Four eyebrow motion kinemes (lifted, lowered, knot, and single movement)
Four eyelid closure kinemes (over-open, slit, closed, and squeezed)
Four nose movement kinemes (wrinkled nose, compressed nostril, unilateral
    nostril flare, and bilateral nostril flare)

Seven mouth movement kinemes (compressed lips, protruded lips, retracted lips,
    apically withdrawn lips, snarl, lax open mouth, and mouth over-open)
Two chin thrust kinemes (anterior and lateral chin thrusts)
One puffed cheeks kineme
One sucked cheeks kineme

The implications of such complex kinesic behavior for language learners who would master the nonverbal system of another culture are staggering. Even Americans cannot *consciously* produce the 33 subtle variations just listed without some instruction. To further complicate matters, kinesicists believe that in addition to the facial displays that are readily visible, there are others that are "micromomentary"—occurring so rapidly that they are invisible to the conscious eye. In one experiment, Ekman flashed pictures of facial expressions on a laboratory screen at speeds up to one-hundredth of a second. People staring at the screen insisted that they saw nothing but a blank screen. But when urged to guess what facial expression might be depicted by an image they perceived subliminally, they were astounded to discover that most of their "guesses" corresponded to the correct expressions on the "unseen" faces.[19] Ekman concluded that we all have the perceptual ability to decode facial messages at one-hundredth of a second but that we have been systematically taught in childhood not to pay attention to these fleeting expressions because they are too revealing.

A device that enables individuals to check their ability to judge facial expressions is the Facial Meaning Sensitivity Test (FMST). Part I requires the taker to match 10 full-face photographs with "The ten basic classes of facial meaning": disgust, happiness, interest, sadness, bewilderment, contempt, surprise, anger, determination, and fear. In Parts II and III, the task involves 30 additional photos with more discriminating categories of facial expression. Dale Leathers contends that by working with the FMST, one can markedly improve both decoding and encoding skills—learning to be more sensitive to the expressions of others and to communicate one's own feelings more accurately through facial expression.[20]

Gaze and Eye Movement   Whether the eyes are "the windows of the soul" is debatable; that they are intensely important in interpersonal communication is a fact. During the first two months of a baby's life, the stimulus that produces a smile is a pair of eyes.[21] The eyes need not be real: a mask with two dots will produce a smile. Significantly, a real human face with eyes covered will not motivate a smile, nor will the sight of only one eye when the face is presented in profile. This attraction to eyes as opposed to the nose or mouth continues as the baby matures. In one study, when American four-year-olds were asked to draw people, 75 percent of them drew people with mouths, but 99 percent of them drew people with eyes.[22] In Japan, however, where babies are carried on their mother's back, infants do not acquire as much attachment to eyes as they do in other cultures. As a result, Japanese adults make little use of the face either to encode or decode meaning. In fact, Argyle reveals that the "proper place to focus one's gaze during a conversation in Japan is on the neck of one's conversation partner."[23]

The role of eye contact in a conversational exchange between two Americans is well defined: speakers make contact with the eyes of their listener for about one second, then glance away as they talk; in a few moments they reestablish eye contact with the listener to reassure themselves that their audience is still attentive, then shift their gaze away once more. Listeners, meanwhile, keep their eyes on the face of the speaker, allowing themselves to glance away only briefly. It is important that they be looking at the speaker at the precise moment when the speaker reestablishes eye contact; if they are not looking, the speaker assumes that they are disinterested and either will pause until eye contact is resumed or will terminate the conversation. Just how critical this eye maneuvering is to the maintenance of conversational flow becomes evident when two speakers are wearing dark glasses: there may be a sort of traffic jam of words caused by interruptions, false starts, and unpredictable pauses.[24]

There is evidence that eye management patterns differ among American subgroups. In poor black families people look at one another less than in middle-class white families. It may even be that the pattern of "speaker looks away, listener looks at" is reversed to become "listener looks away, speakers looks at."[25] If so, this would account for the uneasy feelings that sometimes develop when even the best-intentioned members of the two races try to communicate. Similar differences in eye behavior have been noted between Puerto Rican children and their middle-class American teachers. And in Ohio, teachers of children moving from rural Appalachia to urban centers reported difficulties in adjusting to eye contact patterns in which the children looked down when talking to their teachers. Teachers had to learn that this was a culturally determined respect pattern, not a furtive avoidance signal.[26]

Erving Goffman discusses an American eye management technique that he calls "civil inattention."[27] An interpersonal ritual used in public places, it involves looking at other persons just long enough to catch their eye in recognition of the fact that they are other human beings, then looking away as if to say, "I trust that you will not harm me, and I recognize your right to privacy." When two people perform this ritual on the street, they may eye each other up to approximately eight feet, then cast their eyes down or away as the other passes—a kind of "dimming of lights," as Goffman puts it. Actually, the timing of this act requires considerable subtlety; the individual's gaze cannot be absent, or averted, or prolonged, or hostile, or invitational; it has to be *civilly inattentive,* and one acquires a feel for it without formal instruction.

Two strategies in contrast to the civil inattention courtesy are the deliberate withholding of all eye contact—which has the effect of a dehumanizing, nonverbal snub—and the intense focusing of gaze known as "the hate stare." The author observed an example of the latter several years ago in a church. An obviously unhappy matron, perturbed to find a racially mixed couple seated in a pew near the front of "her" church, walked slowly down the aisle past the couple and fixed them with a baleful glare. So intent was she upon prolonging her hate stare that she maintained eye contact even after passing the couple, which necessitated considerable craning and twisting of her neck. Unable to watch where her steps were leading her, she smacked into a marble pillar with what was to most observers a satisfyingly painful thud.

In-depth studies of eye management in foreign cultures are not readily available. A skimming of differences across cultures reveals that there is great variation in this aspect of communication.[28] British etiquette decrees that the speaker and listener focus attentively on each other. While an American listener nods and murmurs to signal that he is listening, the Englishman remains silent and merely blinks his eyes. Germans tend to maintain a steady gaze while talking. The American shift of gaze from eye to eye and away from the face entirely is not a pattern familiar to Germans. Peruvians, Bolivians, and Chileans consider insulting the absence of eye contact while talking. Arabs, too, share a great deal of eye contact and regard too little gaze as rude and disrespectful. In North Africa, the Tuaregs stare unwaveringly at the eyes during a conversation, perhaps because the eyes are the only part of the body not hidden beneath a swirl of veils and robes. On the streets, Israelis stare at others without self-consciousness. The French are also likely to stare at strangers, as anyone who has ever walked past a sidewalk café can attest. Greeks actively enjoy staring and being stared at in public; when they travel in the West they feel slightly diminished because people do not look at them.

Just why one culture should evolve an eye contact pattern dia-metrically opposed to that of another is not clear. Underlying some avoidance behaviors may be the primitive concept of "the evil eye." Believers feel that an actual substance—a malevolent ray—comes from the eye and influences the person or object it strikes. Witches endowed with the evil eye supposedly leave a thin film of poison on the surface of a mirror when their gaze strikes it. In Naples, even today, priests and monks are thought to possess the evil eye and passersby assiduously avoid their gaze.[29]

Research in kinesic communication has moved from the evil eye to the revealing eye. Eckhard Hess has delineated a field of study that he calls "pupillometrics." His research shows that when people look at a sight that is pleasing to them, their pupils dilate measurably; conversely, when they regard something that is displeasing or repugnant, their pupils constrict. People interacting with others seem to respond to pupil size, albeit at an unconscious level. Hess showed a group of photographs to male subjects, including two ostensibly identical photos of the same pretty girl. In one photo, however, her pupils had been enlarged through a retouching process. The men's responses—measured by increases in the size of their own pupils—were more than twice as positive to the picture with the dilated pupils.[30] No cross-cultural studies on pupillometrics have been reported, but it seems likely that this is a physiological condition that would be observable in all cultures. The differences among cultures would lie in the nature of the sight that was perceived as pleasing or displeasing.

Gestures   Members of the same culture share a common body idiom—that is, they tend to read a given nonverbal signal in the same way. If two people read a signal in a different way, it is partial evidence that they belong to different cultures. In Colombia, an American Peace Corps worker relaxes with his feet up on the furniture; his shocked Colombian hostess perceives the gesture as disgusting. Back in the United States, a university president poses for a photograph with his feet up on the desk; newspaper readers react with affection for "good old President Jones." While Americans use the feet-on-furniture gesture to signal "I'm relaxed and at home here," or "See how casual and folksy I am," neither message is received by a Colombian, who reads the signal as "boor!" An understanding of the role gestures play within a culture is critical to sensitive communication.

Hayes divides gestures into three categories that facilitate discussion: autistic gestures, technical gestures, and folk gestures.[31] Autistic—or nervous—gestures are made by individuals in response to their own inner turmoil and are thus not strictly conditioned by culture. They may take the form of biting the lips or fingernails, cracking the knuckles, jiggling a leg, or twitching a facial muscle. Occasionally, however, they become stereotyped signs for certain attitudes—toe tapping to indicate impatience, thumb twiddling to show boredom—and thus pass into the realm of tradition.

Other movements fall under the heading of technical gestures and include such complex systems of communication as the sign language of the deaf, the gestures of umpires and referees, military salutes, and the signals of music conductors, traffic directors, and radio performers. Technical gestures carry uniform meaning for members of a specialized group and are usually taught formally.

Folk gestures, on the other hand, are the property of an entire culture and are passed on by imitation. Something as simple as the act of pointing is a folk gesture. Residents of Europe and North America point with the forefinger, the other fingers curled under the palm. American Indians, certain Mongoloid peoples, and sub-Saharan Africans point with their lips.[32] Members of these cultures are not taught by their parents *how* to point (although they may be told when *not* to point). They learn by observation—the same way in which they acquire a complete repertoire of folk gestures.

Descriptive gestures include movements used to accompany such statements as "He wound up like this and threw that old ball"; "It swooped down and flew under the bridge"; "She was about this tall." It might seem that these gestures are culture-free, determined simply by the nature of the motion described. Analysis reveals, however, that many descriptive gestures are indeed culture-bound. Reid Scott discusses the gestural background in Mexico for the statement "She was about this tall."

> In parts of Mexico the gesture for indicating how tall something is has three definite cultemes (aspects of culture essential to understanding). The arm held vertically with the index finger extended and the rest of the fingers folded indicates the height of a person. The arm and hand held horizontally, thumb up and little finger down, indicates the height of an animal. The same position, except with palm down, indicates the height of an inanimate object. In most countries, there is only one culteme; it includes measuring humans, subhumans, and all other objects, and it has a single gesture, the last one described, to express it. We can imagine the laughter and even anger that one would cause if he were to measure your dear aunt with the gesture reserved for cows.[33]

A knowledge of the folk gestures of any group provides one way to share in the humor of that culture. A few examples from the American folk gestural system will illustrate the possibilities. The elaborate handshake that began with jazz musicians and spread to other in-groups is today practiced with a kind of gleeful exaggeration by young black males. Mock handshakes are also used to characterize certain professions: the "politicians' handshake," for instance, begins with a great show of false enthusiasm and ends with both parties reaching over each other's shoulders to pick each other's pockets.[34] In some jokes, the humor is carried entirely on the nonverbal band. To illustrate how a stupid person "looks for a land mine," the joke teller covers his eyes with his hand and advances slowly forward, stomping the ground ahead of him with an extended foot. To demonstrate a numskull "hitching in the rain," the jokester makes the usual American hitchhiking signal of the hand with extended thumb, then holds his other hand protectively above it to shelter the thumb from the rain.

Because folk gestures are in circulation, they tend to develop variations in meaning and execution. Nevertheless, they are the gestures that are most profitably learned by those who intend to interact with members of another culture. Whether "learned" means incorporated into students' active kinesic systems so that they can produce the gesture on demand, or merely learned in the sense that they can recognize the meaning of the gesture in its appropriate social context, is a matter of debate among language educators. Jerald R. Green, author of *Kinesics in the Foreign Language Classroom*,[35] believes that the use of gestures adds dimension to language production. "It is neither unrealistic nor unreasonable," he writes, "to expect the language instructor to insist that his pupils use authentic foreign culture gestures whenever appropriate in dialogue repetition." On the other hand, some native speakers—perhaps in a display of kinesic territoriality—feel that it is offensive to see members of a foreign culture using imperfectly the gestural system of a culture that is not their own. Birdwhistell warns that even though a gesture may be produced authentically by a sufficiently skilled nonnative, its performance does not guarantee that the performer is aware of the full range of communicative contexts in which its use is appropriate.[36]

One solution would be for the teacher to draw up a list of gestures in order of their communicative value and teach them in descending order of importance. Gestures associated with greeting and leave taking are critical, since it is difficult to function courteously within any culture without participating actively in these rituals. Gestures used for "yes" and "no," for showing approval and disapproval, and for making and refusing requests would also be useful.

Eisenberg and Smith discuss the variation across cultures in the simple act of attracting the attention of a waiter.[37]

In America, the customer moves his forefinger toward himself, then away from himself, then toward himself again. A Latin American customer would make a downward arc with his right hand almost identical to the American jocular "away with you." The Shans of Burma accomplish the same purpose by holding the palm down, moving the fingers as if playing an arpeggio .... Waiters in India are summoned by a click of the fingers, which on the face of it, is an inconspicuous and efficient gesture. But such a gesture might elicit anger from an American waiter. For us, snapping fingers is the act of a superior asserting power over a menial. As such, finger snapping as a call for service is a violation of the democratic ethos.

Gestures that would be wise to know but not emulate are those considered vulgar or obscene by the foreign culture. Equally important for cross-cultural understanding is a knowledge of those gestures that are repugnant to Americans but regarded as acceptable in other cultures. A quick survey reveals the complexity of emotional response to kinesic interaction. In New Zealand and Australia, the hitchhiking signal used by Americans is tabu. The "O.K." gesture so familiar to North Americans is considered obscene in several Latin American cultures. In Paraguay, signs made with crossed fingers are offensive, but crossing the legs is permissible as long as the ankle does not touch the knee (the leg-cross position preferred by many American men). In Germany, people who enter a row of seats in a theater should face those already seated in the row as they pass in front of them; to turn the back is considered insulting. Korean etiquette decrees that loud smacking and sucking sounds made while eating are a compliment to the host. And although one should never blow one's nose at a Korean table, sniffling throughout the repast is acceptable behavior.

Even within national boundaries, differences in kinesic behaviors exist. Black Americans use the index finger a great deal in gesturing and also show the palm more frequently than do white Americans. Teenage blacks from working-class families move their shoulders much more than their white counterparts.[38] An interesting account of "cut-eye" and "suck-teeth," two gestures known to many black Americans but virtually unknown to whites, is found in the *Journal of American Folklore.*[39] The authors trace the origin of these kinesic signals to Africa. Cut-eye is a kind of visual snub that communicates disapproval and general rejection of the person at whom it is aimed. It involves directing a hostile glare at the other person, then moving the eyeballs down in a sight line cutting across the person's body, another glare, and finally turning the entire head contemptuously away—often to the accompaniment of a satisfying suck-teeth. Suck-teeth by itself is also capable of conveying anger, exasperation, or annoyance. It is made with the lips either pouted or spread out. Air is drawn through the teeth and into the mouth to create a loud sucking sound.

Proxemics   Edward T. Hall, whose book *The Hidden Dimension* deals with the perception and use of space (proxemics), demonstrates that individuals follow predictable patterns in establishing the distance between themselves and those with whom they interact. In each culture the amount of space varies depending upon the nature of the social interaction, but all cultures seem to distinguish the four basic categories delineated by Hall.[40]

Middle-class Americans, for example, have established the following interaction distances within the four categories:[41]

1. *Intimate distance.* From body contact to a separation space of 18 inches. An emotionally charged zone used for love making, sharing, protecting, and comforting.
2. *Personal distance.* From 1½ to 4 feet. Used for informal contact between friends. A "small protective sphere or bubble" that separates one person from another.
3. *Social distance.* From 4 to 12 feet. The casual interaction distance between acquaintances and strangers. Used in business meetings, classrooms, and impersonal social affairs.
4. *Public distance.* Between 12 and 25 feet. A cool interaction distance used for one-way communication from speaker to audience. Necessitates a louder voice, stylized gestures, and more distinct enunciation.

Proxemic distances preferred by Americans do not correspond to those preferred by people of other cultures. Observance of interaction zones is critical to harmonious relations, but because these zones exist at a subconscious level, they are often violated by nonmembers of a culture. The amount and type of all physical contacts—including touching and the exchange of breath and body odors—vary among cultures. One study dealt with the number of times couples touched each other in cafés: in San Juan, Puerto Rico, they touched 180 times per hour; in Paris, 110; and in London, 0.[42] The London couples would be prime candidates for culture shock in an African culture where two people engaged in casual conversation intertwine their legs as they talk.[43]

In general, high-contact cultures (Arabs, Latin Americans, Greeks, and Turks) usually stand close to each other. Low-contact cultures (northern Europeans, Americans) stand farther apart. Barnlund's cross-cultural study of the public and private self in Japan and in the United States points out the dramatic contrasts in proxemic relationships between the two peoples. As a channel of communication, touch appears to be twice as important within the American culture as it is among the Japanese.[44] Although during infancy and early childhood the Japanese foster a closer tactile relationship than do Americans, the situation changes markedly as the child nears adolescence. In one study, a considerable number of Japanese teenagers reported no physical contact at all with either parent or with a friend.[45] The adult Japanese extends the pattern by restricting not only tactile communication but facial and gestural display as well.

The reasons why one culture will prefer a close interaction distance and another demand more space are not clear. Hall theorizes that cultures have different perceptions of where the boundaries of the self are located.[46] Americans and northern Europeans think of themselves as being contained within their skin. The zone of privacy is extended to include the clothes that cover the skin and even a small space around the body. Any infringement of these areas is looked upon as an invasion of privacy. But in the Arab culture, the self is thought of as being located at a sort of central core. "Tucking the ego down within the body shell," as Hall puts it, results in a totally different proxemic patterning. Arabs tolerate crowding, noise levels, the touching of hands, the probing of eyes, the moisture of exhaled breath, and a miasma of body odors that would overwhelm a Westerner. The ultimate invasion of privacy to the Western mind—rape—does not even have a lexical equivalent in Arabic.[47]

In the areas of France that belong to the Mediterranean culture, there is a high level of sensory involvement and a degree of proxemic crowding that would make members of northern European cultures uncomfortable. In sharp contrast, the German concept of self necessitates a privacy sphere with wide boundaries.

KINESIC UNIVERSALS

In the midst of an overwhelming number of gestures whose meanings differ across cultures, scholars are searching for examples of kinesic behavior whose meaning is universal. The so-called nature/nurture controversy finds researchers divided as to whether some expressive behaviors might stem from phylogenetic origins (nature) and thus be common to all mankind, or whether kinesic behaviors are learned from social contacts (nurture) and thus differ from one culture to another.

Birdwhistell, a cultural relativist on the "nurture" side, wrote in *Kinesics and Context* in 1970 (p. 81):

Insofar as we know, there is no body motion or gesture that can be regarded as a universal symbol. That is, we have been unable to discover any single facial expression, stance, or body position which conveys an identical meaning in all societies.

Back in 1872, however, Charles Darwin, arguing from the "nature" standpoint, hypothesized that the headshake to indicate "no" had its origins when the baby, satiated, turned its head away from the breast and emphasized refusal by rhythmic repetition of this sideways movement.[48] (It has since been pointed out, however, that in some cultures the use of the headshake signals "yes.")

A strong contemporary voice for the innate side of the controversy is that of Eibl-Eibesfeldt, who has isolated the "eyebrow flash" as one expressive movement that occurs across many cultures. It is executed by raising the eyebrows with a rapid movement, keeping them maximally raised for about one-sixth of a second, and then lowering them. This maneuver, which signals readiness for social contact and is used mainly when greeting, has been recorded on film among the Europeans, Balinese, Papuans of New Guinea, Samoans, South American Indians, and the Bushmen. Certainly it plays an important role in the American kinesic system. It is suppressed in only a few cultures: in Japan, for instance, it is considered indecent.

Eibl-Eibesfeldt contends that kinesic similarities exist across cultures not only in basic expressions but in whole syndromes of behavior. Such patterns include greetings that involve embracing and kissing (Eibl-Eibesfeldt feels that these are apparently very old since they occur also in chimpanzees), the smiling response, and actions to indicate coyness, embarrassment, and flirting (hiding the entire face, or concealing the mouth behind one hand). Another example is the cluster of actions that express anger, including "opening the corners of the mouth in a particular way," scowling, stamping the foot, clenching the fist, and striking out to hit objects. The anger syndrome can be observed in the congenitally deaf-blind, who have had no opportunity to learn by watching others. In fact, Eibl-Eibesfeldt's studies of these children show that they portray the facial expressions regarded as "typical" when they laugh, smile, sulk, cry, and express fear or surprise, a fact that tends to support the "innate" viewpoint.

Researching facial expressions across cultures, Paul Ekman and associates concluded that "there are a set of facial components that are associated with emotional categories in the same way for all men, since the same faces were found to be judged as showing the same emotions in many cultures."[49] People in Borneo, Brazil, Japan, the United States, and New Guinea all identified the "primary emotions" (happiness, anger, sadness, fear, surprise, and disgust) with a high rate of agreement. Ekman points out, however, that each society has its own display rules that govern when it is appropriate to exhibit or to conceal these expressions.[50]

Ekman is also searching for gestures ("emblems") that carry consistent meaning across cultures. His research in such disparate cultures as the United States, New Guinea, Japan, and Argentina seems to support the hypothesis that there *are* pan-cultural gestures and that they relate primarily to bodily functions such as eating, sleeping, and love making.[51] For example, one widely distributed emblem is the "I've had enough to eat" motion in which gesturers put a hand on their stomach and either pat or rub it. Since food—be it an American hamburger or Japanese sukiyaki—goes predictably to the stomach when swallowed, the logic of the gesture accounts for its universality. On the other hand, more complex activities produce culture-specific gestures. As Davis points out in *Inside Intuition* (p. 77):

> Though the emblem for eating always involves a hand-to-mouth pantomime, in Japan one hand cups an imaginary bowl at about chin level, while the other scoops imaginary food into the mouth; but in New Guinea, where people eat sitting on the floor, the hand shoots out to arm's length, picks up an imaginary tidbit, and carries it to the mouth.

THE ROLE OF KINESICS

While it is clear that all cultures make use of kinesic behaviors in communication, scholars do not agree on the precise nature of the role they play. Scheflen points out that there are currently two schools of thought in the behavioral sciences.[52] The "psychological school" follows the view set forth by Charles Darwin that nonverbal behavior expresses emotions. Most students of language and culture are aware of the emotive role of gesture, posture, and facial expression: drooping shoulder indicates depression; a scowl registers displeasure, etc. The more recent "communication school," including many ethologists and anthropologists, holds that nonverbal behaviors are used to regulate human interaction. Scheflen insists that the two views are not incompatible—that the behaviors of human communication are both expressive and social.[53]

To understand the idea of kinesic behavior as social control, however, one must become sensitive to the nonverbal behaviors that regular—or monitor—social interactions. Ordinarily they are performed so automatically and at such an unconscious level that even those performing them are unaware of their own actions. Some of these monitoring behaviors are probably universal in man and have counterparts in the behavior of animals. Examples of this type of monitoring include:[54]

1. Turning and looking at the source of a disruption (often quells the disturbance)

2. Looking "through" a person who is trying to join a gathering (a signal that he is not wanted)
3. Turning away from someone who is initiating an action (indicates that he will not receive support)
4. Recoiling or flinching from a sudden loud or aggressive display (warns the offender to step back or speak more softly)

Another group of monitors that are less automatic and seem to have evolved from the reactions mentioned above include such facial expressions as those of disgust, boredom, and anger. These monitors are used to provide a running commentary on another's behavior. A monitoring signal of this type common in America is the act of wiping the index finger laterally across the nostrils. It comes into play when someone violates the norms of the group by such actions as lying, using profanity, or encroaching on personal space. This was the kinesic signal used unconsciously by President Eisenhower when he chose to be less than candid during press interviews. He was reportedly warned of the revealing nature of this action so that he could avoid its use thereafter. The anecdote points up the fact that most monitoring acts are carried out without the actor's awareness. It also illustrates a third type of monitoring—self-monitoring—in which those who transgress the social norms perform the monitoring act upon themselves.[55]

Kinesicists are in agreement that nonverbal signals can be more powerful than verbal ones. Verbal signals call for cognitive processing; nonverbal signals operate directly, bypassing conscious analysis and evoking immediate action.[56] Since information can be carried simultaneously on both verbal and nonverbal channels, one is able to negotiate social relationships and supply emotional feedback while exchanging information of a cognitive nature verbally. Emotions, feelings, and interpersonal attitudes are often more effectively expressed by the nonverbal than by the verbal. And while the spoken word does not always convey the truth, kinesic evidence tends to depict reality. As Charles Galloway puts it, "It is to the fidelity of human experience that nonverbal meanings have value."[57]

KINESICS AND PERCEPTUAL EDUCATION

Sapir spoke of nonverbal behavior as "an elaborate and secret code that is written nowhere, known by none, and understood by all." Unfortunately for cross-cultural understanding, the "all" refers only to members of the same culture. Bursack filmed Minneapolis men and women who deliberately tried to express "agreement" and "courtesy" nonverbally in an interview situation.[58] The filmed sequences were studied by citizens of Beirut, Tokyo, and Bogotá. The foreigners were unable to "read" with accuracy the Americans' nonverbal attempts to communicate the two feelings critical to establishing a warm social climate.

We have seen how inextricably movement is linked to meaning. Those who have "learned" a language without including the nonverbal component are seriously handicapped if they intend to interact with living members of the culture instead of with paper and print. Insights into posture, movement, facial expression, eye management, gestures, and distancing as they affect communication not only increase sensitivity to other human beings but deepen inevitably students' understanding of their own kinesic systems.

Research on nonverbal communication is patiently unraveling Sapir's "elaborate and secret code." We know now that in order to really *understand*, we must be able to hear the silent message and read the invisible word. The study of kinesics across cultures must be a crucial part of our perceptual education.

APPENDIX

Suggested Activities for Sensitizing Students to Aspects of Nonverbal Communication

I. *To Make Students Aware of the Scope of the Subject*
    Introduce the term "kinesics" (the study of body motions that are communicative). Ask students to draw up a list of topics that they feel would come under this heading. Combine their lists into one outline on the board. (Their outline will probably be incomplete.) Help them fill it out to include all aspects of kinesics: posture, movement styles, facial expressions, gaze, proxemics (distancing), and gestures (including hand, arm, head, neck, shoulders, torso, hips, legs, and feet).

II. *To Sensitize Students to Their Own Communicative Patterns*
    Give students the following list of questions (from Eisenberg and Smith, *Nonverbal Communication,* p. 8) and ask them to contribute their responses in a class discussion:
    1. Do you ever avoid talking to someone because he speaks too slowly or too loudly?
    2. What are the three most common gestures you make when you speak? Do these gestures say anything about your personality?
    3. How do you know that someone is interested in talking with you when that interest is not verbalized?

4. Under what circumstances do you say what you don't mean? When you do, have you ever noticed yourself telling a lie with your face?

5. Why do you act differently when you are in your own house than when you are in the house of a friend?

6. At what distance does a good friend get "too close"? At what distance does a fellow student, whom you do not know well, get "too close"? Why is there a difference?

7. Have you ever felt hostile or friendly toward someone just because of his appearance?

8. Do you sit in the same chair at home? At school? At work? Have you ever gotten angry because someone took *your* seat? Why?

III. *To Make Students Aware of the Importance of Kinesics*
Pyschologist Albert Mehrabian devised a formula that represents the total impact of a message:

7 percent verbal   (actual word content)
38 percent vocal   (tone, intonation, pitch, stess)
55 percent facial expression

Put this formula on the board, leaving the percentages blank. Ask the students to fill in the percentage of communicative impact made by the verbal, the vocal, and the facial components of an interpersonal exchange. (Remind them that their percentages must total 100 percent.) Put several suggested distributions on the board. Try to arrive at one that most students accept. Then fill in the percentages as revealed by Mehrabian's research.

IV. *To Make Students Aware of the Complexity of Kinesics*
Read Birdwhistell's list of American middle-class movements located in the face and head area (see list p. 123). Ask the students to try to make the movements as you read the list. Elicit discussion on the subtlety of facial expressions and the out-of-awareness aspect of gestural production. Do the students know of any facial expressions or head gestures from the foreign culture not included on the American list?

V. *To Help Students Understand Postural Differences Across Cultures*
Ask for two volunteers to come to the front of the class to demonstrate the postures used in various cultures to represent the emotion of humility (see list p. 120). Begin with the students'

own nonverbal expression of humility. Then ask them to demonstrate the postures of other cultures. In the discussion that follows, ask the students who participated how they felt when assuming the positions: were some postures more awkward (humiliating, embarrassing, etc.) than others? Ask the other students how they felt watching the demonstration.

VI. *To Give Students an Awareness of the Rich Gestural Vocabulary They Possess in Their Own Culture*
Discuss briefly autistic, technical, and folk (including descriptive) gestures. Divide the class into small groups that are to compete with each other. Ask each group to draw up as rapidly as possible a list of the folk gestures of their own culture. Start them off with an example or two. At the end of 10 minutes, have each group take turns demonstrating a gesture while the other groups call out the meaning. No group may repeat a gesture already presented. The last group to give a gesture wins. Point out the surprising number of nonverbal signals known in common by members of the class. Use these suggestions as a checklist:

Snap fingers; tap toe; shrug; flex biceps; shade eyes to peer; draw finger across throat; cross fingers; knock on wood; cross heart; spit on ground (disdain); raise right hand (swear truth); hold nose; limp wrist (homosexual); wave; thumb a ride; shake scolding finger; point to chest (me!); raise eyebrows; wink; slap on back; finger on lips (shhh); point with finger; rub one finger on another, pointing to offender (shame); beckon; thumbs up; thumbs down; peace sign; V for victory; hug self, shiver (cold); wipe brow (hot; narrow escape); stick out tongue; thumbs in ears and waggle fingers; "quotation" signs in air; smack lips; hands on hips; "O.K." symbol; rotate finger in air at side of head (crazy); play imaginary violin while someone tells sad tale; blow on nails, then rub on chest (ego trip); make curvy outline in air with both hands (sexy woman); handshake; throw kiss; rub stomach; cradle head against folded hands; clasp hands above head and shake (victory); bow head; stamp foot; hand up, palm forward (stop!); sign of cross; tap watch (time's up).

VII. *To Make Students Aware of the Cultural Differences in Gestures*
Have several students demonstrate the American gestures for the following list of emotions or directions:

Yes/no; come/go; start/stop; that's good/that's bad; I'm happy/I'm sad; it's over there/it's over here; go up/go down; I like you/I dislike you; bring it here/take it away; be quiet/make more noise; a little bit/a lot; short/long; stand up/be seated; up/down.

Take about 5 minutes to conduct the class without words, using the gestures demonstrated. Then ask the class to imagine that they are in a culture where the meaning of each gesture is exactly reversed: a head nod means "no," a head shake means "yes"; a smile means "I'm sad," a frown means "I'm happy"; etc. Conduct the class for another 5 to 10 minutes using the new gestural code. Or divide the class into small groups to prepare skits showing a segment of social interaction with the new code. Discuss the possibilities for cross-cultural misunderstanding.

VIII. *To Make Students Aware of Proxemic Patterns*
Explain that each individual requires a "personal space bubble" that must not be encroached upon by others. Among Americans, the diameter ranges from 2 to 4 feet and varies according to time, place, and circumstances. (At an X-rated movie the line at the ticket window is more compressed than is the line for a G-rated movie.) As homework, ask students to invade deliberately another person's space bubble without an invitation and to make note of resultant comments and such variables as age, nationality, personality, time, place, and relationship between the interactants. Have them bring to class the next day a brief report on their experiment. Point out that proxemic patterns are to a large extent culturally determined. Discuss the patterns of the foreign culture. Compare with other cultures to give dimensionality.

IX. *To Help Students Acquire an Understanding of the Gestures of the Target Culture*
As a long-range assignment, ask students to develop a gesture inventory. Have them watch for gestures made by native speakers on television, in films, and on the streets, and demonstrate these to the class. Ask them to bring articles and clippings dealing with nonverbal behavior and share them with the class. Urge students to photograph interaction between native speakers. Invite native speakers to class for demonstrations. Insist that students study individual gestures in

relation to communicative context. (No gesture may be "collected" without a description of who, where, why, etc.) At the end of the assignment period ask students to present their gesture inventory as a small-group or individual project. The final product may, for example, take the form of a slide show, a movie, wall charts, learning activity packets, or a scripted pantomime.

NOTES

1. Genelle Morain, speech at Foreign Language Association of Georgia, Macon, 1977.

2. Benjamin Franklin, *Diary,* quoted by Raymond J. Cromier in "A Legacy from the Founding Fathers," *Temple,* fall 1976, 16.

3. Dean C. Barnlund, *Public and Private Self in Japan and the United States,* pp. 12–16, Simul Press, Tokyo, 1975.

4. Gordon Allport, *The Nature of Prejudice,* Anchor Press/Doubleday, Garden City, N.Y., 1958.

5. Ray L. Birdwhistell, "The Language of the Body: The Natural Environment of Words," in *Human Communication: Theoretical Explorations,* p. 213, ed. Albert Silverstein, Lawrence Erlbaum Associates, Hillsdale, N.J.; 1974.

6. Genelle Morain, "Visual Literacy: Reading Signs and Designs in the Foreign Culture," *Foreign Language Annals,* 9 (3), 210–216.

7. Birdwhistell, in *Human Communication,* p. 124.

8. Gordon W. Hewes, "World Distribution of Certain Postural Habits," *American Anthropologist,* 57 (1), 231.

9. M. H. Krout, *Introduction to Social Psychology,* Harper & Row, New York, 1942.

10. Gordon W. Hewes, "The Anthropology of Posture," *Scientific American,* 196 (February), 123–132.

11. Lawrence Wylie and Rick Stafford, *Beaux Gestes: A Guide to French Body Talk,* pp. x–xiii, The Undergraduate Press, Cambridge, Mass., 1977.

12. Ann Banks, "French without Language," *Harvard Today,* 18 (1), 4.

13. Edward T. Hall, *Beyond Culture,* p. 218, Anchor Press/Doubleday, Garden City, N.Y., 1976.

14. Abne M. Eisenberg and Ralph R. Smith, *Nonverbal Communication,* p. 83, Bobbs-Merrill, Indianapolis and New York; 1971.

15. Alan Lomax, *Folk Song Style and Culture,* pp. 235–247, American Association for the Advancement of Science, Washington, D.C., 1968.

16. For the following discussion on interactional synchrony, see Hall, *Beyond Culture,* pp. 61–73.

17. Ralph Waldo Emerson, "Behavior," *The Conduct of Life,* 1860.

18. Ray L. Birdwhistell, *Kinesics and Context,* University of Pennsylvania Press, Philadelphia, 1970.

19. Flora Davis, *Inside Intuition,* pp. 51–52, Signet, New York, 1975.

20. Dale G. Leathers, *Nonverbal Communication Systems,* pp. 26–32, Allyn and Bacon, Boston, 1976.

21. Michael Argyle and Mark Cook, *Gaze and Mutual Gaze,* p. 10, Cambridge University Press, Cambridge, 1976.

22. Ibid., p. 14.

23. Michael Argyle, *Bodily Communication,* International Universities Press, New York, 1975.

24. Davis, *Inside Intuition,* p. 62.

25. Ibid., p. 102.

26. Charles Galloway, lecture at Athens Academy, Athens, Ga., May 1977.

27. Erving Goffman, *Behavior in Public Places,* pp. 83–88, The Free Press, New York, 1963.

28. Examples gleaned from *Intercultural Experiential Learning Aids,* Language Research Center, Brigham Young University, Provo, Utah, 1976; also from David, *Inside Intuition.*

29. Argyle, *Bodily Communication,* p. 247.

30. Ibid, pp. 233–234.

31. Frances C. Hayes, "Should We Have a Dictionary of Gestures?" *Southern Folklore Quarterly,* 4, 239–245.

32. Eisenberg and Smith, *Nonverbal Communication,* p. 76.

33. Reid Scott, *Cultural Understanding: Spanish Level I,* p. 9, Alameda County School Department, Hayward, CA, 1969. ED 046 292.

34. Jan H. Brunvald, *The Study of American Folklore,* p. 247, W. W. Norton, New York.

35. Jerald R. Green, *Kinesics in the Foreign Language Classroom,* ERIC Focus Report on the Teaching of Foreign Languages, No. 24, MLA/ACTFL Materials Center, New York, 1971. ED 055 511.

36. Birdwhistell, *Kinesics and Context,* p. 154.

37. Eisenberg and Smith, *Nonverbal Communication,* pp. 76–77.

38. Albert E. Scheflen and Alice Scheflen, *Body Language and the Social Order. Communication as Behavioral Control,* p. 90, Prentice-Hall, Englewood Cliffs, N.J.; 1972.

39. John R. Rickford and Angela E. Rickford, "Cut-eye and Suck-teeth: African Words and Gestures in New World Guise," *Journal of American Folklore,* 89 (353), 294–309.

40. Shirley Weitz, "Spatial Behavior," in *Nonverbal Communication, Readings with Commentary,* p. 200, ed. Shirley Weitz, Oxford University Press, New York, 1974.

41. Edward T. Hall, *The Hidden Dimension,* pp. 117–125, Doubleday, Garden City, N.Y., 1969.

42. Argyle, *Bodily Communication,* p. 290.

43. Ibid.

44. Barnlund, *Public and Private Self in Japan and the United States,* p. 105.

45. Ibid., p. 106.

46. Hall, *Hidden Dimension,* p. 157.

47. Ibid., p. 158.

48. For this discussion of Darwin and the following views of Eibl-Eibesfeldt, see I. Eibl-Eibesfeldt, "Similarities and Differences between Cultures in Expressive Movements," in *Nonverbal Communication,* ed. Shirley Weitz, pp. 22–27.

49. Paul Ekman, Wallance V. Friesen, and Silvan S. Tomkins, "Facial Affect Scoring Technique: A First Validity Study," in *Nonverbal Communication,* ed. Shirley Weitz, p. 36.

50. Paul Ekman, Wallace V. Friesen, and Phoebe Ellsworth, *Emotions in the Human Face,* p. 179, Pergamon Press, New York, 1972.

51. Paul Ekman and Wallace V. Friesen, "The Repertoire of Nonverbal Behavior: Categories, Origins, Usage and Coding," *Semiotica,* 1 (1), 66–67.

52. Scheflen and Scheflen, *Body Language and the Social Order,* p. xii.

53. Ibid., p. xiii.

54. Ibid., p. 105.

55. Ibid., p. 112.

56. Argyle, *Bodily Communication,* p. 362.

57. Charles Galloway, "Nonverbal: The Language of Sensitivity," in *The Challenge of Nonverbal Awareness, Theory into Practice,* 10 (4), p. 230, ed. Jack R. Frymier, The Ohio State University Press, Columbus, Ohio.

58. Lois Bursack, "North American Nonverbal Behavior as Perceived in Three Overseas Urban Cultures, Ph.D. dissertation, University of Minnesota, 1970.

STUDY QUESTIONS

1. Which type of home, authority-centered or social-centered, best describes the house that you grew up in? What differences are there between yours and the prototype described by Condon and Yousef? Did you have friends whose home was more like the other type?

2. How many different houses have you lived in? If more than one, were there significant differences among them? How are frequent moves both a result of certain American values and a cause of others?

3. Compare the function and role of the various rooms of your house with those of the typical Middle Eastern house. Do corresponding rooms serve the same function with regard to the family and to outsiders? Or are they more similar to those of the German home?

4. Carry out several of the activities suggested at the conclusion of the Morain article, "Kinesics and Cross-Cultural Understanding."

5. To illustrate alternative arrangements of space, describe spatial organizations of classrooms you have been in (position of furniture, room divisions, individual study spaces, group study spaces, etc.). Look at the spatial use in business office settings and grocery stores (the convenience store, the supermarket, the mom-and-pop corner store). What do the arrangements suggest about the users?

6. Eye contact, or lack of it, is one part of interpersonal communication affected by culture. Begin a conversation with a friend. Maintain constant eye contact. Do not let your gaze waver for 2 or 3 minutes. Try to blink infrequently. How do you and your friend feel under these conditions?

7. Begin a conversation with a friend. Have your friend avoid eye contact with you. Keep the conversation going for 3 or 4 minutes. How does each of you feel under these conditions?

VERBAL COMMUNICATION

The following two articles explore different but equally significant aspects of the relationships between verbal communication and culture. Dean Barnlund, in *Verbal Self-Disclosure: Topics, Targets, Depth,* examines the results of a comparative study dealing with verbal interaction patterns of the Japanese and Americans. On the one hand, Americans and Japanese seem to have similar attitudes with regard to the people with whom they can communicate and the topics they can communicate about. However, it is the great difference in the amount of verbal self-disclosure which distinguishes the two peoples. According to Barnlund, this difference in style of verbal communication is a consequence of a difference in values. When one is able to recognize the hidden barrier verbal self-disclosure involves cross-culturally, more effective interaction can take place. In their article, *Communication Overseas,* Szalay and Fisher, in order to investigate the effect of culture on the meanings of words, used a Korean/American comparison. They selected words from the two languages which have accepted direct equivalents in translation. Yet, by asking native speakers to use connotative free associations with each word, the authors show that the connotative meanings of seemingly similar words in the two languages are quite different. Through the use of semantographs, the authors demonstrate that the cultural frame of reference gives subjective meanings to words.

(For further discussion on verbal communication, see K. Sherer and P. Ekman, R. Ramsey, J. Bilmes, S. Ramsey and J. Birk in the bibliography.)

Verbal Self-Disclosure:
Topics, Targets, Depth

Dean C. Barnlund

From *Public and Private Self in Japan and the United States,* by Dean C. Barnlund. Copyright © 1975 by The Simul Press, Tokyo, Japan. Canadian and United States distributor, ISBS, Inc., Portland, Oregon. Reprinted by permission of The Simul Press and the author.

Anyone who stands at an urban intersection or in the lobby of a large office building soon senses some pattern in the migrations of people. There are times when they flow together, congregating in dense masses, and times when they disperse and flow apart. Even within such aggregations there are minor currents: some people seek each other out, others meet by accident, and some consciously avoid each other; there are some who never converse, others who speak briefly, and still others who talk at great length.

If we were to look within these encounters we would find further regularities. Conversations usually begin with rituals of greeting. People prolong the relationship, if they desire, through an exchange of prosaic and predictable commonplaces. These conversational pastimes sometimes extend to more serious talk and a deeper sharing of private thought and personal feeling. Each person contributes remarks that will maintain rapport, disclose his experience, and fulfill his needs. From each encounter flows a mixture of consensus or confusion, trust or suspicion, excitement or boredom, affection or animosity.

Probably there are no more basic questions one can ask of a person or a culture than these: To *whom* does one speak or not speak? About *what* may one talk or not talk? How *completely* is inner experience shared or withheld? Answering each of these questions should help to expose the structure of human relationships and the norms that govern interpersonal communication in Japan and the United States.

PERSON ACCESSIBILITY

In one of the many insightful cartoon episodes of *Peanuts* Lucy declares, "I love humanity! It's people I can't stand!" And so it is with many human beings. No one seeks to talk to every passerby. No one is a friend to everyone. There is simply not enough time or energy to maintain deep relations with all our neighbors. Nor do most people want to do so.

All people are not equally attractive companions. "Interpersonal valence" is a term that reflects the lines of attraction or rejection that develop among the members of any group or society. Each person and each culture generates criteria for the selection of communicative partners. Any personal quality—age, sex, occupation, education, status, power, talent, beauty—may contribute to or detract from the potential attractiveness of another human being.

What part, if any, do cultures play in the selection of conversational partners? Do Japan and the United States favor communication with the same sorts of people? Are members of one culture closer to their parents, and are members of the other closer to their peers? How do these two societies evaluate conversation with females or males, mothers or fathers, acquaintances or strangers?

TOPIC ACCESSIBILITY

How, also, do cultures influence the content of conversations? The catalog of topics that might be appropriate for conversation is infinite. Yet each person develops his own topical priorities and prejudices, ranking subjects according to their attractiveness to him. Some people prefer to talk about work or family life, others to discuss politics or sex. Some prefer "small talk," enjoying an exchange of information about ordinary daily events, while others prefer "big talk," finding greater stimulation in a discussion of larger philosophical issues.

It would not be surprising to find that people are drawn particularly to those with similar interests. A person who enjoys talking about sports and one who likes to discuss music may not be equally enthralled about meeting an olympic medal winner and a member of a chamber orchestra. If someone—out of ignorance or reticence—is uncomfortable talking about existentialism or birth control, he may simply avoid people who are likely to bring up those subjects.

Cultures not only influence the choice of acquaintances, but mediate also the content of conversation. Each society, to some extent, expresses its values by encouraging or discouraging the exploration of certain subjects. Some topics are approved and freely discussed while others are literally forbidden. A society that attaches great value to business, to the arts, or to family life might be expected to promote somewhat different attitudes toward these areas of discourse. At one time or another in history entire cultures have felt it proper or immoral to discuss religion, sex, evolution, politics, race relations, even dress and diet. Are similar topics approved and disapproved in Japan and the United States? Or do they differ on what is proper and improper for people to talk about?

Every person, within his own circle of acquaintances, also forms different kinds of communicative alliances. Friends are seldom alike in their experience, knowledge, talent, or emotional sensitivity. If this is true, then people may discriminate in what they talk about with each of their acquaintances. Financial matters, for example, may be discussed with parents, but sexual problems only with friends. Or once deep attachments are formed, do people explore without limit any subject that concerns them? Do these two cultures encourage selective communication—limiting the discussion of specific topics to specific target persons—or do they encourage unlimited communication with all associates? If they do support topical discrimination, do both societies favor the same topical priorities with parents, peers, or strangers?

LEVEL ACCESSIBILITY

There is another dimension to verbal interaction. It has to do with the depth of talk. No matter what topic happens to be in focus, comments may reflect varying degrees of personalization, the extent to which the self is revealed in any remark. A statement may refer to external realities, the outer public world, or to inner realities, the private world inside our skins. Or it may comment on the relations between these two worlds. Remarks of the first type tell very little about the speaker while remarks of the second type tell a great deal more about the person who makes them. Any message, in short, may be highly self-disclosing or only slightly self-disclosing.

If time were no limitation, every statement could be subjected to this sort of scrutiny. The remark, "You're driving too fast," is a statement about the world outside the self. It claims objective validity. "I get scared going this fast," reflects the inner state of the speaker. The same distinction may be seen in "The company's reorganization plan is sound" compared with "I am excited about my new assignment." The former is a depersonalized judgment, the latter a statement with the self squarely in the center. The mother who says, "The children are going through a difficult phase," and the one who says "I feel inadequate with my children," are conveying quite different information. One tells us about the children, the other about the personal meaning this behavior has for the mother. It reflects her inner experience and informs us as much about her as it does about her children.

In *The Transparent Self* Sidney Jourard emphasizes the difference between people who are "transparent" and those who are "opaque." Some people allow others to know them intimately by often revealing their inner thoughts and feelings, while some hide themselves so others rarely glimpse what they are like inside.[1] Most people, however, are not equally disclosing of themselves on all topics since their emotional comfort and self-knowledge are not equal on all topics. They may speak quite frankly on some subjects, those that seem safest, and speak cautiously or deceitfully on subjects that are dangerous. People are not equally honest with all their acquaintances because it is not common to feel equally comfortable with parents, friends, business associates, and complete strangers.

We might expect that cultures, like human beings, would differ in the level of self-disclosure they feel is appropriate in conversation. They may prescribe different levels of frankness for different topics: heretical religious views were repressed during the Middle Ages just as firmly as racial doubts remain undiscussed in South Africa today. Societies may differ, also, on the degree of intimacy or distance they feel is appropriate for conversations between people and their parents, their friends, their associates, and strangers. Singular levels and forms of self-expression may be cultivated in Japan and the United States.

SELF-DISCLOSURE SCALE

Sidney Jourard and Paul Lasakow have perfected a Self-Disclosure Scale which permits simultaneous measurement of three related variables: topic of conversation, target person, and depth of self-disclosure.[2] For this study the questionnaire was slightly abridged to reduce its length but without altering its basic structure. The form that was used identified six potential communicative partners: Mother, Father, Same Sex Friend, Opposite Sex Friend, Untrusted Acquaintance, and Stranger. The scale enables one to obtain a picture of the relative intimacy of communicative relationships with six persons who occupy significant places in the interpersonal experience of each respondent.

With each target person the respondent is asked to indicate the level of his or her communication. An appropriate symbol is used to indicate the level of disclosure on a variety of topics with each partner. The symbols and their meanings are as follows: 0—Have told the person nothing about this aspect of myself; 1—Have talked in general terms about this item; 2—Have talked in full and complete detail about this topic; X—Have lied or misrepresented myself to this person. From these scores one can easily calculate the relative accessibility of the self to a variety of other people across a number of conversational topics.

The relative depth of disclosure to these target persons was determined on six broad topics commonly discussed in interpersonal encounters: (1) *Opinions* about political, religious, and social issues, (2) *Interests* in food, music, television, and books, (3) *Work* goals and difficulties, special talents and limitations, (4) *Financial* status, including income, savings, debts, and budget, (5) *Personality,* specific assets and handicaps, sources of pride or shame, (6) *Physical* attributes including feelings about one's face and body, illnesses, sexual adequacy. In each critical area five specific questions sought to fix the location of conversational norms and the limits felt appropriate for each of these general topics. The scales have been used successfully over a period of years to study differences in the disclosure patterns of males and females, members of various races, and people belonging to different cultures.

This questionnaire was given to 120 Japanese and 120 American college students. All were single, were between 18 and 24 years of age, and were equally divided between males and females. Each was asked to read the thirty questions carefully, think of a specific person within each target category (Mother, Father, Same Sex Friend, Opposite Sex Friend, Untrusted Acquaintance, Stranger), and report his actual or probable verbal behavior with each. The tests were completed anonymously, and subjects were given unlimited time to finish.

TOPICAL PRIORITIES

What subjects do members of each of these cultures prefer to talk about, or avoid, when they meet? The answers to this question are somewhat surprising. Instead of a cultural difference in topic preferences, the results revealed immense consistency in what is considered an appropriate or inappropriate topic for conversation.

Among Japanese respondents matters of interest and taste were the most fully discussed topics, followed by opinions about public issues, and attitudes toward work or studies. Financial matters, aspects of personality, and feelings about one's body ranked lower. Males and females displayed similar topical orientations, although females ranked work-related questions second while males ranked them third. But this difference was slight and insignificant.

American respondents supplied a very similar, but not identical, pattern of response. Matters of taste and interest again scored as the most appealing subjects, but attitudes toward work and studies scored second. Opinions on public issues ranked third, while financial status, aspects of personality, and feelings about physical adequacy followed in that order. But, again, the difference in the relative ranking of attitudes toward work and opinions about public issues was small. And the degree of cultural consistency was very striking. American males and females agreed completely in their topical preferences.

Hence it appears that there are only small and inconsequential differences between Japanese and Americans (and between males and females) with regard to conversational focus: members of both nations seem to prefer to discuss their tastes in food, books, television programs and films, and prefer to talk less about their personal traits and physical or sexual adequacy.

It might be expected that opinions on public issues, since they are the most remote from the self, might be the most favored topics for conversation. But apparently not. Tastes and interests were. There may be several reasons for this. It may be that matters of taste rarely provoke deep or fundamental conflicts in values, and hence are less likely to produce arguments or friction. Or it may be that such differences, since they need not be reconciled, stimulate curiosity rather than animosity. For whatever reason, they constituted the most likely conversational material in both countries.

Scores on the specific questions that make up the six general areas provide further information on verbal disclosure. Among Japanese the most fully explored questions were those relating to tastes in food, music, reading, television and film. Next most fully discussed were opinions on race and male-female relations. The least popular specific questions dealt with feelings about sexual adequacy, facts about sexual behavior, feelings about the appearance of the body and face, and events that arouse shame or guilt. All but the latter two fall into the broad category of attitudes toward the physical self, and the exceptions relate to the adequacy of the psychic self. Males and females differed only slightly in their response even to specific questions on the scale.

Similarly among Americans the most thoroughly explored specific questions concern taste in food, music, television and film, attitudes on race and career goals. Males and females showed only slight differences even with regard to disclosure on specific questions. Americans and Japanese reflected nearly identical patterns of disapproval for conversations relating to personal and sexual matters. And, again, male and female responses revealed no differences sizable enough to be reliable.

Interestingly the level of talk within each broad area was consistent no matter which specific question was considered. But there was one notable exception to this rule. Questions about sex, for example, appeared under three different topical categories. "My personal opinions about sexual morality" appeared as a question under Opinions on Public Issues, "Facts about my present sex life" appeared under Personality, and "Feelings about my own sexual adequacy" appeared under Physical Attributes. In every case the specific question on sex received the lowest score within the general topic area and, in the last two cases, the lowest scores of any items on the test. This pattern seems to confirm that discussion of the body and its functions is one of the least desirable topics of conversation in both cultures. Sex, even when discussed as a public problem, is seen as a relatively unattractive topic. This may be because it can easily lead to an exploration of attitudes that are highly personal and private. When questions relating to the body and to sexual behavior are set aside, the next lowest specific scores (with the exception of past episodes involving shame or guilt) for both Japanese and Americans referred to money—savings, debts, budgets.

The evidence is overwhelming in support of similar orientations among Japanese and Americans with regard to what is appropriate and inappropriate to talk about. There are slight differences between the cultures on specific questions within the broader categories, but these appear random and inconsequential. Differences between males and females also seem small and, given traditional concepts of their roles, quite understandable.

TARGET PREFERENCES

If conversational topics can be ranked, is there also a hierarchy of conversational partners? Are the people who occupy our interpersonal worlds equally attractive as associates, or do they vary systematically in attractiveness? Does this change according to topic, or does it remain the same regardless of topic? The data obtained from the Self-Disclosure Scale permit these questions to be explored.

A clear hierarchy of target persons emerged from the findings. The Japanese ranked friends highest as communicative partners, parents next, and strangers and untrusted acquaintances last. Within these categories same sex friends were clearly preferred to opposite sex friends, mothers ranked next (scoring nearly as high as friends of the opposite sex), but fathers scored substantially lower. Among the least attractive conversational partners, unknown people were preferred slightly over untrusted acquaintances. While the decline in scores among the most attractive partners (same sex friend, opposite sex friend, mother) was regular, the drop between these and father, stranger, and untrusted person was more precipitous.

All potential target persons scored substantially higher with Americans, but essentially the same hierarchy existed. Friends were communicated with most fully, parents next, and strangers and untrusted people least. Also, the scores decreased gradually and a radical drop did not appear until one reaches the scores for strangers and untrusted people. Again, unknown persons were preferred to untrusted ones.

There are some interesting, though subtle and unreliable, differences in the responses of males and females in both samples. Japanese males appeared to disclose most to male friends, but more fully to friends of either sex than to their mothers. Japanese females disclosed most to the same sex friend, but next to their mothers. There was substantial disclosure to opposite sex friends, but it was less complete than to mothers. Americans, both male and female, communicated more fully with friends of either sex than they did with either parent.

Verbal disclosure to fathers may differ in the two cultures: Americans appeared to communicate almost equally with mothers and fathers; Japanese seemed to differentiate between the amount of disclosure with each parent. Whereas disclosure to American fathers was nearly indistinguishable from other intimates, disclosure to Japanese fathers dropped off considerably and approaches the level of American disclosure with strangers. Americans revealed more of themselves to strangers and untrusted associates, but, like the Japanese, preferred the former to the latter as communicative partners.

Choice of topic and choice of partner would not seem to be independent of each other. They should interact. It would seem reasonable that most people would seek out specific persons when they wish to discuss certain topics, and seek other partners to discuss other topics. But the data from this investigation raise doubts about that presumption, for there was considerable consistency across all topics for all target persons. That is to say, there was little evidence of either avoidance of or emphasis upon particular topics with particular acquaintances. Generally tastes and opinions were the most fully discussed in both cultures with all people. And physical attributes and personal traits were the least discussed, again with all people.

These generalizations may obscure some exceptions to this rule. Some Japanese respondents, for example, seemed to prefer to discuss financial matters with their mothers, next with male friends and female friends. They preferred to talk about bodily characteristics, excepting sexual behavior, with mothers before male or female friends. Among Americans, financial matters seemed more likely to be discussed with mothers, secondly with fathers, rather than with peers of the same or opposite sex. Unlike their Japanese counterparts, Americans did not appear to find discussion of physical attributes easier with mothers or fathers than with the same or opposite sex friend. But evidence of selective communication is too haphazard to be taken seriously.

Thus it appears there is a communicative bias operating in both countries that encourages greater personal disclosure to same and opposite sex friends, favors somewhat less disclosure to parents, and restricts interaction still more with unknown and untrusted people. Each sex seems somewhat to prefer communicating with members of the same sex, but this preference is much stronger among Japanese than Americans. The Japanese seem to differentiate more sharply between communicating with mothers and fathers while Americans seem to perceive both parents as more equally attractive partners.

LEVEL OF PERSONAL INVOLVEMENT

The order of topical priorities and hierarchy of communicative partners seem generally consistent in both cultures. But what is most critical is the depth of personal disclosure that is encouraged within interpersonal encounters. How much of themselves do Japanese and Americans reveal in their conversations? The data obtained from the Self-Disclosure Scale provide a simple and clear index of self-revelation.

The scoring of the Self-Disclosure Scale is such that a score of 0 indicates that respondents "Have told nothing about this aspect of myself," a score of 100 indicates they "Have talked in general terms about this aspect of myself," and a score of 200 indicates they "Have talked in full and complete detail about this item."* Scores falling between 0 and 100 would suggest a low level and between 100 and 200 a high level of self-disclosure. With so broad a range of topics and so

---

*To simplify the presentation of the results on the Self-Disclosure Scale raw scores have been multiplied by 100 to convert them into whole numbers.

diverse a set of communicative partners it would be surprising if scores averaged above 150.

For the Japanese the average level of disclosure across all topics and all target persons was 75. The average disclosure score for Americans was 112. Scores of males and females in both cultures were very similar: Japanese males and females obtained exactly the same scores on self-revelation; Americans showed a slight sex difference, males averaging 113 and females averaging 110. (The small differences in disclosure levels of American males and females is traceable to relatively greater openness of males with strangers.) But these differences were so small they cannot be taken very seriously.

However, it may be more representative of a culture to consider the level of communication only with "trusted acquaintances." Although conversations with strangers may be suggestive of the range of social interaction, it seems questionable to incorporate this figure in appraising the general level of disclosure in daily conversation. Disclosure to untrusted people, too, seems to constitute a special rather than typical instance of personal interaction. A better and more representative estimate of the normal depth of disclosure may be secured by eliminating these two categories of target persons.

When these are omitted from the calculations, the average level of conversation with trusted acquaintances (mother, father, male friend, female friend) rises from 75 to 100 for the Japanese and from 112 to 144 for Americans. A slight sex difference appeared in both samples, but again of such small size as to be discounted.

With regard to overall levels of interpersonal communication the findings seem clear. Interpersonal distance, as estimated by self-disclosure, was substantially greater among Japanese than among Americans. The degree to which persons shared their experience—private opinion and private feeling—was considerably higher among Americans. And this appeared to be true whether potential partners included or excluded unknown and untrusted persons.

For Japanese the average level of disclosure rose to 100 only with trusted acquaintances. This indicates, on the average, that Japanese express themselves only "in general terms" with their closest associates— parents and intimate friends. For the United States the comparable figure was 144. While this figure does not suggest a total sharing of the self, it does indicate a level of expression that varies between talking "in general terms" and talking "in full and complete detail about onself." In order to reach this level approximately half of all communication with intimates would have to involve a full sharing of the self.

The precise boundaries of the "public self" and the "private self" in Japan and the United States may now be estimated using the data on self-disclosure. The generalized models suggested earlier can now be drawn more precisely. (These appear in Figures 1 and 2.) In the typical Japanese the area of the "private self" extends from the "unconscious" to the point at which the person reveals his inner feelings in only "general terms" (100). For the typical American the "private self" extends from the "unconscious" to a point midway between disclosing his inner experience "completely" or in "general terms" (144). Thus the total area of the self accessible to others through communication is significantly smaller in Japan than in the United States. (It is possible to represent the boundary of the public and private self in each topical area—for a culture or an individual—by making the contour of this boundary conform precisely to the profile of scores in each topical area and for each conversational partner.)

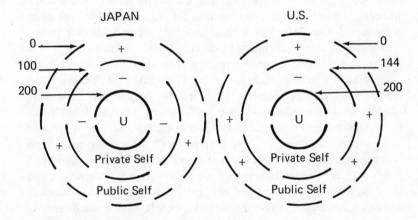

Figure 1   Precise Boundary of Public Self

It is when individual questionnaires are examined that the full impact of these findings is felt. Depersonalized averages tend to obscure extreme cases and blunt somewhat the human significance of these overall figures. Many people reported no disclosure of self on a number of topics; many others reported no instances of deep disclosure to any person. There were more than a few, especially among the Japanese sample, whose average level of self-expression was not near 100, but closer to 0, who on *nearly all topics* and with *nearly all people* reported they "Have told the person nothing about this aspect of myself." As one data processor remarked while scoring some of the questionnaires, "Have these people ever revealed anything about themselves to anyone? Are they known to any other human being at all?" This is a stronger indictment of Japanese conversational manner than that offered by Robert Guillain, but it is similar in tone. He notes that the Japanese enjoy social contacts, but contacts that are more pleasant than deep: "Beyond polite phrases, the Japanese speaks very little, particularly about himself."[3]

The avoidance of frank or full disclosure of interior experience is reflected not only in the findings of this study but in many commentaries on social behavior in Japan. James Moloney, for example, remarks that "There are vast areas of behavior about which the ordinary Japanese may be unwilling to talk freely."[4] Conversation, according to Bernard Krisher, is founded on an "economy of words," with couples often spending a lifetime together without ever discussing their feelings with one another.[5] There appears to be strong cultural resistance to excessive verbalization and a compensating reverencing of silence and less explicit forms of expression. Many Japanese aphorisms reflect this cultural attitude. Talkative persons, for example, are characterized as resembling a "paper carp in May." Like these inflated banners, talkative people consist only of huge open mouths with nothing but air inside.

If verbal disclosure among Japanese is restricted, and is consistent with cultural attributes such as "reserved," "cautious," "evasive," and "silent," so is the extent of verbal expression among Americans more uninhibited and equally consistent with cultural traits such as "talkative," "frank," and "self-assertive." If one society favors a "restrained self," the other favors an "unrestrained self"; where one encourages "contraction," the other encourages "expansion." Those in the United States who are inarticulate, verbally vague or clumsy with words, and those unwilling to contribute or express their views, have limited influence. Status and respect are accorded people with unusual capacity for defining problems and mobilizing support for their solution. An appetite or aptitude for expressing the self verbally seems differently valued in these two cultures.

LEVEL OF DISCLOSURE BY TOPIC

Interpersonal encounters move through a more or less patterned sequence. People talk first in more formal ways. The subject matter is more distant than self-revealing (Tastes). Gradually, after an appropriate period of exploratory testing, conversants move to more personal levels of talk (Opinions, Work). Finally, as mutual trust grows between them, they may drop their defenses and exchange more private feelings (Personal and Physical). Not only does the topical focus change with time, but also the level of disclosure deepens on each topic. If so, the findings of this study suggest that among Japanese this is often an incomplete process; the topical progression is interrupted earlier and is less often carried to the point of deep mutual sharing. Though the same overall pattern undoubtedly appears in American conversations, they seem to move more quickly and more consistently to the final stages. Clearly neither culture always completes this process; each favors some restriction upon the sharing of inner meanings.

The average level of verbal disclosure can easily be computed for each topical area. The figures presented in Table 1 reinforce the earlier conclusion drawn from overall averages. Americans showed a consistently higher level of self-revelation on all topics. In fact, their level of disclosure on the least appealing topic in both cultures equaled or surpassed the level of disclosure of Japanese on all but the most preferred topic. That is, Americans shared nearly as much of themselves with regard to physical and sexual adequacy as the Japanese did with regard to their preferences in food, music, reading materials, and television programs.

Table 1   Average Disclosure on Conversational Topics

	Japanese	American
Average Disclosure on All Topics (To All Persons)	75	112
Average Disclosure on All Topics (To Intimates)	100	144
Average Disclosure by Topic (To Intimates):		
Interests/Tastes	126	163
Work/Studies	113	162
Opinions on Public Issues	107	151
Financial	96	143
Personality	90	129
Physical	69	113

Again, individual patterns of communication within specific topics were revealing, and convey some of the uniqueness of the responses. What often appeared among both Americans and Japanese might be called "communicative blanks." Though most respondents talked with some intimacy to some people on some topics, there were areas of private experience that were blotted out completely. Some, for example, avoided discussing illness or debts or sex with anyone, while others avoided conversations that touched upon race relations or Communism or work handicaps. (Somewhat surprising was the finding that Americans disclosed slightly more to each other on the subject of sexual standards than on the subject of Communism.) It seems, then, that some people confine interaction to well-worn conversational ruts, often avoiding alternative topic material. Both healthy and symptomatic communicative patterns may be identifiable in these individual profiles of self-disclosure.

LEVEL OF DISCLOSURE TO SIGNIFICANT PERSONS

Finally, we may examine the relation between levels of disclosure and the persons with whom one converses. As noted earlier, both countries tended to rank potential communicative partners in similar ways. The precise averages for disclosure to all target persons, trusted target persons, and each of the specific persons identified in this study are presented in Table 2.

Table 2   Average Disclosure to Target Persons

	Japanese	American
Average Disclosure to All Partners (All Topics)	75	112
Average Disclosure to Intimates (All Topics)	100	144
Average Disclosure to Specific Target Persons:		
Same Sex Friend	122	157
Opposite Sex Friend	103	153
Mother	100	138
Father	75	126
Stranger	27	58
Untrusted Acquaintance	22	38

Again, the overall level of disclosure, regardless of whether all target persons or only trusted ones are included, was substantially lower among the Japanese than among the Americans. On the whole, the Japanese talked only in the most general terms even with their own parents and closest friends. The overall average for Americans with all target persons, including unknown and untrusted people, exceeded the level of personal exchange of Japanese in even their most intimate relationships. The figures for specific target persons, of course, elaborated this general trend. The extent of personal disclosure for the Japanese was roughly similar for male friend, female friend and mother, but then dropped sharply. For Americans the communication levels with male friend and female friend were nearly identical, and similar for father and mother. The level dropped more sharply only with strangers and untrusted people.

Yet it is important not to overlook the diversity that lies behind cultural norms. In both samples there were some who communicated deeply with their mothers, but others who communicated with them superficially. If some discussed a wide set of topics with their closest friends, there were others who were more discriminating about what they talk about with their same or opposite sex friends. Where some did not explore any topic with strangers in depth, others appeared to be more open with strangers than with their own parents. Still, despite such individual variability, the consistency within each cultural group was striking and the contrast between them was substantial.

DISCLOSURE TO FATHERS

Disclosure to fathers appeared to constitute a special instance of interpersonal communication. According to Jourard there is less sharing of the self with fathers than with mothers and peers in many cultures. If so, our data did not confirm that conclusion among Americans, but strongly reinforced that generalization among Japanese. There was substantially less disclosure to fathers than to any other intimate associates inside or outside the family. Americans apparently shared their private thoughts and feelings nearly as much with strangers as Japanese did with their own fathers. These findings tend to substantiate the saying that there are four things Japanese fear most: earthquakes, thunder, fire, and fathers. The inclusion of fathers on a list of purely physical occurrences appears to be more than accidental. At any rate the evidence supports Benedict's characterization of Japanese fathers as "depersonalized objects" and Doi's description of Japan as a "fatherless society."

A study of the communicative orientations of high school students corroborates these results. With regard to the question "With whom can you share your troubles most freely and frankly?" Japanese students ranked in order of attractiveness "mothers," "intimate friends," "older brothers and sisters," "younger brothers and sisters," and "fathers." When asked to identify the person with whom they shared the least communicatively, fathers were the nearly unanimous choice. These students reported saying little to their fathers beyond "Good morning" and "Goodnight." In contrast, mothers were the persons with whom the most was shared conversationally.[6]

When asked to identify the chief role of their father among those of "Friend," "Teacher," "Adviser," "Boss," "Partner," or "None of these," Japanese college students rarely chose "Friend." Many found none of the terms really suitable in describing his role. Among those who did, most preferred "Boss" or "Adviser." Only 11 percent regarded him as a "Friend."[7] Hiroyoshi Ishikawa reports a similar sentiment reflected in college students' perceptions of their fathers. They described him as "alone" or "isolated," a remote figure surrounded by forbidding walls that reduced conversation to commonplaces.[8]

CONCLUSION

Conversation is an activity sustained by two or more persons who use their private experience as a resource on which to build some sort of human relationship. The kind of relationship, of course, depends on their desire and capacity to maintain a deep or shallow linkage with each other. The findings of this study, reflected in the accompanying visual summary [Figure 2], suggest there is both universality and distinctiveness in the verbal style cultivated in each culture. (Comparisons along any dimension can be made simply by glancing down the columns to compare the extent of disclosure with each communicative partner, or across the rows to contrast the level of disclosure on each topic.)

These charts reveal that both cultures cultivate a similar set of attitudes toward people who are the potential receivers of messages. As communicative partners, peers are preferred to parents, parents are preferred to strangers. Within these categories there is a slight preference for same sex over opposite sex friends, but a more marked preference, especially in Japan, for mothers over fathers. Neither culture encourages verbal intimacy with strangers. Both societies also promote similar orientations toward a wide range of topics. In both, people tend to talk more about their tastes, opinions, and work than about their financial affairs, personal traits, and physical or sexual adequacy.

But here the similarity ends. These two countries appear to differ sharply in the depth of conversation they feel is appropriate in interpersonal encounters. Among Japanese there is substantially less disclosure of inner experience while among Americans substantially greater disclosure on all topics and with all persons. Where the former share their private thoughts in only a general way, among the latter these are revealed much more completely. Americans, for example, reveal themselves more completely on the most superficially explored topics

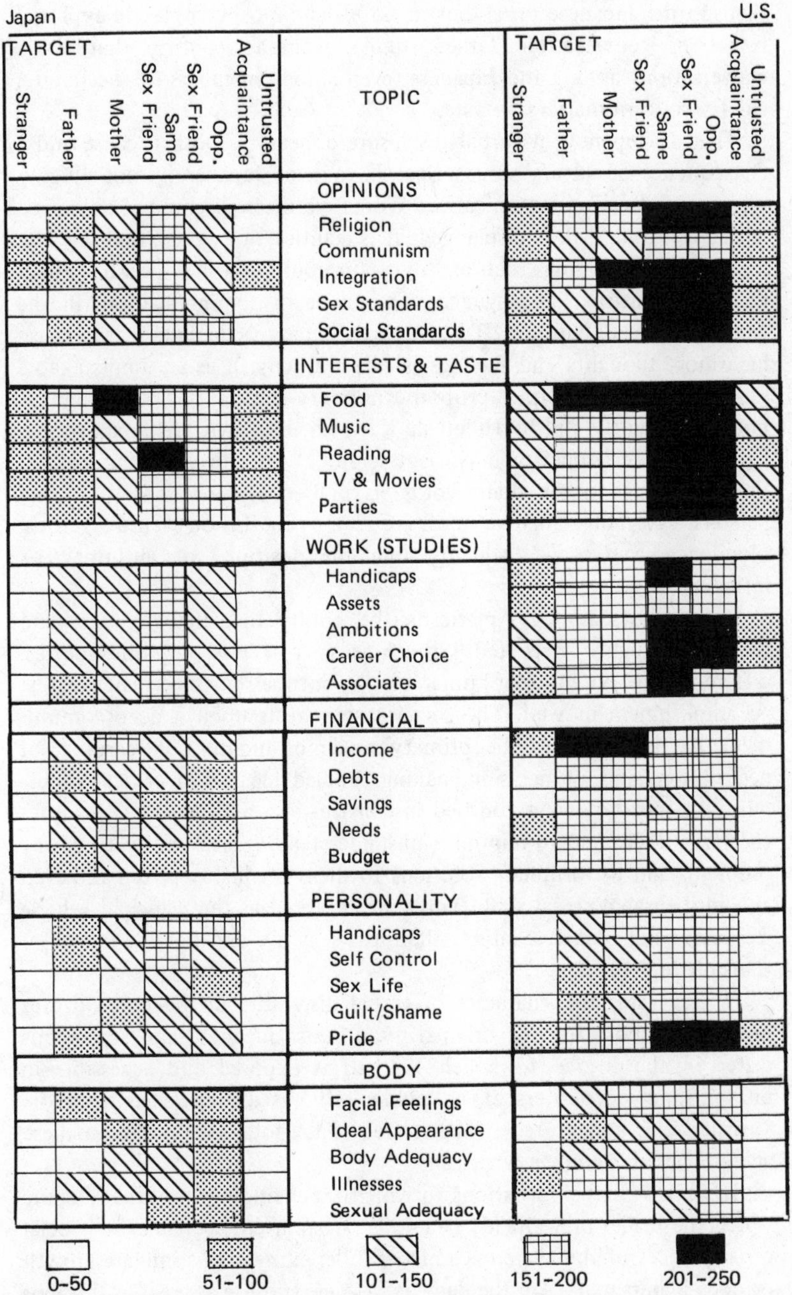

Figure 2 Summary of Topic, Target, and Level of Disclosure

than do the Japanese on all but the safest and most completely explored topics of conversation. Other studies seem to confirm that many conversations among the Japanese, even among members of the family, chiefly concern matters of taste.

This discrepancy in verbal disclosure appears as both a cause and a consequence of cultural values. Speech, to many Japanese, is not a highly regarded form of communication. Words are often discounted or viewed with suspicion. Talk is disparaged. It is realities, not words, that regulate human affairs. Sayings such as "By your mouth you shall perish" reflect this basic mistrust of language as a vehicle of communication. In the words of Inazo Nitobe, "To give in so many articulate words one's innermost thoughts and feelings is taken among us as an unmistakable sign that they are neither profound nor very sincere."[9] This thought is put more bluntly still by Hidetoshi Kato when he says, "In Japan speech is not silver or copper or brass—but scrap."[10] Intuitive communication, through means other than words, is praised and revered. Articulate persons, especially talkative ones, are seen as foolish or even dangerous. Eloquence can even disqualify one for positions of authority or influence.

In contrast, among Americans the ability to articulate ideas and feelings is highly respected. Speech is seen as not only the species-differentiating potential of human beings, but the source of their greatest accomplishment as well. The social system rests upon a deep commitment to discussion as the primary mode of inquiry, of learning, of negotiation, and of decision making. Valued ideals and critical procedures are nearly always codified in constitutions and contracts in order to clarify them and to minimize misunderstanding. An ability to define problems and to formulate solutions to them is a highly prized and even an indispensable social skill. Words are regarded as the principal vehicle for preserving human contact, the most sensitive and flexible means of transmitting experience.

In any case, the character of verbal disclosure in the two cultures provides support for the original hypothesis: Japanese and Americans differ in the degree to which the self is exposed and accessible in interpersonal encounters. The "public self" as distinguished from the "private self" constitutes a smaller area of the total self among Japanese and a larger area among Americans.

There are further questions to which these findings point, and some which the reader may already be asking: What are the personal and social consequences of this difference? Does fuller expression stimulate growth or does it impair it? Are the dangers of overexposure as great as those of underexposure? Is someone capable of communicating at deeper levels likely to communicate better interpersonally or interculturally? These questions can be explored, but first it would be helpful to know more of the character of nonverbal interaction and of the prevailing forms of defensive communication in these two cultures.

NOTES

1. Sidney Jourard, *The Transparent Self*, Van Nostrand, Princeton, 1964.

2. Sidney Jourard and Paul Lasakow, "A Research Approach to Self-Disclosure," *Journal of Abnormal and Social Psychology*, 56 (1958).

3. Robert Guillain, *The Japan I Love*, Tudor Press: New York, n.d., p. 11.

4. James Moloney, *Understanding the Japanese Mind*, p. 126, Philosophical Library, New York, 1954.

5. Bernard Krisher, "Who Are the Japanese?" *Newsweek*, July 17, 1972, pp. 12-13.

6. Keiko Hida, Shizue Nomonto, and Midori Shigeta. "Family Communication." Research Project, International Christian University, 1968.

7. Miwako Kaihara, "A Comparative Study of Selected Communication Patterns in Japan and Costa Rica." Senior Thesis, International Christian University, 1972.

8. Hiroyoshi Ishikawa, "Father Is Complicated Person," *Japan Times*, Jan. 1, 1973.

9. As quoted in Bernard Rudofsky, *The Kimono Mind*, p. 157, Tuttle, Tokyo, 1971.

10. Hidetoshi Kato, "Mutual Images: Japan and the United States Look at Each Other," paper presented at the Conference on Intercultural Communication, International Christian University, 1972.

Communication Overseas

Lorand B. Szalay and Glen H. Fisher

Reprinted by permission of Lorand B. Szalay, Institute of Comparative Social and Cultural Studies, and Glen H. Fisher, Foreign Service Institute. This material has been reproduced for instruction purposes at the Foreign Service Institute, Department of State. The graphic material has been provided by the Institute of Comparative Social and Cultural Studies, Inc., 4430 East West Highway, Suite 900, Washington, D.C. 20014.

When we travel abroad or undertake an overseas assignment, we expect some degree of communication problems. Our attention is fixed on the foreign language itself, on language lessons, and on how much English will be spoken. But the mistake most of us make is to assume that our problems in communication stem only from language differences, and that the problem can be resolved by completing a language course and learning how to translate our English thoughts into the appropriate foreign language.

We do realize, when we consider communication in a sense broader than language, that difficulty in getting meaning across is not limited to those who must speak across a language barrier. There are breakdowns in communication within our own country, and even within our own families where there is no language difference. Yet in using a foreign language or an interpretation, we dismiss our problems not too thoughtfully by simply saying "it loses something in translation." If our concern is really communication, the obvious question is: "Just what is it that is lost?"

Although our modern advances in communications technology have been impressive, and even revolutionary in nature, our understanding of the human dimension in communication is relatively limited. As communication involves ideas, images, and symbolic meaning, communication problems arise in any situation in which the life experiences of the communicators are not the same. These differences can range from simple matters of age and sex to living in differing cultures and speaking in entirely different languages.

Thus, while speaking and understanding the local language in a country we visit are certainly useful, one has to go beyond the words themselves and accepted translations to become aware of a complex series of psychological processes which, in final analysis, determine the course of human communication. The mechanical process of sending communications signals is comparatively simple: Signals emitted by the sender are picked up and decoded by the receiver. This, however, is only the first step in a very complex, psychological process of human communications. Whether the words we use faithfully perform their intended communication function depends mainly on the subjective reaction they elicit in the mental processes of the listener. If in decoding the signals the receiver attaches the same meaning to the words as the speaker had in mind when he used them, then the communication is a success. Usually it does not work out this perfectly. The communication is often only a partial success as the result of some degree of discrepancy between the psychological meanings attached to the words by the communicator and the receiver, respectively. The factors which impinge on psychological meaning can be varied and profound.

Important differences in effective meaning occur even at the primary levels within a society. When adults talk with their teenagers about the drug scene, the success of the discussion will depend greatly on the adults' ability to talk about drugs in a way that carries meaning in terms of adolescent concerns, interests, and actual experiences—and vice versa. In other words, the critical factor in this communication process is the subjective meaning which each attaches to the word "drug." The dictionary meaning is of limited use: "A substance with medical, physiological effects." This does not take into account the fact that adults and teenagers bring their own world of experiences and associations into the meaning of the word. Nor, for that matter, does it show how Christian Scientists, drug addicts, and physicians define the word from their own subjective experiences. The meaning of the word, then, is determined in large part by each person's characteristic *frame of reference.*

Further, there are additional ways to convey subjective meanings along with the choice of words, for communication in everyday life is normally a face-to-face verbal interaction process which is supported by many nonverbal elements. These include a variety of feedback mechanisms such as gestures, facial expressions, tone of voice, and the context of the interaction itself. Most of this goes on largely spontaneously and without conscious direction, although the whole speaking and listening process is highly complex and involves sophisticated communications skills. The speaker must be able to read all types of cues which indicate his listener's reactions, agreement, disagreement, lack of understanding, and so forth. With this ability he is able to choose a strategy in manipulating all the subtle factors which will convey his meaning. Every day we use these skills as a matter of course, and a good communicator learns to empathize enough with his listener to sense which approach will be effective. A successful salesman or politician, for example, develops almost a sixth sense to know what to emphasize to a potential customer or client, or what meaning or connotation to signal to achieve the desired impression. By experience, the salesman learns to adjust his sales pitch to the frame of reference of each type of customer.

The objective then, whether sought with conscious intent or not, is to capture the frame of reference. Even within a single country one finds groups of people whose frames of reference differ greatly. In these cases we are often able to communicate reasonably well, as both speaker and listener are familiar with these differences as a matter of normal experience and are able to shift frames of reference to accommodate the difference. But when we must communicate with people whose culture is foreign to us, the range of differences grows, and we are less prepared, on the basis of direct, firsthand experience, to cope with the mental framework confronting us. Therefore, a new communications task is involved simply to comprehend the subjective meaning of the words used in communication after the translation is made. Still greater effort is needed to read the nonverbal cues. And to the extent that subjective meanings reflect differences in underlying philosophy, assumptions, world view, or habits of logic, the complexity of the task is compounded.

CROSS-CULTURAL COMMUNICATION:
A PROCESS OF ADAPTING TO NEW FRAMES OF REFERENCE

In adjusting to an overseas communication situation, the first problem we must overcome is "egocentric bias." This involves the tacit assumption that if we say something that makes good sense to us, it should make sense to everyone else—a bias that is about as unrealistic as it is widespread. In some cases in our own culture, as when talking to children

or to mental patients, we are more aware that our statements may not be
automatically understood. But on the whole, our failures to communicate in our own society have not been dramatic enough to modify our
conviction that what we are saying is based on a type of universal
validity. Without previous foreign travel, one is hardly attuned to
recognizing his own egocentric bias or—perhaps better for this discussion—ethnocentric bias. And foreign experience does not necessarily
disabuse a person of this bias unless he is sensitized to some degree to
note more specifically the kind of communication problems which rise
out of cultural differences.

People in every country of the world develop their own particular
interests, perceptions, attitudes, and beliefs—that is, a characteristic
frame of reference within which they organize and interpret their life
experiences. How much people in a particular country differ from
Americans in this regard is hard to judge. The psychological factors
involved are difficult to define, observe, and predict. Nevertheless, tuning
in on this difference is essential to communication across a language
barrier.

That language and its meaning are so much a function of culture is
understandable, for language is one of the most fundamental systems of
culture and human society. It serves its purpose as it provides the means
to express, share, and transmit the ideas and experiences of the people
who practice the corresponding culture. Thus anthropologists have
suggested that making a transition from one language to another actually
involves going from one culture world to another. They further have
noted the close association between language structure and content and
characteristic habits of perceiving and reasoning on the part of its native
speakers. **How much particular language forms determine or limit
patterns of thinking and perceiving is much debated, but disassociating
language from some cultural context is a cognitive impossibility.**

A MODEL FOR CONTRASTING
CULTURAL FRAMES OF REFERENCE

If, as we have shown, communication is fundamentally a psychological
process, we need something more than the usual dictionary technique for
establishing the effective meaning of words and phrases. To translate
with optimum communication we need more than an English-Spanish
dictionary, for example, or an English-Japanese phrase book. Psychological meanings are not those found in dictionaries. In contrast to the
limited dictionary meaning based on convention and formal rules of use,
psychological meaning refers to the entire subjective reaction elicited by

a particular concept. This subjective association can be thought of in terms of components, of which one would naturally be the dictionary meaning. For example, "education" is "the process of schooling," but many other meanings would be attached to "education" based on what activities it involves, how it is valued, what purposes it serves. These components, which vary in saliency or "dominance," would determine which aspects of education are considered most important to the individual and therefore deserve special attention from the viewpoint of analyzing the communication process. If, for instance, you were urging technical education on people whose concept of education emphasized the social prestige of law and medical degrees, your communication would fall short of the mark.

Let us follow this sample word "education" in a further example in order to demonstrate the way in which these meanings can be conceptualized and charted to make this kind of analysis more explicit—to build a picture of what is involved in analyzing varying components of meaning, and varying dominance of these components. Consider the differences in psychological meaning which our word "education" would have for a priest and a football coach, confining the contrasts to American society for the moment. Based on what is commonly known of these two occupations, we can assume that they will agree on the importance of some of the possible components of meaning, and disagree on others, or at least assign differing importance to them. They would probably agree on school attendance, but disagree on the most desirable types of schools or curricula. They may agree on character development as a part of education, but the priest might more likely stress morality and the role of the church in the nurturing of character, while the coach might be more concerned with discipline, physical fitness, training, fame, desire to win fairly, and the like in building character.

To visualize this divergence in frames of reference, a visual aid is available in the techniques which have been used in an analytical approach called Associative Group Analysis (AGA). This is a word-association technique which, among other products, produces "semanto-graphs," as will be demonstrated below. When the technique is applied cross-culturally, the procedure is to select statistically valid sample groups of native speakers of the two languages concerned, and ask them to respond by free association to stimulus words in their respective languages—such as "socialism," "father," or "education" for the English speakers and the accepted translations for the other language group. When these methods are carefully applied and the results are analyzed, it is possible to chart salient differences in the components of subjective meaning, and differences in dominance or strength of these subjective meanings. Note how a semantograph would chart the differing frames of reference for the priest and coach above, even without a language barrier (see Figure 1).

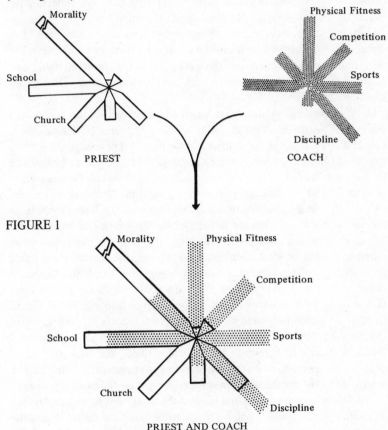

FIGURE 1

PRIEST AND COACH

In Figure 1, we see how the composition of the subjective reactions of the priest and coach to "education" compare in schematic form. The length of the bars expresses the importance and the strength of particular meaning components. The longer the bar, the more important that aspect or association with education is to that person. When the bars coincide and are long, both persons share and give importance to that component. Such provides the basis for easy communication between the priest and the coach. Nonshared elements, i.e., bars which do not coincide or agree in length, tend to increase the difficulty of communication.

This illustration shows the combination of subjective meaning reactions as well as the formal dictionary component. The subjective elements derive from the frame of reference of the person interpreting "education." For the priest, education contains strong religious elements (morality, virtue, church). The coach's subjective concept, reflecting his frame of reference, emphasizes sports, competition, and training. Combined, these two frames of reference form a *semantograph.* The radial direction of the bars is arbitrary, with the stronger components for one frame of reference on the left, the other on the right, and accommodation made for overlapping connotations or subjective meanings.

It is important to note that when this method is used in research work, the components are isolated by a free-association method. Therefore, this serves as evidence to which a knowledge of normal experience or cultural background can be added to gain an understanding of the contrasting frames of reference involved in a communication process. The above illustration suggests an additional important hypothesis: If the subjective, psychological meanings of individual words or themes such as education are influenced by the major components of a person's frame of reference, we may also expect these subjective meanings to tell us something about a more general characteristic frame of reference which would supply meaning for other words and themes in other communication situations. Thus the coach might carry over some of the same or consistent meaning components into his psychological reaction to words like "school," "teacher," or "sports." If this is tested and found to be the case, we find that something of an enduring and repetitive frame of reference has been described, and that this would allow one to predict that these meaning components would have a bearing in other instances in what we might call an "education domain."

All this becomes complicated beyond the intentions of this discussion. In technical application this approach is the basis for research into the contrasting meanings of translated language. It is also being used for developing lexicons which allow one to look up the meaning components for key words and phrases, to note the cultural context consistent with the psychological meanings presented and appreciate the consistency in frames of reference from one subject to the next.

Empirical research in this direction has only begun. But the logic of the approach itself may provide a useful intellectual orientation for anyone working with a foreign language and concerned with communication rather than merely accepted translation. Therefore, the following comparisons of American and Korean meanings are presented as samples of the kind of results obtained when the AGA analysis is applied in an actual communications research project. In this case they provide insight into the nature and scope of cultural differences which affect communication between native speakers of English and Korean. The key words and phrases presented here are drawn from an extensive project. The explanation of the analytic technique and computations may be found in the large prototype communication lexicon which was produced covering social, national, and motivational domains.

Empirical research is needed to achieve the level of analytic completeness attempted in the samples which follow, something which is out of the question in routine communications situations. However, much is to be gained by carrying around in one's head a picture of a semantograph—circles, bars, components, and all—as a reminder of what one is searching for when learning or using a new language, for it is in recognizing the existence of differing patterns of underlying meaning that the full dimensions of a cross-cultural communication process can be seen.

In order to convey to the reader the nature and range of cultural meanings, two groups of themes, one on family and one on political systems, will be presented.

"FAMILY"

To illustrate some consistent cultural trends in the area of "family," the analysis of the following four themes is presented: FAMILY, FATHER, FILIAL DUTY, and ANCESTORS.

FAMILY
Summary of Main Components of Cultural Meanings

1. CHILDREN, BROTHER, SISTER (U.S.: 593; K: 737). This component reflects preoccupation with *siblings* (K: 251) and *children* (U.S.: 133; K: 19) and is stronger for Koreans, although it is also weighty for the Americans. Both groups think more in terms of brother and sister rather than *son* and *daughter*.

2. RELATIVES (U.S.: 218; K: 465). Koreans pay a great deal of attention to various *family members* (K: 168) and *relatives* (K: 104; U.S.: 83), especially those belonging to the older generation: *grandmother* (K: 61; U.S.: 13) and *grandfather* (K: 74; U.S.: 8).

3. HAPPINESS, FUN (U.S.: 166; K: 183). FAMILY as a source of emotional satisfaction is about equally emphasized by Americans and Koreans: *happiness* (U.S.: 94; K: 58), *harmony* (K: 74), and *fun* (U.S.: 29).

U.S. and Korean Meanings
FAMILY
가 족

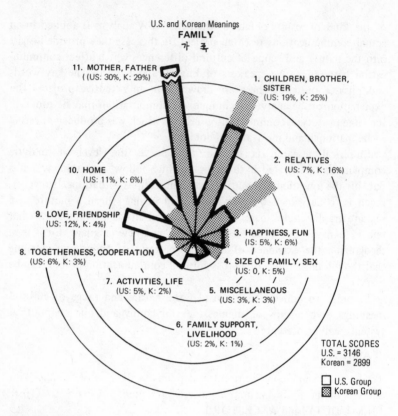

11. MOTHER, FATHER
((US: 30%, K: 29%)

1. CHILDREN, BROTHER, SISTER
(US: 19%, K: 25%)

2. RELATIVES
(US: 7%, K: 16%)

10. HOME
(US: 11%, K: 6%)

9. LOVE, FRIENDSHIP
(US: 12%, K: 4%)

8. TOGETHERNESS, COOPERATION
(US: 6%, K: 3%)

3. HAPPINESS, FUN
(IS: 5%, K: 6%)

4. SIZE OF FAMILY, SEX
(US: 0, K: 5%)

7. ACTIVITIES, LIFE
(US: 5%, K: 2%)

5. MISCELLANEOUS
(US: 3%, K: 3%)

6. FAMILY SUPPORT, LIVELIHOOD
(US: 2%, K: 1%)

TOTAL SCORES
U.S. = 3146
Korean = 2899

☐ U.S. Group
▨ Korean Group

U.S. GROUPS

The main emphasis is on the nuclear family: MOTHER, FATHER, and CHILDREN. RELATIVES receive less attention. Beyond the people included in the U.S. image of the FAMILY, emotional ties and life conditions receive increasing attention. LOVE and FRIENDSHIP are the important ties accounting for the climate in the HOME, involving TOGETHERNESS, shared ACTIVITIES, and HAPPINESS.

KOREAN GROUPS

In the Korean's image of FAMILY, the role of parents, MOTHER AND FATHER, is about as pervasive as in the American's image. Nonetheless, CHILDREN and also RELATIVES occupy a more important part of this image for Koreans than for Americans. They emphasize more the older and the male members of the FAMILY (*father, grandfather, brother*). The emotional climate, HAPPINESS, and harmony are given distinct attention. There is some concern expressed with the SIZE OF THE FAMILY.

4. SIZE OF FAMILY, SEX (U.S.: 15; K: 136). Koreans show stronger concern with the family size, sex differences, and *family planning* (33).

6. FAMILY SUPPORT, LIVELIHOOD (U.S.: 58; K: 28). This is a small, primarily U.S. component, in which the family *car* (40) represents the largest response.

7. ACTIVITIES, LIVING (U.S.: 147; K: 62). The common events, activities, and shared family experiences play a somewhat greater role in the U.S. image: *dinner, reunions, outings, picnics, vacations.*

8. TOGETHERNESS, COOPERATION (U.S.: 192; K: 77). This component further reinforces the impression of stronger U.S. emphasis on family unity, on living and working together: *togetherness* (U.S.: 89), *close* (U.S.: 31), *unit* (U.S.: 25). The Koreans mention family *cooperation* (34), *dependence* (10), and *intimacy* (10).

9. LOVE, FRIENDSHIP (U.S.: 367; K: 120). The emotional ties of *love* (U.S.: 184; K: 91) and *friendship* (U.S.: 82) apparently play a stronger role in the U.S. image of the family. The emphasis on friendship appears to be especially characteristic of the American group.

10. HOME (U.S.: 111; K: 49). This strong, primarily U.S. component is consistent with the content of the previous components emphasizing love, togetherness, and shared life.

11. MOTHER, FATHER (U.S.: 951; K: 840). This is the strongest component for both groups. *Mother* (U.S.: 328; K: 287) appears to have a slightly greater role for Americans, while the *father* (U.S.: 257; K: 318) is slightly more emphasized by the Koreans. There are also more U.S. references to *wife* (U.S.: 203; K: 36), which reflects that a greater percentage of the U.S. subjects were married at the time of the testing.

FATHER
Summary of Main Components of Cultural Meanings

1. HOME, FAMILY, RELATIVES (U.S.: 324; K: 331). In both images there is a strong component expressing that father is a part of the *home* (U.S.: 131; K: 112) and *family* (U.S.: 83; K: 23). While family is a narrower concept for Americans, it involves a more extensive network of relationships for the Koreans: *uncle, nephew, grandfather, ancestor.*

2. MAN (U.S.: 112; K: 301). The Koreans greatly emphasize the manliness of the ,father (*male* 260, *man* 41). What this exactly means becomes more apparent from some of the following categories.

3. LEADER, PROTECTOR (U.S.: 140; K: 204). For the Koreans the father is *master of the family* (108), who because of his role and age assumes an elevated position. This leadership role receives much less emphasis from the U.S. groups (*leader* 49, *head of house* 29).

4. RESPECT, FILIAL DUTY (U.S.: 103; K: 172). The idea of *respect* for the father (U.S.: 80; K: 61) is shared by both groups. *Filial*

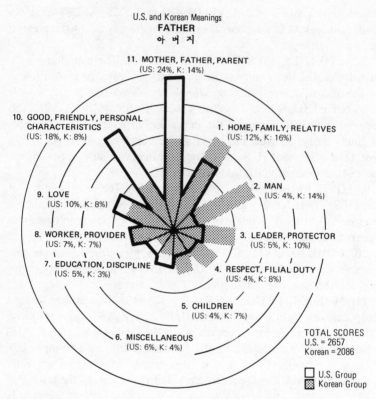

U.S. and Korean Meanings
FATHER
아 버 지

11. MOTHER, FATHER, PARENT
(US: 24%, K: 14%)

10. GOOD, FRIENDLY, PERSONAL
CHARACTERISTICS
(US: 18%, K: 8%)

1. HOME, FAMILY, RELATIVES
(US: 12%, K: 16%)

2. MAN
(US: 4%, K: 14%)

9. LOVE
(US: 10%, K: 8%)

8. WORKER, PROVIDER
(US: 7%, K: 7%)

3. LEADER, PROTECTOR
(US: 5%, K: 10%)

7. EDUCATION, DISCIPLINE
(US: 5%, K: 3%)

4. RESPECT, FILIAL DUTY
(US: 4%, K: 8%)

5. CHILDREN
(US: 4%, K: 7%)

6. MISCELLANEOUS
(US: 6%, K: 4%)

TOTAL SCORES
U.S. = 2657
Korean = 2086

☐ U.S. Group
▨ Korean Group

U.S. GROUPS

The U.S. image of FATHER shows a few differences in emphasis. His relationship to MOTHER is emphasized as the critical tie underlying the American family. His most outstanding characteristics are that he is GOOD and FRIENDLY. LOVE is the prevalent tie. He is a WORKER and PROVIDER and has an important role in EDUCATION and in maintaining DISCIPLINE. In this sense he is a LEADER and PROTECTOR.

KOREAN GROUPS

In the Korean context, FAMILY implies an extended network of relatives. The elevated position of the FATHER in this network derives apparently from his traditional role as the master of the family. This idea is supported by the high cultural values placed on men (manliness) and age (elderliness). From the part of the children, this role is accepted with the attitude of FILIAL DUTY. The image of FATHER conveys the idea of authority and strength, which, as the reactions show, does not preclude love.

duty (79) and dignity (20), however, constitute characteristically Korean values of considerable importance.

5. CHILDREN (U.S.: 102; K: 146). In both the American and Korean context, the image of the father involves having children. The

weight of the Korean component is somewhat heavier. The father-son relationship is emphasized by both groups.

7. EDUCATION, DISCIPLINE (U.S.: 132; K: 72). The role of the father in the education of his children is about equally emphasized by both culture groups. Nonetheless, the idea of *help*, being *helpful* (50) is emphasized by the American groups. The responsibility of disciplining the children is also closely associated with the father by Americans.

8. WORKER, PROVIDER (U.S.: 196; K: 144). The role of the father as *working* (102) to support his family is especially strong in the American perception of father. The Koreans show much recognition of the *hardships* (46) involved in earning enough *money* (47) for living.

9. LOVE (U.S.: 276; K: 172). FATHER has an especially strong emotional component for the U.S. group (*love* 223). The Korean references to *love* (99) are less weighty but still sizable. The Koreans mention separation from their father (*wish to see* 55); the Americans mention *missing* (26) their father.

10. GOOD, FRIENDLY, PERSONAL CHARACTERISTICS (U.S.: 477; K: 157). Americans view the father in a relationship based on *friendship* (U.S.: 70; K: 10) and *fun* (U.S.: 26) and describe him as *good* (106), *kind* (53), and *strong* (39). The Koreans characterize the father in terms of *sternness* (44) and *graciousness* (28).

11. MOTHER, FATHER, PARENT (U.S.: 629; K: 293). One of the most important aspects in the American image of father is his relationship to *mother* (U.S.: 346; K: 189). This suggests the American focus on the nuclear family is built on the close dualistic ties of father and mother, in contrast to the Korean concept of family, which involves extended family ties.

FILIAL DUTY
Summary of Main Components of Cultural Meanings

1. PARENTS, MOTHER, FATHER (U.S.: 56; K: 1004). This largest Korean component involves especially heavy references to *parents* (461) in general and to *father* (219) and *mother* (226) in particular. References to *grandparents* (98) are distinct but less sizable.

2. SON, DAUGHTER, FAMILY (U.S.: 38; K: 317). Heavy Korean references to *son* in particular suggest that this attitude toward the parents involves at least tacitly the son more than the daughter. *Ancestors* and *ancestor worship* (34) are also a part of FILIAL DUTY to the Koreans.

3. SINCERITY, RESPECT, LOVE (U.S.: 138; K: 277). This is again primarily a Korean component. While the U.S. groups emphasize *love* (53), the Koreans focus on *sincerity* (88) and *respect* (70).

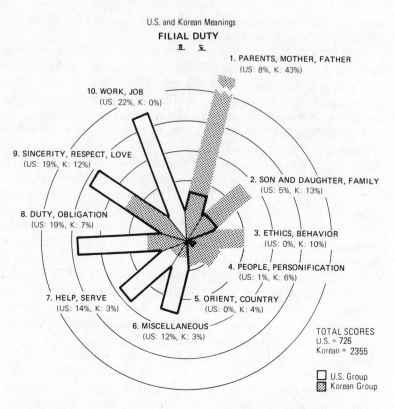

U.S. and Korean Meanings
FILIAL DUTY
孝 도

1. PARENTS, MOTHER, FATHER
(US: 8%, K: 43%)

10. WORK, JOB
(US: 22%, K: 0%)

9. SINCERITY, RESPECT, LOVE
(US: 19%, K: 12%)

2. SON AND DAUGHTER, FAMILY
(US: 5%, K: 13%)

8. DUTY, OBLIGATION
(US: 19%, K: 7%)

3. ETHICS, BEHAVIOR
(US: 0%, K: 10%)

4. PEOPLE, PERSONIFICATION
(US: 1%, K: 6%)

7. HELP, SERVE
(US: 14%, K: 3%)

5. ORIENT, COUNTRY
(US: 0%, K: 4%)

6. MISCELLANEOUS
(US: 12%, K: 3%)

TOTAL SCORES
U.S. = 726
Korean = 2355

□ U.S. Group
▨ Korean Group

U.S. GROUPS

For Americans this theme is generally unknown and relatively meaningless. With its rudimentary denotation, it refers to the attitudes of LOVE, *responsibility,* and *obligation.* As an activity, it suggests HELP, mainly menial performance. The idea of DUTY elicits strong identification with WORK, JOB. As is apparent, the U.S. interpretation of FILIAL DUTY is preconditioned mainly by its component parts ("filial" and "duty") and is little related to the original concept.

KOREAN GROUPS

As the four times larger score expresses, this concept is more culturally meaningful for the Koreans. It refers to a particular relationship toward the PARENTS by the children: SON AND DAUGHTER. This relationship involves the attitudes of SINCERITY and RESPECT as well as the virtues of *loyalty, obedience, service,* and *sacrifice.* It has its historic roots in the Confucian ETHICS with contemporary implications for PEOPLE and their interpersonal relationships.

4. ETHICS, BEHAVIOR (U.S. 0; K: 232). The largest response, *Confucius* (48), reflects the ethical origin of this concept. Other strong associations were *courtesy* (24), *piety* (29), and *honesty* (18). No U.S. reference was made to this ethical-religious component.

6. DUTY, OBLIGATION (U.S.: 138; K: 167). The strongest Korean duties are *loyalty* (54) and *obedience* (50); for the U.S. groups, *responsibility* (45) and *obligation* (25) score the highest.

7. PEOPLE, PERSONIFICATION (U.S.: 7; K: 143). This predominantly Korean component focuses on characterisic personifications of this virtuous attitude. *Sim chong* (51) is mentioned as a classical symbol of filial piety, since she sacrificed her life for this cause.

8. ORIENT, COUNTRY (U.S.: 0; K: 83). The Koreans express their awareness that FILIAL DUTY is fundamentally an oriental concept.

9. HELP, SERVE (U.S.: 129; K: 69). The American emphasis is on *help* (33) and *menial* work (28); the Koreans stress the idea of *serving* (37), *sacrifice* (9), and *devotion* (9).

10. WORK, JOB (U.S.: 135; K: 0). This purely U.S. component indicates that duty has a strong English connotation of *work* (93) and manual labor.

ANCESTORS
Summary of Main Components of Cultural Meanings

1. FOREFATHERS, GRANDPARENTS, RELATIVES (U.S.: 546; K: 824). This is an especially strong Korean component with almost exclusive concentration on the male lineage: *grandfather* (420), *great grandfather* (77), *forefather* (125). The U.S. group refers more to family with emphasis on grandparents, both *grandfather* (126) and *grandmother* (47).

2. RITES, VENERATION, WORSHIP (U.S.: 39; K: 384). This primarily Korean component expresses semi-religious attitudes and behavior such as *veneration* (84) and *respect* (34). These are manifested in *rites* (198), having religious, ethical foundation in Confucianism.

3. GRAVE, DEAD (U.S.: 91; K: 233). This predominantly Korean component also is related to the ceremonial aspects of ancestor worship and respect: visiting the *graves* (106). This component indicates that ancestors are an active part of the Koreans' daily lives.

4. LEGENDARY FIGURES (U.S.: 0; K: 144). References to famous personalities of history and legend are exclusively Korean.

6. PREHISTORIC MAN, APE (U.S.: 73; K: 35). The main U.S. focus is on ancient and subhuman predecessors to man as identified by disciplines such as anthropology and zoology with regard to phylogenetic evolution: *Adam* (10), *cave man* (19), *Neanderthal* (13), *Java man* (11).

7. HISTORY, TRADITION (U.S.: 152; K: 84). The U.S. emphasis is on *history* (69) and historical heritage (*Mayflower*); the Korean is more on *tradition* (28) and *custom* (5).

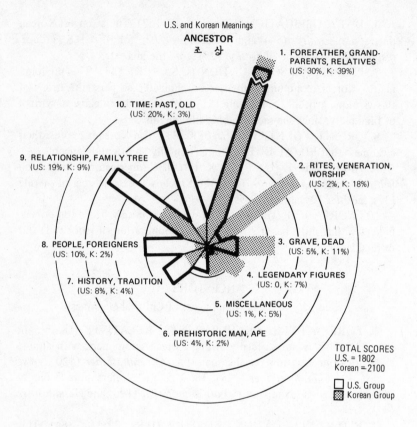

U.S. and Korean Meanings
ANCESTOR
조 상

1. FOREFATHER, GRAND-
   PARENTS, RELATIVES
   (US: 30%, K: 39%)

10. TIME: PAST, OLD
    (US: 20%, K: 3%)

9. RELATIONSHIP, FAMILY TREE
   (US: 19%, K: 9%)

2. RITES, VENERATION,
   WORSHIP
   (US: 2%, K: 18%)

8. PEOPLE, FOREIGNERS
   (US: 10%, K: 2%)

3. GRAVE, DEAD
   (US: 5%, K: 11%)

7. HISTORY, TRADITION
   (US: 8%, K: 4%)

4. LEGENDARY FIGURES
   (US: 0, K: 7%)

5. MISCELLANEOUS
   (US: 1%, K: 5%)

6. PREHISTORIC MAN, APE
   (US: 4%, K: 2%)

TOTAL SCORES
U.S. = 1802
Korean = 2100

☐ U.S. Group
▨ Korean Group

U.S. GROUPS

As a primary meaning, ANCESTOR refers to progenitors, particularly GRANDPARENTS and *great grandparents*, with emphasis on consanguine RELATIONS–deceased relatives belonging to the FAMILY TREE. More distant in the past are those Americans who played a major part in HISTORY (*Mayflower*) and also FOREIGNERS, the immigrants from other countries and continents. ANCESTOR also refers to an even more distant category: PREHISTORIC MAN, APE. This explains why the American attitudes toward ANCESTORS are weak and mixed, while the dimension of TIME: PAST, OLD acquires salience.

KOREAN GROUPS

As expressed by the substantially higher score, this theme is more dominant for the Korean groups. It refers to FOREFATHERS, with emphasis on male predecessors. The Koreans also show concern with the VENERATION of ANCESTORS, involving moral, religious principles and attitudes frequently labelled as "ancestor worship." As overt manifestations this includes services at the GRAVE, RITES. All the ideas related to this concept are viewed as an element of the Korean cultural HISTORY, TRADITION. Ancestors are not old, forgotten relatives, but command contemporary influence and recognition as an active part of the daily lives of Koreans.

8. PEOPLE, FOREIGNERS (U.S.: 187; K: 33). This primarily U.S. component contains numerous references to *people* (85) and foreign nations—*Europe* (10), *Ireland* (24), *Germany* (15)—reflecting the multinational background of Americans. The only Korean response refers to ANCESTORS as *human beings* (33).

9. RELATIONSHIP, FAMILY TREE (U.S.: 335; K: 196). The U.S. focus is on *relatives* (216) in the sense of consanguinity, as is reflected by the *family tree* (48) and *descendants* (52). Comparable Korean reactions refer to *ties* (25), *generations* (55), and *genealogy* (58).

10. TIME: PAST, OLD (U.S.: 354; K: 59). This is mainly a U.S. component emphasizing the time dimension of the *past* (97), an idea not entirely free from connotations of remoteness and irrelevance— *long ago* (32), *unknown* (6).

Trends of Cultural Interpretation in the Area of Family   There are some consistent response trends which reveal culturally characteristic patterns of family structure, role relations, as well as value orientations.

The U.S. focus is on the father and mother. This is also true for the Koreans, but they place greater emphasis on children than do the Americans. Emphasis on the father and mother suggests a horizontal relationship, while emphasis on parents and children suggests a fundamentally vertical relationship. The Koreans' description of the father as master, leader, and head of the family indicates the father's roles within the Korean family.

Sex differences produce strong role differentiation between mother and father within the Korean family where maleness and age constitute preferential status. There is consistently more emphasis on male relatives and on the older generation by Koreans than by Americans.

The generally stronger emphasis on relatives by the Koreans reflects that the extended family is more characteristic of the Korean culture while the nuclear family limited to parents and children is more characteristic of the American.

The organizational characteristics of the family predispose different types of relationships between the members of the family. The Americans emphasize love and friendship as the main family ties. This implies that the existence of the American family is dependent on the personal feelings the members attach to each other. On the other hand, the fact that the Koreans place less emphasis on feelings suggests that the Korean family is a more stable, institutionalized unit, whose permanence is taken for granted.

Compared to Americans, the Koreans refer more to filial duty and respect, which suggests more traditional ties and interrelations that involve subordination rather than equality. The greater Korean emphasis on tradition is consistent with their strong concern with ancestors—another case in which Koreans see a superior (ancestor) and subordinate (Korean individual) relationship. The similar type of relationship between the Korean parent and child is consistent with the idea of education as a strong function of the Korean family.

The Americans make consistently heavy references to goodness and kindness and features of likability and sociability. For the Americans, the idea of home is especially central, which is a framework for living together—working, providing as well as entertainment and fun.

"POLITICAL SYSTEMS"

Three themes have been selected on "political systems" to show how Koreans and Americans perceive important political concepts differently. They are GOVERNMENT, CAPITALISM, and SOCIALISM.

GOVERNMENT (See page 183 for chart.)
Summary of Main Components of Cultural Meanings

1. NATION, COUNTRY, PEOPLE (U.S.: 183; K: 512). This largest Korean meaning component suggests that the most salient aspect of the GOVERNMENT is that it represents the *nation* (216). The focus here is not on the faithful representation of the will of the people, but on government as a symbol of the nation, protecting the country's interests and enhancing its prestige. For the U.S. group, however, GOVERNMENT is closely related to the *people* (U.S.: 134; K: 124).

2. PRESIDENT, EXECUTIVE BRANCH (U.S.: 187; K: 473). The most important element of the government is the executive branch, headed by the *president* (U.S.: 76; K: 173), which receives especially emphatic attention from the Korean groups.

3. LEGISLATIVE, JUDICIARY BRANCHES (U.S.: 143; K: 167). The main difference between the two cultural groups is that the American references to legislative bodies include *Congress* (80), *Senate* (34), and *House* (12); the Koreans refer only to the *National Assembly* (118), which is unicameral.

5. POLITICS (U.S.: 108; K: 99). The U.S. group appears to pay more attention to *politics* (U.S.: 59; K: 31) and *elections* (U.S.: 39; K: 22). At the same time, the Koreans pay distinct attention to the *government party* (34) and its *opposition* (12), which represent an alien notion to the independent U.S. party system.

6. ARMED FORCES (U.S.: 126; K: 16). This distinct component is characteristic of the American groups. It shows that the Americans perceive the armed forces as a part of the government.

Main Meaning Components for U. S. and Korean Groups

GOVERNMENT

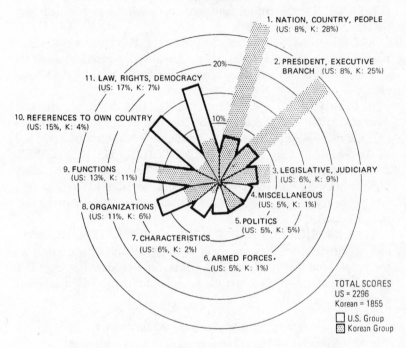

1. NATION, COUNTRY, PEOPLE (US: 8%, K: 28%)

2. PRESIDENT, EXECUTIVE BRANCH (US: 8%, K: 25%)

11. LAW, RIGHTS, DEMOCRACY (US: 17%, K: 7%)

10. REFERENCES TO OWN COUNTRY (US: 15%, K: 4%)

9. FUNCTIONS (US: 13%, K: 11%)

8. ORGANIZATIONS (US: 11%, K: 6%)

7. CHARACTERISTICS (US: 6%, K: 2%)

3. LEGISLATIVE, JUDICIARY (US: 6%, K: 9%)

4. MISCELLANEOUS (US: 5%, K: 1%)

5. POLITICS (US: 5%, K: 5%)

6. ARMED FORCES (US: 5%, K: 1%)

20%

10%

TOTAL SCORES
US = 2296
Korean = 1855

☐ U.S. Group
▨ Korean Group

U.S. GROUPS

A central idea expressed by this cultural group is that the GOVERNMENT exists for the people and must provide LAW, RIGHTS, and DEMOCRACY for the individual. The American group is well aware of the complex, differentiated structure of their government (ORGANIZATIONS, AGENCIES–OFFICIALS). The executive branch seems most representative of the government, followed closely by the legislative; only slight mention is made of the judicial branch. The CHARACTERISTICS of government are more negative than positive. The ARMED FORCES are also considered to be a part of the U.S. government.

KOREAN GROUPS

NATION, COUNTRY, PEOPLE, the largest Korean meaning component, suggests that GOVERNMENT is conceived at a collective, national level. The Korean idea of GOVERNMENT seems to be centered around the executive branch—more specifically, on the president and his cabinet. The government is thus fundamentally identified by its top leadership as representatives of the nation. This idea of leadership embodies offices more than personalities. The functions of the government are expressed mainly in terms of administration, management, and policymaking.

7. CHARACTERISTICS (U.S.: 137; K: 42). The Americans are especially concerned with the size (*big, large* 26) and strength of the GOVERNMENT; the critical sentiments outweigh the positive (*corrupt, red tape, inefficient, injustice*).

8. ORGANIZATIONS (U.S.: 256; K: 121). This component reflects strong concern with the bureaucratic, administrative organizations of the government. It is nearly twice as large for the American as for the Korean groups.

9. FUNCTIONS (U.S.: 303; K: 208). This category reflects a somewhat stronger U.S. concern. The largest U.S. responses are *taxation* (79) and *rule* (64); the largest Korean response is *administration* (87).

10. REFERENCES TO OWN COUNTRY (U.S.: 335; K: 66). This is the second largest American category, probably because of the heavy response *U.S.* (271). The concept of "U.S. government" represents a high-frequency idiom which establishes a close connection between U.S. and government.

11. LAW, RIGHTS, DEMOCRACY (U.S.: 393; K: 139). The central idea of this largest U.S. component is that GOVERNMENT stands for the people, for their personal legal rights, for freedom. The large U.S. response *law* (102) implies that the power and activities of a democratic government are controlled by law.

CAPITALISM (See page 185 for chart.)
Summary of Main Components of Cultural Meanings

1. MONEY (U.S.: 169; K: 398). This primarily Korean category suggests that the financial aspects of CAPITALISM are the most salient: *money* (U.S.: 129; K: 336), *capital* (U.S.: 21; K: 21).

2. OWN AND OTHER NATIONS (U.S.: 236; K: 315). For both groups, the country most representative of the idea of CAPITALISM is the *United States* (U.S.: 211; K: 205). Koreans also make sizable references to their own country (76).

3. RICH AND POOR (U.S.: 6; K: 309). By contrasting richness (118) with poverty (37) this large Korean component carries negative connotations. It has more social than economic implications of inequality.

4. DEMOCRACY, FREEDOM (U.S.: 94; K: 232). In this primarily Korean component, a close connection is seen between CAPITALISM and the political ideals of *democracy* (U.S.: 27; K: 132): *freedom* (U.S.: 67; K: 39), *equality* (K: 20), *rights* (K: 15).

5. NATION, COUNTRY, SOCIETY (U.S.: 90; K: 143). CAPITALISM is viewed as an economic system characteristic of particular countries. This component is slightly stronger for the Korean than the U.S. groups.

Main Meaning Components for U.S. and Korean Groups

CAPITALISM

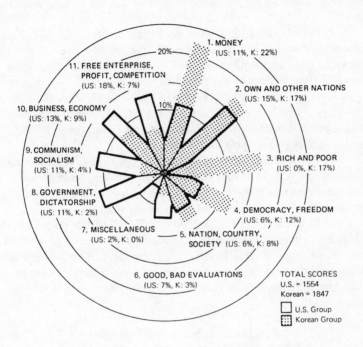

1. MONEY (US: 11%, K: 22%)

11. FREE ENTERPRISE, PROFIT, COMPETITION (US: 18%, K: 7%)

10. BUSINESS, ECONOMY (US: 13%, K: 9%)

9. COMMUNISM, SOCIALISM (US: 11%, K: 4%)

8. GOVERNMENT, DICTATORSHIP (US: 11%, K: 2%)

7. MISCELLANEOUS (US: 2%, K: 0%)

2. OWN AND OTHER NATIONS (US: 15%, K: 17%)

3. RICH AND POOR (US: 0%, K: 17%)

4. DEMOCRACY, FREEDOM (US: 6%, K: 12%)

5. NATION, COUNTRY, SOCIETY (US: 6%, K: 8%)

6. GOOD, BAD EVALUATIONS (US: 7%, K: 3%)

TOTAL SCORES
U.S. = 1554
Korean = 1847

☐ U.S. Group
▦ Korean Group

U.S. GROUPS

The combined focus on NATION, COUNTRY, SOCIETY, and particularly on OWN AND OTHER NATIONS, suggests that for the U.S. groups the large-scale, systemic aspects of CAPITALISM are the most prevalent. Their OWN NATION is the foremost representative of CAPITALISM. FREE ENTERPRISE, PROFIT, COMPETITION are the main operational principles of the system, which is based on THE ECONOMY, BUSINESS and MONEY. Components with sociopolitical content such as DEMOCRACY, FREEDOM and RICH AND POOR have low salience. For Americans, CAPITALISM is mainly an economic concept.

KOREAN GROUPS

The Koreans have not only an economic but also a highly sociopolitical conception of CAPITALISM. The categories dealing with NATIONS (OWN AND OTHER NATIONS and NATION, COUNTRY, SOCIETY) suggest that Koreans also think of CAPITALISM as a system characteristic of specific nations. They view the United States as the main representative of CAPITALISM and, to a lesser extent, also associate their own country with CAPITALISM. Their heavy focus on DEMOCRACY, FREEDOM and on the strong contrast of the RICH AND POOR indicates that for Koreans CAPITALISM has more sociopolitical connotations than for Americans.

6. GOOD, BAD EVALUATIONS (U.S.: 105; K: 50). Responses indicating positive evaluation of CAPITALISM are mostly American (*good, ideal, needed*); the negative, mostly Korean (*corruption, cruel, unfair*).

8. GOVERNMENT, DICTATORSHIP (U.S.: 169: K: 30). This is almost exclusively a U.S. component, particularly stressed by U.S. workers, who apparently view their government as capitalistic or as promoting the interests of the capitalists.

9. COMMUNISM, SOCIALISM (U.S.: 167; K: 65). For both groups there is a strong contrast between CAPITALISM and *communism*. Although the CAPITALISM-*socialism* contrast is also strong for the U.S. groups, it appears negligible for Koreans.

10. BUSINESS, ECONOMY (U.S.: 201; K: 169). This component indicates that CAPITALISM is primarily an economic system, which to the Americans operates on the principles of free enterprise, profit, and competition. The Koreans emphasize economy more.

11. FREE ENTERPRISE, PROFIT, COMPETITION (U.S.: 283; K: 130). Concern with the economic principles fundamental to CAPITALISM is reflected in this largest U.S. component. The Koreans show relatively little interest in or awareness of these principles. Outside the U.S., the meaning of CAPITALISM is primarily excessive control of government.

SOCIALISM (See page 187 for chart.)
Summary of Main Components of Cultural Meanings

1. DEMOCRACY, EQUALITY (U.S.: 22; K: 323). This strongest Korean component shows that the Korean groups view and evaluate SOCIALISM in the context of democratic principles, especially *equality* (U.S.: 16; K: 46) and *freedom* (K: 51). For the U.S. groups this context is negligible.

2. NATION, RACE (U.S.: 21; K: 67). This is a small and primarily Korean category. The Korean response *race* (14) is used in the sense of ethnic national identity.

3. IDEA, BELIEF (U.S.: 59; K: 45). This small component indicates that the U.S. groups view SOCIALISM more as a matter of *belief* (42), while for the Korean students, it is more a *theory* (24).

4. CAPITALISM (U.S.: 55; K: 39). This is a small but distinct response category. Capitalism, perhaps even more than democracy, represents a partial opposite of SOCIALISM. This interpretation is supported by the small response *anticapitalism*.

6. PROGRAMS, ISSUES (U.S.: 145; K: 107). Social and economic programs, such as *welfare* (U.S.: 32) and *social security,* receive the most

Main Meaning Components for U.S. and Korean Groups

SOCIALISM

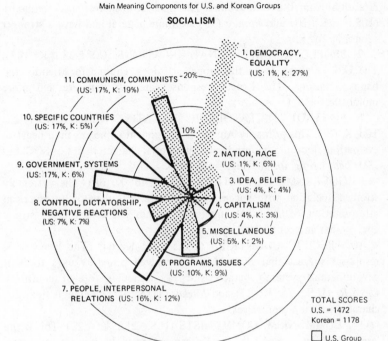

1. DEMOCRACY, EQUALITY (US: 1%, K: 27%)

11. COMMUNISM, COMMUNISTS (US: 17%, K: 19%)

10. SPECIFIC COUNTRIES (US: 17%, K: 5%)

9. GOVERNMENT, SYSTEMS (US: 17%, K: 6%)

8. CONTROL, DICTATORSHIP, NEGATIVE REACTIONS (US: 7%, K: 7%)

2. NATION, RACE (US: 1%, K: 6%)

3. IDEA, BELIEF (US: 4%, K: 4%)

4. CAPITALISM (US: 4%, K: 3%)

5. MISCELLANEOUS (US: 5%, K: 2%)

6. PROGRAMS, ISSUES (US: 10%, K: 9%)

7. PEOPLE, INTERPERSONAL RELATIONS (US: 16%, K: 12%)

TOTAL SCORES
U.S. = 1472
Korean = 1178

☐ U.S. Group
▦ Korean Group

U.S. GROUPS

There is clear evidence that the meaning of SOCIALISM is complex and controversial. First of all, the Americans strongly identify socialism with COMMUNISM. However, among the SPECIFIC COUNTRIES mentioned, there are more non-Communist than Communist countries. Fundamentally, SOCIALISM for the U.S. groups refers to a political system run by a strong centralized GOVERNMENT, which carries heavy connotations of CONTROL, DICTATORSHIP. However, it is also associated with active socioeconomic PROGRAMS and denotes friendly INTERPERSONAL RELATIONS as well.

KOREAN GROUPS

As shown by the lower total scores for the Korean groups, the theme SOCIALISM may be less meaningful than for the U.S. groups, but it is no less controversial. It shows similarly strong association with the two major competing doctrines (DEMOCRACY AND COMMUNISM). The students identify it more with COMMUNISM, the workers and peasants with DEMOCRACY. Accordingly the students mention mostly Communist COUNTRIES and express more negative attitudes (CONTROL). There is no indication of concern with an extensive role of the GOVERNMENT. References to economic PROGRAMS are more general, and they do not include specific programs; for example, those comparable to Medicare.

attention from the U.S. groups. The main Korean responses *economy* (U.S.: 7; K: 20) and *money* (23) are more general and have a stronger economic focus.

7. PEOPLE, INTERPERSONAL RELATIONS (U.S.: 230; K: 143). The U.S. emphasis is on the proper attitudes required for friendly and happy relations. The Korean responses are less concrete and more moralistic.

8. CONTROL, DICTATORSHIP, NEGATIVE REACTIONS (U.S.: 106; K: 79). This primarily American component expresses their negative evaluations focusing on oppressive, dictatorial characteristics of SOCIAL-ISM: *bad, wrong, unfair, oppression.*

9. GOVERNMENT, SYSTEMS (U.S.: 246; K: 68). The extremely strong association with *government* (140) reflects that in the American interpretation SOCIALISM implies a system characterized by strong government and centralized power.

10. SPECIFIC COUNTRIES (U.S.: 256; K: 64). The heavy U.S. responses suggest that SOCIALISM is viewed primarily as a form of governmental system characteristic of particular foreign countries. *U.S.S.R.* (U.S.: 75; K: 27) and *England* (U.S.: 92) emerge as the most characteristic representatives.

11. COMMUNISM, COMMUNISTS (U.S.: 252; K: 223). This is the largest U.S. and second largest Korean category. It shows a very close relationship between SOCIALISM and *communism* (U.S.: 144; K: 136). However, this does not mean that the two themes are synonymous, as distinct differences appear in other categories.

Trends of Cultural Interpretation in the Area of Political Systems   There are some consistent trends of interpretation within this problem area of "political systems" as well. The U.S. groups place consistently greater emphasis on government. Government has a higher dominance for Americans; it is a key issue in viewing socialism as well as capitalism. These systems are apparently perceived as implying first of all a particular system of government. Government control and dictatorship appear as especially central concerns for the Americans.

For the Koreans government appears to be more a national issue than a matter of power and political organization. Their references to nation, race, and president are consistently stronger, whereby it has to be mentioned that race is a reference to their own ethnic national identity. There is a Korean tendency to capitalize on high offices and on the executive branch with less emphasis on the other branches, functions, organizations.

Americans emphasize generally more functions, organizations, and the political process, while there is a stronger Korean emphasis on political isms and ideology.

Similarly, Americans stress consistently more human rights, people, and economic principles of free enterprise and competition; the Korean emphasis is generally more on society and social principles. An exception to this rule appears to be in the case of capitalism, but even here the heavy Korean references to money, rich, and poor appear to have not only economic but social and political connotations as well.

The preceding comparisons of U.S. and Korean meanings show that there are distinct differences as well as similarities between the two cultures. Themes representing important concerns for Americans do not always represent equally important concerns for the Koreans. Nonetheless, some words (or themes) seem to have broad universal meanings, such as FATHER and FAMILY. These themes show relatively large areas of agreement between cultures. On the other hand, there are concepts that are more characteristic of specific cultures, such as FILIAL DUTY or ANCESTORS. These themes with relatively little cross-cultural overlap show greater cultural differences.

Generally, the more concrete concepts such as FATHER and FAMILY retain a similar meaning for both cultures, while more abstract themes such as FILIAL DUTY or SOCIALISM show greater cross-cultural variation. Moreover, even if there is a universally agreed upon core meaning, as in the case of FATHER, there will still be differences in the subjective meanings of the word for each culture. Even though the biological meaning of FATHER (i.e., the male progenitor) is universal, the subjective meaning also involves his roles, relations, and functions as head of the family, educator, and provider, which differ from culture to culture. In certain cultures, for instance, the mother's oldest brother is the head of the family, provider, and educator, while the biological father is only an occasional guest. Thus, psychological or cultural meanings of even such fundamental concepts as father and mother are also dependent on the broader framework of interpersonal relations.

Furthermore, the more a concept refers to interpersonal relations, the greater will be the differences in cultural meanings. In instances where the concept denotes primarily relationships that are largely culture-specific, as in the case of FILIAL DUTY, it becomes a question of whether the original Korean word and its U.S. translation really represent the same concept. The relationship referred to by the concept FILIAL DUTY is so fundamentally characteristic of the Confucian philosophy that without conveying this, the label FILIAL DUTY naturally remains meaningless to an American; or worse, it becomes filled with character-istically U.S. interpretations: for example, "duty" implying menial jobs, work.

At first glance, the meaning differences shown by the single specific examples may appear discouraging, suggesting there is often a gap between what we want to say and the meanings other people really attach to our translated message, even if the translation is precise according to the dictionary. Such meaning differences also suggest that learning the foreign language will not make us effective communicators unless we also learn the cultural meanings of the foreign words. Because a reasonable fluency in a foreign language requires learning at least a couple of thousand words, it would appear that learning these subtle, psychological differences is a hopelessly demanding task.

However, by considering the larger, more general areas as a whole, the problem of cultural differences becomes more manageable. There is no need to learn all the single psychological differences in meaning related to each word of the vocabulary.

First, there are some common trends in the U.S. and Korean interpretations of these specific themes. A component that appears important in the interpretation of one word tends to emerge with similar importance in the interpretation of related words. For instance, the fact that the extended family is a characteristic social structure in the Korean culture emerges clearly from the large number of relatives mentioned in the context of each word analyzed on "family." The Americans, on the other hand, consistently had a narrower focus on parents and children— the nuclear family. The consistency of findings across the themes from the area of family therefore suggest that information from a sample of themes representing a particular problem area can be extended to other themes from the same area.

In order to obtain general knowledge in the most economical way, groups of words representing several important fields of concern can be used. From the findings based on single themes, consistent trends of cultural interpretations will emerge.

The preceding examples show that words are not isolated and independent units of language but organized elements of the culture's frame of reference. Psychological meanings both depend on and faithfully reflect the important dimensions of this frame of reference.

USING CULTURAL MEANINGS TO COMMUNICATE EFFECTIVELY

The important question is how to systematically organize such knowl-edge so that it becomes useful to people trying to familiarize themselves with another language and culture. Because the information is on meanings, the construction of a new type of dictionary seems to be a logical solution.

In this new concept, a communication lexicon differs fundamentally from a conventional dictionary in that it is not designed for word-by-word translations. Its purpose is to describe the cultural frame of reference through its natural units of meaning, which happen to be the natural units of the language as well. It contains information on well-established images, patterns of thought, and attitudes characteristic of the people of a particular culture. To approach a particular problem area, the lexicon can indicate (1) how to select themes of dominant concern within a given problem area and (2) what to emphasize and in which context to discuss it so that it will communicate, that is, bear on the experiences and concerns of a particular foreign people.

The practical problems encountered while abroad are countless and often unforeseeable. Thus it would be impossible to anticipate all the potential problems in communication and interaction and to provide a specific solution for each. However, a general approach toward improving communications is outlined below.

First, we must realize that cultural differences do exist and that we cannot assume the translations of our ideas in another language will convey the same meaning. The objective, concrete meanings may be understood, but it is the subjective meanings associated with the ideas that will actually determine how effective our communications will be. Naturally, this works both ways. Just because a representative of another country speaks English fluently does not mean there will not be communication problems.

Second, it is the culture and life experiences that produce different patterns of thinking, or frames of reference. The cultural frame of reference influences the meanings of the words that the native speaker uses to communicate his ideas.

Finally, the culture can be studied through the meanings of words used to communicate within the culture. By analyzing the psychological meanings of words representing those concepts that are most important to a people, we can focus on the natural priorities of a particular culture and equip ourselves with data of fundamental relevance and broad applicability. We will then possess the important information about a particular cultural frame of reference that will enable us to communicate effectively with that people.

STUDY QUESTIONS

1. Rate your own responses to the items on the Self-Disclosure Scale (see Figure 2 of the Barnlund article). Do you find that you are more like the typical American or more like the typical Japanese? If you were considering a particular friend of either sex as the target for your self-disclosure, would it make a difference in your responses if you considered a different friend?

2. Have a parent or older person respond to the Self-Disclosure Scale of Barnlund (see Figure 2). Do their responses differ? If so, in what categories? How would you account for the differences, if any? Give the Self-Disclosure topics to a friend of the opposite sex. Are the results similar or different when compared with your responses? If they are different, in what areas? Can you explain why there might be a difference?

3. What do Barnlund's findings imply about the ease or difficulty with which Japanese and Americans can become close friends?

4. What other examples can you think of, besides the meaning of "education" to a priest and a football coach, of words that might have different connotations for different groups of English speakers?

5. How might a lack of understanding of the cultural differences reflected in word connotations pose a barrier to effective communication between a Korean and an American? Can you give a specific example?

6. Besides "filial duty," another expression frequently used in Korean culture is "filial piety." What is your understanding of this expression? What is a dictionary definition? Why does the notion of "filial piety" have little significance for an American? How do you think filial piety would be expressed or shown?

7. In an activity similar to the one in the Szalay-Fisher article, ask four of your American friends to make free associations with the expression "human rights." Is there any consensus on its connotations for them? If you can, ask nationals from other countries to respond in the same manner. Why are there differences and/or similarities of the connotations when compared with the American responses?

8. If Asian cultures are often low contact, low context cultures, Italian, Spanish, and Slavic cultures are considered high contact, high context cultures. How can you see this in their speech habits, gestures, dress, family structures, social spaces, and marriage and funeral rites?

ROLE EXPECTATIONS

Understanding of role expectations in a foreign culture is a critical factor in minimizing communication interference. Raymond Gorden examines the role expectations and attitudes of Colombian hosts and Peace Corps volunteers who lived with the families during their assignments in Latin America. He shows how misunderstandings arose when expected behavior patterns and culture cues were misread by both Colombian nationals and American visitors. The source of this miscommunication stems from conflicting role expectations on the part of both the guest and members of the family, and different uses of formal customs of courtesy. From a very different perspective, Kathleen Newland assesses role expectations through the prism of the mass media. She takes a hard look at the impact of media in different cultures in defining role expectations for women. Her conclusion is that the media tend to reinforce traditional stereotypes rather than to instill greater understanding for the newly evolving roles of women. In fact, in many cultures, including the United States, the media portray women as weak and passive. The image often has strong sexist overtones in that it is completely at odds with the reality of women. Transmittal of such role models can lead to great misperceptions of role expectations for women not only within one's own culture but also across cultural boundaries.

(For further discussion on role expectations, see E. C. Carterette and M. P. Friedman in the bibliography.)

The Guest's General Role in the Family

Raymond L. Gorden

From "The Guest's General Role in the Family," in *Living in Latin America: A Case Study in Cross-Cultural Communication* by Raymond L. Gorden, copyright © 1974 by National Textbook Company. Reprinted by permission of National Textbook Company.

It is quite obvious from the talks with the students and Peace Corps trainees that to be "a member of the family" is a very good thing in the minds of the American guests. Yet when we begin to see the meaning of "member of the family" in terms of specific behaviors and motivations, we find considerable ambivalence both in the North American guest and in the Colombian host as to whether they want the American to be "a member of the family." The high value placed upon this phrase by both guest and host seems to be based upon a mutual desire of each to be sociably acceptable to the other and to be viewed as accepting by the other.

THE AMERICANS' AMBIVALENCE[1]

The Americans' ambivalence seemed to be a conflict between a desire for emancipation from the older generation (or a desire for independence) and the desire for some special support, help, and advice needed while in the foreign environment. In short, there was a strong tendency for the American guest to accept such restrictions, advice, or supervision only when it gave him the support he felt he needed. When he did not feel the need, he tended to reject the aspects of his role in the family that were restrictive, made demands, or involved obligations. He was more interested in the aspects that entitled him to considerations, services, rights, and privileges.

This was not only because he was basically human but also because the mechanisms of social control that generally operate within our own society to get us to accept obligations as well as rights do not operate immediately upon the sojourner in the host culture. The degree to which a person accepts both the obligations and the rights connected with his role is an index of his integration into a particular group of culture.

Seventy-six percent of the students said they felt like members of the Colombian family, yet 35 percent of that group said that it was quite difficult for them to exchange ideas with their family. Of course, this in itself is not a clear contradiction, since some of them may find it difficult to exchange ideas with their own families in the United States. However, it is highly doubtful that they could feel like real members of the family when only 12 percent said that they did take the initiative in discussions with the family. Even though 77 percent said that the family did respond when they took the initiative, still 60 percent preferred to spend most of their free time with Americans. This particular group of 49 American students lived with Colombian families, took courses from Colombians in Spanish, and might have felt a need to reduce the pressure of the constant speaking of Spanish by seeking out their American friends in their free time. Of course, this is not totally consistent with wanting to be a member of the Colombian family.

The height of this ambivalence between wanting to be independent and needing some help is shown when we compare the fact that 70 percent said they preferred to meet people on their own initiative and 35 percent said they felt that the host family should open more social doors for them. Forty-seven percent said they think that CEUCA, the sponsoring American organization, should open more social doors for them. Thus there is evidence that they were not completely satisfied with the amount of social interaction they have been able to have with Colombians, and yet they did like to feel that they were capable of independently making the social contacts they wanted.

One of the most important locks on the social doors the American guest would like to open he often places there himself. This is the general image of social unacceptability projected by some of the Americans: The guests "acted like they felt superior to Colombians"; they were "generally thoughtless of others"; they did not "dress appropriately for the occasion"; they gave the impression that "they did not care about their reputation among the Colombians"; they "did not bathe frequently"; some of them "smelled bad at times"; and "they do not greet people properly."

Most of the negative images projected by the American guests were products of their own behavior patterns in a context of ignorance of the foreign cultural patterns, yet the interviews with the Americans showed that only rarely did a guest say there was any connection between his own behavior and the closed social doors. Those who thought that the sponsoring American organization should do more to help them socially usually thought that they merely needed help in making the initial contact with a certain kind of Colombian. The doubtful assumption seemed to be that they would know how to take advantage of the opportunity.

Whatever may be the forces of mutual attraction, it seems that there are also forces of mutual repulsion that derive their strength from the simple basic fact that tension and anxiety generated in cross-cultural interaction can be reduced by simply separating the actors, temporarily stopping the interaction. If this is true, the American guest's ambivalence about accepting the role of full-fledged family member is understandable, and the general direction of the solution is to learn how to interact with members of the foreign culture without producing anxiety and tension.

Basically, the American guest's ambivalence is generated by the conflict between his desire to be *independent* of the older generation, especially of his own parents; yet he is more *dependent* because he is in a foreign culture.

Other types of ambivalences develop when the American discovers that the price of being "a member of the family" is more than he would like to pay as he begins gradually to perceive the *obligations* of a family member of his own age. The *gringas*, particularly, may feel that the restrictions and supervision to which they are subjected as a member of the family make them long for dormitory life again.

The Colombian hosts also have ambivalences regarding the American guest's role in the household.

THE COLOMBIANS' AMBIVALENCE

The Colombian hosts, like the guests, also tended to be ambivalent about the proper role of the American living in their home. We have already seen that they think that a principal motivation for taking *norteamericano* guests is "to earn extra money," yet 87 percent of the señoras said that the American should be treated "like a member of the family" and none said they should be treated "like a guest who pays." Logically, since paying is important and since treating them "like a member of the family" also seems to be important, we would expect a fairly large portion of the señoras to have chosen the fourth response, "like a mixture of these." Yet only 9 percent chose this response in spite of the fact that the Americans were usually treated like some combination of a family member, special guest, and boarder.

This apparent contradiction is resolved to some extent when we analyze the spontaneous remarks of the señoras explaining why they preferred to treat the Americans as members of the family. First, it was clear that most of the señoras prided themselves in being good hostesses who can make anyone in the home feel comfortable. Seventy-four percent of the señoras volunteered the idea that the American should be treated like a member of the family so that he would feel more comfortable. Another 14 percent volunteered that it would also make the family more comfortable. The remaining 11 percent said that if they treated the American like a member of the family, he would in turn treat their own children in the same way.

Being a "member of the family" means not only that the person should be comfortable (in the Colombian way, of course) but also that he should assume certain responsibilities of a family member of the same age and sex. The señoras felt that the American should make his own bed neatly, keep his room orderly, leave the bathroom tidy, hang his towel out in the sun to dry, come to meals (lunch and dinner) on time, etc. There are additional responsibilities such as giving gifts on certain occasions, greeting and introducing people, paying one's way, and helping with household chores on special occasions.

Just as some of the American guests hope to carve out a role for themselves which has all the advantages and none of the disadvantages of the role of family member, some of the señoras also would like to have all the advantages of a family member who can "take the place of the son or daughter" but who has other advantages one's own son or daughter would not provide.

A large majority of the señoras preferred a North American to a Colombian guest if both paid the same amount. This may seem strange, since a Colombian could actually play the role of "member of the family" much more accurately than could the North Americans. Their reasons included the cross-cultural contact benefits (e.g., learning English) and that the North American would be less bother to the señora than a Colombian.

It was not easy for some of the señoras to articulate *why* or *how* the North American would be less bother. "More trustworthy" included a variety of statements such as "more honest," "dependable in paying what he owes," or "more sincere." "Easier to handle" meant that they thought the American guest was more docile because he felt insecure in the foreign setting and would need help and advice. "More respectful" meant both that North Americans were not so rebellious toward the older generation in general, but more often it meant that the North American male would be more respectful toward the señora, and the female would be more respectful toward the señor than would be a Colombian university student. "Less demanding" in some cases meant that the Colombian guest paying the same amount would demand more special services than an American. "More independent" often meant that the North American was more capable of getting around on his own initiative and would not be so dependent upon the family for his social life. This is in contrast to "too independent," which referred to a person who was not attached to the family and who did not have a warm relationship with the señora. "Males less fresh" usually meant that they viewed the Colombian male as more amorously aggressive, which might constitute a problem for the señora.

Many of the señoras felt that the *gringas* needed less supervision than would a Colombian girl of the same age, which is consistent with the idea of "less bother." To measure the extent of this belief among the host señoras we later asked whether they felt that the *colombiana* or the *gringa* guest would require the most supervision. Forty-one percent felt that the *gringa* should be supervised less strictly than the Colombian daughter; 4 percent felt they should have *more* strict supervision; 55 percent felt that the *gringa* should have the same amount of supervision.

MISCOMMUNICATION ABOUT THE GUESTS' ROLE IN THE HOUSEHOLD

The American guest did not know precisely how to play the role of either "guest" or "member of the family." He did not know how a member of a Colombian family would be treated. Some felt that they were being treated like a special guest rather than a member of the family *because* orange juice and coffee were brought to their bedroom at breakfast time. In several of the homes this is a practice, particularly for the señora or daughters in the home. Other Americans felt that since the Colombians were polite in their greetings and forms of address, they were not treating the American like a member of the family when in fact they were.

The American guests' underestimate of the number of señoras who *think* the American should be treated as a guest could be a reflection of the señora's own ambivalence or of a discrepancy between her idea of how they *should* be treated and how she actually treated them.

> They treat me sort of like a family member but more like a guest because they always make sure I get the best food and often do special favors that the other kids wouldn't get.

> They expected me to help around the house like a member of the family, yet
> if I broke something they made me pay. Also, if you stay a few days longer
> into the vacation period they make you pay extra.

Miscalculation also results when the American guest tries to discover whether he is being treated like a member of the family with respect to a certain issue by observing how a Colombian family member is treated. In doing this he may fail to compare himself with a Colombian of the same age and sex. For example, "I am reprimanded if my room is disorderly although I clean it myself, change the bed and make the bed, while the kids in the house leave such things to the maid and are a hundred times more disorderly than I."

This sounds like evidence of discrimination, but in interviewing this host family it was discovered that "the kids" with whom the American college student was comparing himself were boys seven and nine years old.

In families where there are no members of the guest's age and sex, the guest cannot discover what is appropriate for himself by observing the others. The female guest cannot always assume that if the señora does a certain thing or has certain privileges or duties, the *gringa* should behave in the same way. Nor can the *gringo's* observations of the señor's behavior be a reliable guide, because parents and children occupy a different role and status in any household.

Even though a large minority of the señoras felt that the *gringa* should be less strictly supervised than a *colombiana,* a much larger portion (91 percent) of the American guests felt that the señora expected to exercise less supervision over the *gringa.* Usually the *gringa* was not aware that the señora was quite distraught because of the difficulty in exercising what she felt was adequate supervision. The American girl who tended to take her freedom and independence for granted often felt that she was bending over backward to meet the demands of the culture, but the señora was mainly aware of the shortcomings, particularly those that might damage her reputation.

We also saw a gap in communication in that only 7 percent of the señoras said that they had no preference for a Colombian versus an American guest if the amount paid were equal, but 36 percent of the guests thought their señora felt this way. There was an assumption among many of the Americans that the host families were being paid much more for board and room than could have been collected from a Colombian. In some cases this was because the student did not know how much the señora was paid but *assumed,* since he had paid into the Program the same board and room fee he would have paid on his home campus, this total amount was paid to the host family. He did not realize that a large portion of the cost of board and room in the foreign country went into locating and selecting the host families and in dealing with the developing problems of adjustment between host and guest.

Another possible reason for the American guests' reluctance to think that the señora would actually prefer an American if the pay were equal is that they found it more difficult than did the señoras to see reasons other than money for the señora's taking an American guest. For example, when the guests were asked why their señora might prefer an American, none of them had the idea that the señora would feel that the American would be less bother than a Colombian guest. All of the reasons they could give were in the cross-cultural experience category.

Another area of miscommunication was revealed in the fact that many guests did not realize the extent to which the host families would support their role as student. Some guests felt that there was a conflict between their role as student versus family member. The Americans reported in the interviews that their host family wanted them to skip classes for a day or two in order to take a long weekend trip with them, and they worried that the family would be insulted if they did not go. We asked the señoras, "If you were planning a trip over a long weekend and you invited your American guest to go with you, should he be willing to miss classes for two days if he really wanted to go? " Then the guests were asked to indicate how they thought their señoras would answer the question.

The guests greatly underestimated the proportion (79.5 percent versus 4.5 percent) of the señoras who felt the guests should not miss classes to go on a trip. A few of the señoras volunteered the comment that they should come on the trip because they should not stay in the house without the family there, particularly if the guest were a *gringa*. We cannot explain why more Americans did not realize how the señoras felt about interfering with their studies, nor do we know that their saying that the "studies come first" was not simply a polite excuse to leave the foreign guest behind. To take him might have caused overcrowding if they were driving, or the American might not have intended to pay his way to the extent expected by the host, or the Colombian family may have wanted some time away from the foreign guest they see every day. The student may also have been hopefully rationalizing his own desires to escape from his studies by saying that the family would be insulted if he put his studies above a long weekend trip with them.

FORMAL CUSTOMS OF COURTESY

The North American can easily give a Colombian the impression that he does not want to meet people or participate in social events because he does not observe the social rituals that are so important in Latin America. Even after the guests begin to sense the vital importance of these "superficial customs," he still may not know how to do them correctly.

The host-family señoras feel that they can separate the sheep from the goats among American guests by whether they make the proper polite responses such as greeting, introducing, and thanking people. None of the señoras interviewed took a neutral position on whether their particular American guest was polite in this respect. The señoras felt that the Americans' weakest point was in knowing how to greet people. To some hosts this meant that the guest did not know how or when to shake hands.

Shaking Hands   To the Colombians the Americans seemed to have some reluctance to shake hands.

> His customs were typically North American. Even in the way he greeted you. You know the Americans don't like this thing about shaking your hand.

> As an advisor to the North Americans as foreign students here in Colombia, I tell them that the only time they don't shake hands on greeting someone is when both hands are broken. It is difficult to impress them with the importance of this simple act.

Although there is a difference in the amount of handshaking that is customary in different regions of the United States,[2] in general the *bogotanos* tended to shake hands much more than the North Americans were accustomed to. The American at first had to force himself to shake hands with even 10 people when he arrived and left a dinner party, for example. The American college student's tendency to minimize the greeting rituals is even more emphasized when he is abroad where he feels unsure about the language and the accompanying actions. At first it takes considerable effort on the American's part even when he understands what the *bogotanos* expect. In time it becomes a habit and, when he returns to the United States, he catches himself extending his hand in many situations when it is not expected.

Here are some of the ways in which handshaking is different from the practice in most parts of the United States.

Shake hands more frequently. The probability that two North Americans will shake hands upon meeting depends upon (among other things) how recently they have seen each other. It is clear that the time lapse that requires the "reshaking" of hands is much shorter in Colombia than in the United States. For example, on entering the home of a friend or acquaintance it is expected that you shake hands even though you may have seen the person only a few minutes before.

Shake hands with more people. On entering a place where a social or business gathering is taking place you shake hands with each person, up to as many as 20 persons. In very large groups of 50 or more, it is customary to stop at each small group and shake hands with each person present.

Shake hands on more occasions. The North American is less inclined to shake hands when he leaves a group than when he arrives. Colombians shake hands as frequently upon leaving as when arriving.

Men do not wait for women to take initiative. When a man greets a woman, he does not wait for the woman to offer her hand because it is customary for women to shake hands on all the same occasions as would a man.

The woman-to-woman handshake is different. It is a custom for women to shake hands with women, particularly after the first time they have met, in a style different from the man-to-man or woman-to-man handshake. They frequently shake hands by simultaneously grasping each other's right forearm. If the North American girl first experiences this without any prior warning, she may be surprised.

> I went to this party at a relative's house where there were several Colombians I had met once before. The hostess shook hands with me like this [grasping forearm], and I thought maybe she was blind and had missed my hand or something.

> The first time I went to a party I was lucky because I had a chance to observe my señora welcoming guests to our home and noticed that she shook hands with the men one way and with the women another. Of course I didn't know how general this was, but then when I went to another house party I was on the lookout for it.

> For the first month or so I didn't realize that I wasn't shaking hands right, but I noticed a bit of fumbling confusion sometimes as our hands met. Then later I discovered that this was because I grabbed their hand before they could get past mine to clasp my arm like they do. I just never thought that they would shake hands with a man one way and with a woman another.

The man-to-man handshake is less vigorous. The American men also had a problem with the manner of shaking hands even though it is essentially the same act as in the United States. Many of the Americans were accustomed to a vigorous grasp and felt that many of the *bogotanos* had an insipid handshake: "You'd think some of these men are sick from the way they shake hands. It is like holding a dead fish. It's hard to believe that they mean it. They are certainly not very enthusiastic."

Similarly, some of the *bogotanos* interpreted the American's vigorous handshake as another expression of his feeling of superiority: "The Americans say that we are so concerned with *machismo,* in trying to prove our masculinity, but when they shake your hand they seem to be engaging in some kind of contest to prove that they are stronger."

In the eyes of some *bogotanos* both the American's reluctance to shake hands and his "aggressive" manner when he does so can contribute to that image, shared by many host families, that the American thinks he is superior to the *bogotano*. At the same time, the American can get the impression that the *bogotano* is not warmly enthusiastic about meeting him.

These differences in handshaking customs may not exhaust the whole range of differences,[3] but they include the most common cross-cultural dissonances encountered by the Americans and Colombians.

Thanking Colombians   A majority of the señoras thought that the North American guests knew "how to thank a person for a favor." Significantly, none took a neutral position on this issue. Again this shows the tendency for the host to put his guest clearly in either the positive or negative category with respect to his manners. We must, however, make a distinction between knowing how and actually doing it. If a Colombian thought his guest did know how but did not thank him properly for a favor, he concluded that the American did not appreciate the favors done **for him. This interpretation is consistent with the fact that despite the majority who agreed that the American knows how, only half agreed that** "they appreciate the favors they receive."

In the depth interviews with the señoras we found a few hints as to what was lacking in the American's attempt to thank them.

... and we took her on a picnic at Zipaquirá, went to the Salt Cathedral, took her to the market to take pictures, and then went to show her Villa de Leiva which is a long trip so we stayed overnight in Villa. When we got back home, all she said was "gracias"!

He was interested in seeing some of the sights in Bogotá, so we went to Monserrate on the cable car, went through the museum of the Quinta de Bolívar, to the Cathedral, the Plaza de Bolívar, and the Plaza de la Constitución and even to the market which we never would go to, but he wanted to see it. We went to lunch at the Casa Vieja and returned home at about seven. When he got home, he just said "gracias" and that he was tired so went up to his room.

The key to the problem is expressed concisely in the phrase "all he said was 'gracias.' " This is enough if someone has just lent a person a match, but not adequate in the cases of larger favors. The following excerpts from the señoras' interviews give a strong stamp of approval to the guest who shows his appreciation more profusely.

... he wasn't a typical American in this way. He had very good manners. He was well brought up. For example, we invited him to the soccer game, then went swimming at the Club Militar and then to dinner at La Chesa. He was very appreciative. He said, *"Qué buena la excursión! Fue sumamente interesante para mí. Fue muy amable de su parte el haberme invitado. Es el dia más especial que he tenido aquí en Bogotá. Muchísimas gracias por todo.* "

He seemed to always appreciate little things we did for him. He was so different from the first student who would just say "gracias" in a very dry way.

It is not strange that the host does not teach the guest how to show his appreciation, because the role of host would preclude appearing to demand profuse thanks. If the guest does not do some equivalent favor for the host, he cannot learn by observing the example of the host's reaction to a favor. The breakdown in communication is facilitated by the señora's assumption that the guest knows how to express appreciation but does not feel any appreciation in a particular instance.

Greetings   The *bogotano's* feeling that the North Americans did not "greet people properly" was also related to the Americans' failure to say either "hello" or "goodbye." It was not necessary to ask the señoras specifically whether the American guest greeted people properly. It was clear that this was such an essential factor in their judgment of the American that in the depth interviews they would mention the greeting problem when they were asked questions such as: "What kind of a person was your last guest? " The responses most frequently given could be categorized into different dimensions of etiquette such as greeting people properly, thanking people, giving of gifts, and paying one's way.

Well, in general the American girls never say hello. I think it is only natural to greet people when you come into the house but they never do.

They never came to say hello and sometimes we were here. That bothered us.

Some of the Americans that came were very badly brought up in that they would not greet you.

Sometimes we would have parties and introduce them to my friends too. But later when you meet them again they do not even say hello to you. Maybe they don't remember us.

This last statement may involve much more than the simple reluctance to greet people. It may be due to a situation that typically confronts any foreigner who is new in the community. When he goes to any group function, he may be the only stranger to the group, while all the members are strangers to him. They have only one new face to remember while the foreigner has many. Nevertheless, there is considerable evidence that the American did tend to greet people less frequently and to be less formal or profuse when he did greet them.

The fact that the *bogotanos* appreciated those guests who did not "behave like typical Americans" can be seen in the following positive statements coming from the host señoras:

He was very polite and nice. He used to say hello and when he left the house he would say goodbye.

Ricardo would usually say hello and goodbye but some days he forgot it. That was very different from Russ who would even look for me to say goodbye. It was a big difference.

Whenever she would come in and there were people here, she would greet everyone and stay a little while before she went upstairs. She said goodbye in a very friendly way. All my friends liked her very much.

When there were people here she would come and would say hello as if she were a member of the family.

The majority of the señoras preferred that the American guest seek them out to greet them even in the routine daily return to the home. The proportion who preferred to be sought out rises when the American returns after sightseeing on Saturday afternoon, and all the señoras felt the guest should greet them upon returning from a two-day absence. The señoras, as *dueñas* of the home, not only considered it polite, but also liked to know when the American was in the house just as they would like to know when one of their own children or their husband returned.

The Use of Adiós   The word *adiós* as a greeting was a source of mutual puzzlement between Colombians and North Americans. For example, the American was puzzled when he met a Colombian acquaintance on the street who simply said, "Adiós," and continued walking. The American in this case tended to think of *adiós* as being part of the leave-taking ritual, and therefore not to be used between two people as they approach each other on the street. In English the Americans would say, "Hello," "Hi," or "Good morning," and *adiós* seems to be inappropriate. Actually, the Colombian uses *adiós* in those situations where two people are going to pass each other without stopping, or if they do not wish to be detained. In effect it combined the idea of *hello* and *goodbye* in one word.

The Colombians, in turn, were puzzled by the North American's use of *adiós* as a parting formality. The American seemed to think of it as meaning simply *goodbye*; therefore, after he had spent the evening with a group he would say only, "Adiós," and leave. This was not enough. It was considered cold unless some phrase were added such as *mucho gusto de verte, que estés muy bien,* or *saludos en tu casa.* The incorrect interpretation of the use of *adiós* in these two situations was a source of mutual irritation.

Greeting Versus Leavetaking   The North American guests were sometimes confused by the use of *"Buenos días! " "Buenas tardes! "* and *"Buenas noches! "* to mean both hello and goodbye depending on the situation. A majority of the Americans seemed to think of these phrases as equivalent to "Good morning! " "Good afternoon! " and "Good evening! "[4] and therefore equal to a form of hello but not goodbye.

> When she said, *"buenos días"* I thought she had just arrived or that she thought I had just arrived. I felt that I had been talking to her in the group of Colombian students just before we went into the classroom, but when she said *"buenos días"* I was a bit confused because I thought I must be wrong in thinking she was the one I had just talked to. Later I realized that this was because I interpreted the *buenos días* to mean good morning in the sense of hello not goodbye.

> It took a while before I was sure that *buenos días* alone would not tell you whether they were saying hello or goodbye. It depends upon what else they say, if anything.

Inquiring About the Family   When greeting a married person who is not accompanied by the family, it is always polite to ask about the spouse and children. This is automatic with the *bogotanos* but takes practice for the North American.

Using Titles   In greetings, as in any form of direct address, it is customary to use the person's title. Never should we say, *"Buenos días, Martínez,"* or *"Buenas tardes, José."* It is much more polite to say *"Buenos días, señor Martínez,"* or *"Buenas tardes, don José."* The feminine equivalents of *señora* and *doña* are used in the same way. A specific degree such as *licenciado* can be used also.

In cases where someone has a professional status, the last name is often preceded by *doctor*. A student addressing a professor should always use the title *profesor* or *doctor* before the last name. *Doctor* is used much more generally than in the United States to refer to anyone with education or higher status. In Bogotá anyone with a college education may be addressed as *doctor*. To avoid confusion we must refer to a physician as *el médico* not *el doctor*. The lower class and the *campesinos* often address anyone in a higher socioeconomic class as *doctor*, which often surprises the American undergraduate student.

Of course, when using titles in indirect address the definite article is added, as in *la señora, el doctor*, but there is a very important exception to this rule in the case of *doña*. We should never refer to a woman as *la doña* which would mean "the madam" of a house of prostitution to some Colombians. This would severely shock a *bogotano* even though he knew it was not intentional on the part of the American. In some contexts it could appear to be quite intentional and would damage the American's image by lending credence to the idea, "Americans don't care about their reputation among Colombians."

The North American is often at a loss in addressing a nun or priest in Spanish. In general the priest should be *Padre* in direct address and *el padre* in indirect address parallel to the English *Reverend* and *the Reverend.* On some occasions the form *su reverencia* is also used. In addressing a nun the form *madre* or *hermana* is used depending on the nun's order and her position in the hierarchy. It is always safest to call her *madre* since this is the higher status. When possible the American should be alert to follow the lead of the Colombians in the particular situation. The Bishop is addressed as *su excelencia.*

Some of the Americans who were from Protestant or Jewish background found it very difficult and unnatural to use these forms of address which in their minds was like calling a stranger father, mother, or sister. Others felt that it implied some theological commitment on their part to Catholicism Those who thought of it as simply a title to designate one's function in society did not find these titles difficult to use.

Introductions　　It is a common practice for someone who is about to make an introduction to ask, *"¿Ustedes no se conocen? "* Then if one or both say, *"No tengo el gusto,"* one of three things might happen. The two may shake hands and give their names simultaneously. The person making the introduction may add, *"Quisiera presentar a mi amigo,"* or *"a mi primo,"* or *"a mi esposa,"* without giving the name, and the pair shake hands and give their own names simultaneously. The person making the introduction may give both names and they will shake hands. The first two forms are very common, but they make it very difficult for the American to hear the other person's name which is being given just as he gives his own name to the Colombian. Yet the system is often advantageous in that the introducer may not remember a person's name at the moment; so he can simply say, *"Quisiera presentar a mi estudiante,"* and then it is up to the two persons to give their own names, which allows the introducer to learn the person's full name. If the introducer uses the third form, he must not only be sure he has the correct name but must also remember to use the title with the article to indicate indirect address, *"Quisiera presentar al doctor García."*

Even though many of the American guests understood the correct forms of introductions, they were still considered aloof in situations that called for introducing themselves. For example, a guest would arrive home at 5:00 P.M. and find some strangers at the house in the living room. Since the señora was not with them at the moment, he might pass by them with a simple "Buenas tardes," as he headed for the stairway without stopping to introduce himself or giving the visitors a chance to introduce themselves. The *bogotano* hosts felt that the American guests failed to introduce themselves at times when it was considered appropriate. This was not due to the guest's general reluctance to introduce people, because a majority of the hosts felt the guest did very well in introducing his friends to the family.

Another aspect of the introduction situation that bothered some Colombians and gave the impression of the American's being aloof was what we might call the "hit-and-run" tendency. Instead of seeing the introduction as a prologue to a pleasant friendly chat, the American would immediately try to leave.

> for example, you would introduce him to your friends and he would say "hello" very kindly, but then he would immediately try to leave the situation.

> She came home that afternoon and I introduced her to some people in the living room and instead of sitting down and taking a moment, she just said, *"Con su permiso,"* and went upstairs to her room.

The lack of this knowledge could result in the American giving the impression that he is "aloof and superior" if he did not stay or that he was a "pushy intruder" if he did.

Using *tú* **Versus** *usted*   The English speaker often has difficulty in deciding between the use of the formal *usted* and the familiar *tú* forms of pronouns. Historically, he has lost his choice between *you* and *thou* and feels an added burden in making this decision when speaking Spanish. He has the linguistic problem of knowing both forms of pronouns and verb conjugations plus the more complex nonlinguistic problem of sensing when to use each.

He often arrives in Latin America with the idea that there is one simple consistent pattern for the use of these two forms. To the contrary, it is highly probable that this usage pattern varies from one region to another, from one social class to another, and according to other more subtle differences in the social situations in which the conversations take place.

The Americans were confused about the proper use of the familiar form. Some had obtained contradictory ideas from different Colombians they had asked for advice.

In general, *tú* was used when the señora addressed her husband, her children, and when her children addressed her. Most señoras used *usted* to address their maids. However, there is enough lack of unanimity to confuse the Americans. The señoras who chose the "other" category were almost all of two types—those who said they used both *tú* and *usted* depending on the occasion and those who used *su merced* instead of *tú*.

There is a possibility that the form used with children would depend upon their age. It was suggested by one respondent that with smaller children they used *usted* and for older ones *tú*. The exceptions to the general pattern are enough to shake the security of the American trying to learn the pattern.

The fact that most of the señoras used *tú* in addressing their children, and most of the children addressed their mothers in this way, would lead us to predict that these same señoras would expect their American guests to address them with *tú* since a large majority of them also expect the American to act "like a member of the family." To test this idea, which is very relevant to the American's role in the family, we asked the señoras about the conditions under which *tú* should be used between the guest and the host. We distinguished between the different sex combinations of host and guest and tried to determine how soon the *tú* relationship could be established. Then to determine the amount of guest-host communication on this point, we asked the American guests how they thought their particular señora would answer the questions.

In all four relationships the guests erred in the direction of assuming that they should never use *tú*. More of the Americans than the Colombians thought it was necessary to wait until after a certain relationship was established. Fewer Americans than Colombians felt that *tú* should be used from the beginning. The proportion of hosts choosing each category correlates mainly with whether the relationship is between persons of the same sex or opposite sexes. More say not to use *tú* when it is between opposite sexes.

When we ask whether the American guests were correct in perceiving the hosts' preference for *tú,* one clear pattern emerged. The American guests consistently underestimated the hosts' preference for using *tú* with their American guests. Fewer Americans expected *tú* to be used from the beginning, and more of them thought it should never be used than did the Colombians. This could be another factor supporting the Colombians' image of the "superior American" who does not want to be "a member of the family."

In some cases this unfortunate image was avoided when the señora took the initiative in directly instructing the guest.

Three days after I was here I was told to address everybody as *tú* because we were a family.

The señora said to me "You are a member of the family and you are not going to address us with *usted*!!"

My family told me that I was a member of the family and was to address them as *tú*.

The lack of unanimity regarding the appropriate use of *tú* was also graphically demonstrated by the fact that of the four Colombian interviewers who interviewed most of the *señoras,* one always used the familiar form in the interview. When I asked her why she did this, she said, "in order to get their confidence." Other interviewers with the same educational background and socioeconomic status used the formal *usted* in all interviews.

In view of these inconsistencies, it is highly probable that there are not only regional and social class differences in the use of the familiar form, but also there may be a historical trend toward the use of only one of the forms or a breaking down of the rigid distinction between their use. In any event the simple one-sentence explanations of the use of the familiar form, still found in Spanish textbooks for English speakers, seems too simple to accurately reflect the realities in Bogotá.

Three salient results emerged from this exploratory study which are relevant to the central problem of communication barriers: There was no unanimity among these señoras regarding the appropriate use of the familiar form; the American guests often did not know when they were expected to use the familiar form and so failed to use it in situations where it was expected by the hosts; this failure was often interpreted by the Colombians as a symptom of the American's desire to remain aloof from the family.

If the Colombian did not directly suggest using *tú,* the American was often at a loss to know what to do. In some cases they were aware that the hosts had started using *tú* in addressing them, but they did not know whether this was a dependable sign that they should also begin to use *tú.* When one American tried to advise another on the problem, confusion would often result.

My Colombian sister told me that in Bogotá *usted* is used more with close friends and *tú* with acquaintances and strangers.

In my (Colombian) family, I would feel uncomfortable using *tú* with either the señor or the señora unless they asked me to. The girl should with the señor only if she completely trusts him and doesn't feel that it would embarrass the señora. They are starting to use *tú* much more with me but I won't with them until they ask me.

Here in Bogotá, it seems to me that you only use *tú* with your boyfriend. Even within the family they use *usted* with each other.

In Colombia *tú* is used less frequently than in Mexico. For example, even my (Colombian) twin brothers use the *usted* form. So I think it is better to treat it as a grammatical thing than as a personal reflection.

It is clear that a more thorough study should be made of the use of *tú* to determine the causes of this variation and search for dependable tactics for the American to use in specific situations to select the appropriate form of address.

NOTES

1. The data for this section are based on a questionnaire designed and administered by Miss Hermena W. Evans who was in charge of housing the CEUCA students with Colombian families in Bogotá.

2. For example, the New Englander is much less likely to shake hands than the Texan. The New Englander's pattern is more like that in England today, while the Texan's is more like that of the Mexican or Colombian.

3. The use of the *abrazo* and styles in between the standard handshake and the *abrazo* such as men grasping the other's upper arm or shoulder with the left hand while shaking with the right have not been discussed.

4. Some thought of "Good evening" as meaning hello and "Good night" as meaning goodbye.

Women in Words and Pictures

Kathleen Newland

The mass media, printed and broadcast, are probably the most pervasive influences on attitudes and opinions in the modern world. Access to mass media, is, in fact, one of the defining characteristics of modernity. Other, more powerful forces may exist within a given region or culture, but on a global basis, in terms of sheer numbers reached, other forms of communication cannot compete with the words and pictures carried in newspapers, television and radio broadcasts, large-circulation magazines, and commercial advertising. The ways women are presented, misrepresented, or unrepresented in the mass media strongly affect people's notions on woman's place, as it is and as it ought to be.

A recent UNESCO report concluded that "the media can exert their influence in many ways, for example, by presenting models, offering social definitions, encouraging stereotypes, conferring status on people and behavior patterns, suggesting appropriate behaviors, indicating what is approved and what disapproved, and in several other indirect ways..." Although technical knowledge of how mass-media messages are transmitted to their human targets abounds, the UNESCO report makes it clear that knowledge of how human beings digest and react to those messages is lamentably sparse. The steps that connect media exposure and personal behavior remain a mystery. A few ghastly instances of life imitating art have occurred, such as juvenile crime copying some televised atrocity. Yet most studies seem to indicate a less direct link between the image presented in print or on the air and the attitudes and actions of the audience.[1]

An audience may be influenced by the media to abandon stereotypic thinking, but the media may also reinforce conservative or even reactionary predilections. Unfortunately for women, the latter is most often the case. Research suggests that the media have more power to reinforce existing views than to instill new ones. People tend to respond to and remember what is consistent with what they already believe and to ignore information that conflicts with their beliefs. Attempts to overcome that conservative bias are relatively uncommon, found mostly in media controlled by governments with a strong interest in social change.

Where a socially conservative bent is compatible with the interests of those who control the media, be they public or private powers, the media's treatment of women is narrow. In newspapers, on television, on the radio, and in magazines, woman's world is limited to home, family, fashion, and gossip. Women rarely appear in "hard news" coverage—a fact that reflects not only women's general exclusion from decision-making positions, but also the news industry's narrow view of newsworthiness. In entertainment programs and popular fiction, women figure as passive, dependent creatures with few concerns outside the domestic or the romantic. As the target audience for much of the advertising in the mass media, women are manipulated, bullied, and patronized. Straightforward appeals to their common sense and real needs are rare, and recent responses by the media to changes in women's lives and aspirations are both tentative and long overdue.

The influence of the mass media can only be expected to increase. For one thing, ever-increasing numbers of people have access to them; literacy campaigns are enlarging the range of the print media (though for millions more women than men printed media remain inaccessible because of illiteracy). For another, telecommunications technology is making it possible to reach more and bigger audiences with broadcasts. In social terms, however, the technology has not fulfilled its promise. The sophistication of communications hardware has escalated at a dizzying rate, but *what* is communicated—especially as it concerns women—has scarcely changed since kings and queens kept foot messengers in their employ.

WHOSE NEWS?

The nature of news reporting makes it difficult to describe a development as diffuse and many-faceted as the contemporary change in women's roles. Reporting emphasizes the concrete and the particular rather than things abstract and universal; elaboration of the context of an event and its implications is secondary to the requirements of who, what, when, where, and why. Reaching for concrete and particular illustrations of a complex social movement inevitably produces distortions. It brings to mind the tale of seven blind men describing an elephant: the overall impression differs depending on which particular piece of reality one is grappling with at the moment.

Feminist discontent with news coverage tends to focus on three different complaints: the depiction of women as second-class human beings, the underrepresentation of women and women's issues in routine coverage, and the distortion of the women's movement itself. This is not to say that some reporting of women's issues has not been fine and sensitive. But the many abuses, belittlements, oversights, and distortions cannot be denied.

The most obvious complaint concerns the portrayal of women in news reports. The tendency to include irrelevant information about a female newsmaker's appearance and family status, information that would not be reported about a man in a similar situation, remains strong. Some American newspapers have become more self-conscious about this practice, but it is still pervasive. In February 1977, the *Christian Science Monitor* carried a news story about France's new minister of consumer affairs in which the official was described as resembling "an impeccably groomed directress of some couture house rather than the prototype of a top-ranking female economist or the class intellectual who generally turns out in horn-rimmed spectacles, baggy skirt, and baggier stockings."[2] This not-uncharacteristic report (written by a woman, incidentally) is doubly offensive, first for overemphasizing physical appearance, and second for implying astonishment that a woman of achievement could be stylish.

The depiction of women in the press can be even more harmful when it goes beyond physical appearances and visits judgments on women's behavior. Yayori Matsui, one of the few female senior reporters on a major Japanese newspaper, contrasts the Japanese press's treatments of two tragic cases, each involving the death of a young mother. In one, a hairstylist with a young child was torn between her attachment to her job and social pressure to quit working in order to be a full-time house-wife. She eventually committed suicide. The headlines of the story reporting her death read "Female Stylist, Unwilling to Give Up Her Fashionable Occupation to Care for Her Child, Burns Herself to Death," and "Woman Ruined by Her Own Selfishness." Nowhere was there any criticism of the social attitudes that drove a working mother to such desperation. In the second case, an impoverished mother of five starved to death, while struggling to feed her children as best she could. In contrast to the earlier case, the press eulogized this woman as a model of maternal self-sacrifice—but again, it never questioned the social grounds for such a tragedy in a country as affluent as Japan. According to Matsui, the Japanese press regularly evinces hostility toward women who transgress traditional boundaries and approval toward those who remain firmly inside them.[3]

No aspect of news coverage is more frustrating than the low visibility of women and women's concerns in news reports. In part, this news vacuum reflects the fact that so few powerful positions are held by women. In a country like Denmark, where one-quarter of the cabinet is female, it is likely that women will make the news on a routine basis. But women's "low profile" is also a product of the socially conditioned definition of news. Women are at their most newsworthy when they are doing something "unladylike," especially arguing with each other. Since the complex and powerful changes in women's daily lives—how they make their livings, raise their families, spend their money, and so on—are difficult to reduce to a discrete news item, most coverage of women's issues is linked to an event, which may be contrived (like a march or demonstration) precisely for its ability to attract news coverage. Such events are often controversial, and tying news coverage to them has made the processes of change seem more controversial than they really are.

Coverage of the feminist movement as such has been particularly subject to distortion. The most enduring image of the women's movement comes from misconstrued reports of the "Miss America" demonstration of 1968; at that demonstration, brassieres, girdles, false eyelashes, and such were tossed into a "freedom trash can" and a sheep was crowned Miss America. But bra-burning is what was reported, and bra-burning is what was indelibly imprinted on the public consciousness.[4]

The nascent women's movement in Japan meets with pronounced hostility from the press. Linguistics professor Sachiko Ide describes the way newspapers write about the actions of women's groups: "These actions are always described by stereotyped expressions such as the color words *kiiroi koe,* "yellow voice," and *akai kien,* "red yells." These color words as modifiers of action have connotations of an irrational, emotional, sometimes hysterical atmosphere, and do not convey a serious or reasonable image."[5]

Something of the attitude of the Japanese press must have rubbed off on a *New York Times* reporter who filed an extraordinary story from Tokyo in July 1977, heralding the collapse of the women's movement in

Japan. "Japan's women's liberation movement has folded," the story began. It went on to describe the disbanding of a small, marginal women's group, *Chipuren*, which it described as Japan's "only major women's liberation group" and the theatrical tactics of the group's leader, Misako Enoki. The article concluded that "without Miss Enoki, who has become a symbol to many through Japan's pervasive mass media, the women's liberation movement here is expected to virtually disappear for the foreseeable future."[6]

The article brought waves of protesting letters from feminists in Japan, who pointed out that many other women's liberation groups were flourishing in Japan and that *Chipuren* was a fringe group that had been made a sort of pet by the establishment reporters because its actions were so easy to ridicule (its members, wearing white jumpsuits and pink helmets, held public demonstrations against unfaithful husbands) and its leader was so photogenic and obviously confused. (After dissolving her matriarchial political party, she agreed to "retire" to keep her house for her husband.) Even the Ministry of Labor felt called upon to object to the *Times* story. That an article displaying such profound ignorance could appear in a newspaper respected for accuracy and objectivity justifies some of the suspicion feminists feel toward the establishment press.

Although news stories that misrepresent the women's movement continue to appear, some news organizations are growing receptive to news about women's issues. At the international level, UNESCO and the UN Fund for Population Activities are helping establish regional feature services for news about women around the world. The first of these, covering Latin America, began operating in January 1978. Its intention is to produce for international distribution about two hundred articles per year on women's changing roles in the family, in society, and in the development process. A similar news network is being formed in the Caribbean. The hoped-for result of the project, according to UNESCO, is a worthy objective for any news organization: it is to make sure that "the image of women projected will be closer to the realities of society in a process of change."[7]

THE WORLD OF WOMEN'S MAGAZINES

Maria, the heroine of a popular Latin America serial romance, begins her career much as millions of her real-life sisters begin theirs. Born of poor, Indian parents on the high mountain plateau, she migrates, innocent and optimistic, to the capital city. She goes to work at the bottom rung of the social and economic ladder—as a domestic servant.

Her mistress is harsh; the young medical student she falls for is charming but weak and cowardly. Seduced and abandoned, she bears a child. Fending for herself and her baby is a desperate struggle.

Up to this point, Maria's story is achingly typical. But Maria gets lucky. In her valiant efforts to better herself, she meets a kind, handsome, and clever schoolteacher who is impressed by her bravery and goodness. At his urging, she learns to sew. Blessed with innate talent, good fortune, and the teacher's encouragement, Maria makes it—first as a seamstress, then as a dress designer. Her success knows no bounds. She marries the teacher, takes her place in the international firmament of high fashion, and lives happily ever after: elegant, wealthy, famous, loved.

Although it started off as a television soap opera, *Simplemente Maria* gained its widest following as a *fotonovela,* a serialized romance-magazine in which photographs are captioned like comic book illustrations. In this format, which even the barely literate can follow, *Simplemente Maria* won a huge audience among working-class women in almost every Latin American country. In Lima, enrollment in sewing classes soared along with Maria's fortunes. Domestic servants, the largest occupational group of women in Latin America, were among Maria's most ardent devotees. When a group of social scientists asked Lima's servant women about their career aspirations, or what they would like their daughters to be, a single chorus drowned out all other replies: dressmaker.[8]

In many ways, *Simplemente Maria* typifies a genre of women's magazine fiction. The stories, and the magazines that carry them, both reflect and inform their readers' feelings about appropriate behavior for women. The subjects they deal with are the classic components of women's traditional domain: home, family, beauty, and fashion, and—above all—romance. Although this list constitutes a truncated view of women's concerns, discussion of these topics does interest most women. More at fault for the values they promote than the subjects they treat, the traditional magazines depict the ideal woman as dependent and utterly home-centered, capable of finding real satisfaction only in service and submission to others.

The usual run of fiction in the traditional magazines is even more conservative than the editorial content. Cornealia Butler Flora's study of women's magazine fiction in the United States and Latin America showed the values of the two cultures to be quite consistent. The qualities of the ostensibly desirable fictional heroine all manifested passivity: the Everywoman of popular fiction is humble, virtuous, and dependent; weak, submissive, and tolerant of a sexual double standard.

Sixty-nine percent of the plots in Flora's sample were resolved in a way that reinforced female dependence and passivity. In over half of the Latin American stories, one of two plot devices was used: a too-independent heroine found happiness in submitting at last to a dominating man; or an erring man was inspired to abandon his wicked ways by the example of a patient, loving woman who never nagged or reproached him.[9]

These stories depict women in a deeply reactionary way. They do more than misrepresent women; they also lure their readers into a fantasy world of false standards and easy solutions. In this fictional world, happiness comes not out of one's own efforts but via the miraculous intervention of a handsome man. The source of problems is always personal, never born of oppressive social conditions. Marriage is a woman's ultimate goal, childbearing a reward or a resolution rather than a serious responsibility. Saintly self-sacrifice is a women's only heroism, while pride and ambition are follies best outgrown. By promising every women that her prince will someday come (even if only in the guise of a husband whose ardor is miraculously rekindled), escapist stories divert women's energy into daydreams and thus perpetuate passivity.

Some of the traditional women's magazines boast enormous audiences. *McCall's*, the largest in the United States, sells 6.5 million copies of each issue, while *Ladies' Home Journal* and *Good Housekeeping* reach 6 million and 5 million readers, respectively.[10] Yet the continuing popularity of the old standbys has not killed interest in new women's magazines. Rather than catering to the full-time housewife, the new magazines are aimed at the income-earning, decision-making woman. Some of these publications are far from feminist, or only superficially so—they invoke women's changing lifestyles, often in practical terms, but on an individual, material basis. Another group of the new periodicals, seriously feminist, address themselves to the collective awareness and common problems of women.

The line between the two types of "new woman" magazines can be hard to draw. Even some of the hearth-and-hairdo titles have changed to satisfy a different kind of reader. In its fiction *McCall's,* for example, now depicts working women—even working mothers—in a more sympathetic light than it did when few U.S. adult women held jobs. In July 1976, twenty-six American women's magazines, including many of the most traditional (such as *Bride's, Modern Romances,* and *Ladies' Circle*), and the three largest-selling, all ran articles discussing the Equal Rights Amendment. In France, the glossy home-and-fashion magazine *Marie-Claire* started publishing a feminist insert called

Femmes in 1977. Bound into the center of the parent magazine, *Femmes* includes articles about sex-discrimination lawsuits, jobs, and feminist books, while *Marie-Claire* features recipes, grooming tips, celebrity interviews, and the like. Many of the traditional publications have come to include more articles of interest to working women, such as features on day care or on time-saving recipes.[11]

While the traditional periodicals have been making some adjustments, magazines for the "new woman" have been doing well. In a financial climate in which starting a new magazine constitutes a risky business venture, some newcomers have turned in strong performances, attracting both readers and advertisers. Advertisers in particular have flocked to magazines like *Cosmopolitan,* whose feminism (if any) is purely incidental; yet *Cosmo* and its kind are popular with many young women, who work, live alone, and spend hefty sums on clothes, cosmetics, travel, and entertainment. Japan's *More: Quality Life Magazine* is one of this genre, with regular writing on the accoutrements of the "new woman's style"—gourmet cooking, interior decorating, travel, and male-female relationships.

Distinctly unliberated is the obsession displayed by most of these newer magazines with the art of attracting and manipulating men. One characteristic particularly distinguishes them from their predecessors: a casual, almost mercenary attitude toward sex. Their concept of a woman's ultimate goal has not changed—to get a man, it remains—but the woman's arsenal has expanded. No longer is the way to a man's heart simply through his stomach. At its most extreme, represented by *Viva* and *Playgirl,* this class of journalism represents a sad capitulation to the male ethic. Reporter Laura Shapiro asked a spokeswoman for *Playgirl* what was feminist about the magazine and got the answer, "We make men into sex objects."[12]

The middle ground of the new women's magazine market is occupied by publications that lack an explicitly feminist editorial policy but, nonetheless, emphasize women's changing roles, lifestyles, and opportunities. The editor of the new Japanese magazine *Watashi wa Onna (I Am Woman)* denies that the genesis of the magazine lay in the 1970s' new wave of feminism. The reasoning was purely business-like: a drop-off in readership for the traditional periodicals and an obvious market for journals with more serious content. So *Watashi Wa Onna,* feminist or not, carries articles like "Independence from Marriage," "The Revolution in Sex Consciousness," and "Towards a New Understanding among Women." In the United States, *Working Woman* is equally uncommitted to feminist ideology but emphasizes women's career concerns and the management of a busy life that includes a substantial commitment to work as well as to friends, fashion, and entertainment. Advice columns on legal and financial matters, health, and diet also number among *Working Woman's* regular features. The magazine emphasizes individual effort rather than social change. The appeal of this formula is bankable: the magazine had 200,000 readers before the end of its second year.[13]

Many new, explicitly feminist magazines cannot match the circulations of the traditional publications. Reasons include the lack of financial resources for most of the feminist magazines, the non-commercial orientation of many, limited access to conventional distribution channels, and, in some cases, a deliberate appeal to a narrow audience. *Famille et Developpement*, for example, published in Senegal for French-speaking West Africa, has a circulation of only 20,000—though it is probably read by ten times that many people by the time the copies are lent, traded, resold, and passed along. While not exclusively a woman's magazine, *Famille et Developpement* has published hard-hitting articles on prostitution, birth-control pills, female circumcision, polygamy, and sex education. Its independent editorial policy may be partly explained by the fact that the magazine accepts no paid advertising; it is foundation-supported. Since its debut in 1975, every issue has sold out, and the journal is said to have an impact belied by its small circulation.[14]

Ghana's *Obaa Sima (Ideal Woman)* shares with *Famille et Developpement* the problems of publishing for a small literate audience—but it is well established in its seventh year of publication. The magazine's fifth anniversary editorial reviewed some of its policies:

> Through these columns, we have brought to the notice of the whole nation (especially the woman) some of the laws and customs which are not in the interest of women, for example, the existing laws on inheritance and intestate succession.
>
> We have called for the abolition of such laws and asked for progressive national laws on inheritance and we have reason to believe that something is going to be done about them.
>
> We shall continue to draw the attention of our readers and the whole nation to all matters which will improve the status of women in our society and we know that our readers will help us in this. . . .[15]

Because they run articles that address serious problems in a serious manner and because they hire editors and writers who do not flinch from controversy, magazines like *Obaa Sima* and *Famille et Developpement* have an impact on attitudes and policies that affect women.

Most literate countries with well-developed media markets now support at least a few small feminist magazines and newspapers. Germany has at least two dozen; in the United States, such publications must number in the hundreds. A few of them have won readerships broad enough to qualify them as organs of the mass media. The grandmother of them all, in a sense, is *Ms.* magazine, published in New York. The first feminist periodical to achieve true commercial success, its circulation in its seventh year reached nearly half a million. *F.*, a French feminist magazine launched early in 1978, is using highly professional promotional techniques to attract a wide audience. *F.* will address itself to serious women's issues but adopt a moderate tone. The hope is that it will strike a sympathetic chord in French women who are well-educated, aware, but not radical. Its founder, Claude Servan-Schreiber, deliberately dissociates the magazine from France's leftist, militant Movement de Liberation des Femmes. "Militancy," she claims, "isn't profitable."[16]

For women, the ultimate value of mass-circulation feminist magazines goes far beyond the financial interests of the backers. Such publications speak both to their readers and to other, more traditional publications: the message is that the audience interested in serious discussion about the world of real women is growing. Because of this, that world and the world of women's magazines may be approaching a closer correspondence.

RADIO—A MEDIUM FOR THE MASSES

To the more than one-third of the world's women who are illiterate, newspapers and magazines mean little. Fewer than a fourth of all women ever see television. The medium with by far the largest audience globally is radio. Radio can reach even the most remote and inaccessible settlements; broadcasting is flexible, low cost, and technically simple. Receivers, especially transistor radios, are easy to operate, durable, and inexpensive. From the listener, radio requires no special skills other than the ability to comprehend the broadcast language. For many millions of the poor, the isolated, and the illiterate, radio provides a window on the world.

In many countries, radio is used to reach rural adults with practical information and educational programs. Colombia has more than 250 radio broadcasting stations; Brazil has nearly 600. All-India Radio broadcasts around the clock in all of India's major languages and some fifty dialects. The government there has also subsidized the purchase of community radio receivers. Virtually every country in the world today has at least one radio station, and most of the world's regions lie within at least one station's broadcast sphere.[17]

Owing to their lower literacy rates, more limited access to formal education, lack of leisure, and lesser mobility, women have even more to gain from radio than men. In Egypt, for example, women make up an estimated 70 percent of the audience for literacy courses broadcast over radio. In a pilot educational radio program in Iran, it was found that for every student organized into listening "classes" (comprised mostly of men), four women followed the programs privately at home.[18]

Programming designed especially for women in poor countries tends to stress domestic skills and child care almost to the exclusion of anything else. So far, too little use has been made of radio to assist women with less traditional pursuits. Realistically, though, providing for home and family remains a large part of women's work and worry. Where radio programs present practical advice that helps women to do their jobs better or more easily, the programs are enthusiastically received.

Some of the most successful of these practical programs coordinate radio broadcasts with the work of extension agents, either hired or volunteer. The broadcasts lend authority to the agents, and the agents can elaborate points made during the broadcasts, illustrate or demonstrate the techniques recommended, and answer questions that arise in connection with the programs.

CARE started one such project in South India in 1977, employing slum women to work with their peers in a multimedia project emphasizing nutrition, health, and family planning. Part of the project was a popular radio soap opera, in which the adventures of a typical slum family illustrated practical solutions for problems concerning children's nutrition and common illnesses, sanitation, immunization, male and female sterilization, deworming, and vitamin A requirements. The program generated many requests for information beyond that presented in the program; the extension agents were prepared to answer them, and CARE provided some of the needed medical services and food supplements.[19]

Although generally a success, the CARE project also illustrates some of the limitations of practical education through mass media. Among the perennial problems that came up were women's lack of control over family income, their secondary role in family decision making (even in matters concerning their own health), and the scarcity of basic facilities such as sewage treatment and potable water. If CARE had not made food and medical treatment available on the spot, many of the women reached by the radio and other media might have been unable to act on the advice they received. As it was, doing so was sometimes impeded by lack of cooperation and understanding from their husbands.[20]

Given the usual absence of special services like those provided by CARE, the best that most broadcast programs can do is to help people make optimal use of the resources at hand. One radio network has been engaged in this sort of effort for more than thirty years: Colombia's Accion Cultural Popular (ACPO), or *Radio Sutatenza* as it is popularly called after the small town where it was founded by a young priest. Latin America's most powerful rural educational radio system, ACPO reaches nearly 500,000 rural Colombians and unknown numbers of people in neighboring countries. ACPO provides no equipment or financing except for educational materials—books and a weekly newspaper. Its action campaigns are based on local needs and local resources; the listeners must plan and carry out the projects themselves.

Some of ACPO's programs are designed specifically for women, and women benefit indirectly from many others. A campaign to improve homes focused on how to build a simple kitchen so that women would no longer have to bend over a smoky fire built around three stones on the ground. The building of local aqueducts in conjunction with another media campaign improved village water supplies. A recent campaign has been carried out on the theme of "responsible parenthood"—though *Radio Sutatenza*, affiliated with the Catholic church, does not advocate modern contraceptive techniques.[21]

Besides broadcasting educational material (as well as news, entertainment, religious, civic, and cultural programs), ACPO trains people. Some of the volunteers who lead the local radio "schools," where the peasants gather in small groups to follow the basic education courses, are chosen to go to one of ACPO's training institutes. There, they are familiarized with radio-school organization, schooled in community-development methods and, at the more senior levels, given management training. Today, the majority of these volunteers are women. Of the more than 12,800 people trained at the institutes so far, nearly half are women—an extraordinary proportion for a conservative society in which women are hardly ever allowed to go away to school, much less to assume leadership positions.[22]

Although some argue convincingly that its heydey has passed, *Radio Sutatenza* has shown how much radio can accomplish when people's real needs are addressed and their participation stimulated. The system taps the collective spirit of the community and diffuses the personal risk attending innovation by lending its prestige and authority to development projects. The system's operation also demonstrates, however, that women's needs are unlikely to be fully answered by a system controlled by others who place their own interests ahead of women's. In the case of *Radio Sutatenza*, Catholic dogma is given precedence over women's need for reliable modes of contraception. The uses of any medium are determined by those who own or control the medium. Influence in the mass media is distributed in much the same way as are other forms of power in society.

TELEVISION

Television is not the most pervasive medium on a worldwide basis, but it is arguably the most compelling. In the relatively affluent countries where television has become truly a mass medium, people devote more of their waking hours to watching TV than to any other activity except work. In societies as disparate as the United States and the Soviet Union, children spend as much or more time watching TV as they spend in school.[23]

Third World countries are rushing headlong to join the television age, often with unanticipated consequences. For television changes the way people live in some fundamental ways. It may change the way they think as well, and it certainly changes what they think about. The world as portrayed on television—especially if much programming is imported—differs markedly from the viewer's real world. A huge discrepancy exists between the broadcast image and the reality of women's lives.

A person brought up on television could end up with some distorted notions about women. For example, an American viewer who thought that television accurately reflected reality would gather from watching television that only one-third of the population was female (though in fact more than half of all Americans are women), for only one-third of the characters who appear on television are female. The viewer would get the impression that about 20 percent or so of the labor force was female (though in reality 46 percent of the American labor force is female), because only a fifth of the working people seen on television are female. On television, women seem to have a shorter lifespan than men, since most TV women are in their twenties or thirties while the men quite often survive into late middle age. In the real world, American women outlive American men by about six years.[24]

To be sure, the televised world is not the one we inhabit. The "facts" are all wrong. But when it comes to portrayal of character, conflict, personal relations, problem solving, and so forth, American television's mirror of women's reality is even more distorted. The content of U.S. television programming has been analyzed during the mid-seventies by both public and private groups, including the U.S. Commission on Civil Rights, the Corporation for Public Broadcasting, the American Association of University Women, and the United Methodist Church.

Their monitoring projects have produced remarkably consistent results: most TV women are economically and psychologically dependent, deceitful, incompetent, indecisive, foolish, and cruel or competitive toward other women. Women rarely occupy positions of authority and are often portrayed unsympathetically when they do. They are much more likely to have their problems solved for them by a man than to solve their own or someone else's problem. The television woman's flaws are typically presented as being cute and funny, as if womanly charm equals a kind of social retardation. The adorable nitwit is a damaging and lowly role model for women and girls, yet they see few positive alternatives on the television screen.[25]

Social pressures have produced some changes in U.S. television programming. The mid-seventies saw a trend toward showing more lifelike people in more plausible situations, toward allowing programming on controversial issues, and even toward giving a few strong, credible female characters prominent roles. Some of the standard bearers of this trend, like "The Mary Tyler Moore Show" and "All in the Family," proved immensely popular. But few would argue that the changes went far enough in these shows or in their spin-offs. Men continue to be overrepresented by a three-to-one margin in prime-time television programs.[25] Women continue to be subordinate, professionally and emotionally, to men.

A more recent trend in prime-time programming may increase the number of women on American television but can only reinforce their status as sex objects: in the late seventies, the number of what network executives frankly refer to as "girlie shows" was on the increase. Under pressure from both audiences and federal regulators to tone down the violence on television shows, the networks have responded by substituting sexy women for violent men in their "adult" programs.

The success of one such show, *Charlie's Angels*, generated a rash of imitators featuring gorgeous young women in various glamorous occupations with their sexual charms constantly on display. In the 1978 viewing season, the three female private detectives of "Charlie's Angels were joined by the three stewardesses of "Flying High" and the two investigative reporters of "The American Girls." Among the backup pilot programs readied for 1978 were "The California Girls" (lifeguards), "Cheerleaders," "El Paso Pussycats" (more cheerleaders), and "She" (a female James Bond type). Network executives must believe that they possess a winning formula.

U.S. audiences reacted to the banality of the 1977 television season by watching less television. Prime-time viewership in the autumn of 1977 was 3 percent below the level of a year earlier, a small decline but enough to cause alarm in an industry that has grown steadily since its earliest years.[27] The networks' attempts to win back the viewers with a lavish display of feminine pulchritude and a little more explicit sex may improve ratings for a time, but TV audiences may well find television sex can be every bit as banal as television violence.

The bias of U.S. television finds echoes in sexual stereotyping on British, French, Japanese, and Latin American TV, indeed, on most TV. (Television in China and the Soviet Union has a didactic flavor that does not permit "sexploitation." Significantly, both countries import almost no TV from the West.) The portrayal of women on American television, however, looms large in a discussion of worldwide patterns for one compelling reason: the United States exports programs to all but a handful of TV broadcasting countries, and it is by an overwhelming margin the largest exporter in the world. The image of women presented on U.S. television is nearly as ubiquitous as television itself.

The predominance of the United States in television program exports is explained mostly by the size of its domestic market. Until the early sixties, more television sets were found in the United States than in the rest of the world. In 1978, 96 percent of all American homes had at least one set—more than had private bathrooms. The size of this audience assures that domestic showings pay production costs. The programs can then be sold abroad for a marginal price that is usually set according to the number of viewers served by a foreign buyer. Usually, the smaller the network, the more economical it is to buy American; so local productions cannot possibly compete financially. In Jamaica, for example, it costs twenty times as much to produce a local show as it does to broadcast one made in the United States. Imported programs are a compelling alternative for any country that lacks a well-developed infrastructure in the performing arts, a body of trained technicians, or money for local productions.[28]

Since foreign sales of U.S. programs are handled by many distributors, total sales figures can only be roughly estimated. According to a UNESCO report published in 1974, between 100,000 and 200,000 hours of U.S. television programming are sold to foreign clients each year. The closest competitor, Britain, sold no more than 30,000 hours abroad. France followed with 15,000 to 20,000 hours per year. Apart from these three, only a handful of countries export more than 1000 hours per year. Thus most countries with high ratios of imported to domestic programming show a great deal of American television (see Table 1).[29]

When a broadcasting system buys U.S. television programming, it also buys the American version of the feminine mystique—a view of women that may be even more out of tune with the purchasing country's

Table 1 Estimated Imports of Television Programming, Total and from the United States; Selected Countries

Country of origin	Imports as share of total, percent	Imports from United States as share of total, percent
United States (commercial)	1	NA
Canada (BC)	34	28
Western Europe:		15-20
United Kingdom (BBC and ITV)	13	12
Latin America:	—	33
Chile	55	40
Colombia	34	24
Dominican Republic	50	25
Guatemala	84	50
Mexico (Telesistema)	39	33
Uruguay	62	40
Eastern Europe:	—	—
Soviet Union (Cent. 1st)	5	0
Bulgaria	45	—
Poland	17	—
Yugoslavia	27	11
Asia and the Pacific:	33	17-20 (excluding PRC)
Australia	57	30
China	1	0
Japan (NHK General)	4	2
Republic of Korea	31	28
Malaysia	71	36
New Zealand	75	44
Philippines (ABC-CBV)	29	19
Near East:	50	—
Egypt	41	29
Lebanon (Telibor)	40	20
Yemen PDR	57	14
Africa:	48	—
Ghana	27	—
Nigeria	63	—
Uganda	19	—
Zambia	64	—

Source: UNESCO, Reports and Papers on Mass Communications, No. 70, 1974.

society than it is with American life. A few countries, Britain and France among them, have deliberately reduced their consumption of American television in protest of the violence contained in the imported programs. (One BBC study found that the 20 percent of prime-time programming imported from the United States contained 50 percent of all the violence in BBC broadcasts.) Broadcast authorities would do well to give equally careful consideration to the sexual content of television imports (whatever their source), judging whether the image of women presented is in the public interest.[30]

Domestic productions should receive the same scrutiny. Television is, for increasing numbers of people, a major source of information about the world. Since its distortions are all too often accepted as reality, those who control the medium must see to it that television does not delude people with powerful false images of women. Thus far, that responsibility has been sadly neglected.

BEHIND MEDIA BIAS AGAINST WOMEN

The entire weight of sexism in society is behind the mass media bias against women. This is not to say, however, that the media merely reflect public attitudes passively. Newspapers, magazines, radio, and television also shape opinion. They provide information selectively and play favorites among different kinds of people. Perhaps most important, media executives determine which issues gain the attention of the public, secure in the knowledge that media coverage both signifies and conveys importance.

Most of the people who set policy, write copy, and make daily decisions in the news, entertainment, and advertising industries are men. This imbalance poses a problem of perspective, at the very least. Concern for and sensitivity to matters that affect women particularly are most likely to be found among women themselves; so go the dictates of experience and simple self-interest. Lack of this concern and sensitivity is one source of the media's bias against women. As one senior, female advertising executive put it, it is a challenge for industry professionals "to subject their own personal assumptions about society to the kind of objective appraisal they are trained to do so well."[31]

The answer to the perspective problem is an obvious one: hire more women in the media. Yet, while in many countries the numbers of women employed in the media have risen over the past few years, women are still a small minority among both print and broadcast professionals, especially in senior positions. Among British senior journalists in 1975, for example, only 10 percent of those with at least 10 years' full-time working experience were women. In Denmark, where almost all media employees are unionized, only 15 percent of active members of the journalists' union are women. Both of these countries, however, compare favorably with Japan, where not even 1 percent of the staff writers on daily newspapers are women.[32]

In broadcasting, women professionals are similarly scarce. The Canadian Broadcasting Corporation (CBC) is fairly typical of its counterparts: in 1975, three-quarters of all its employees were male, and in management-level jobs men's share was 93 percent. Out of 1425 job titles within the CBC, men held 1086 exclusively. Because television careers carry glamor and prestige as well as high salaries, the competition for jobs is unusually tough. Women have generally found easier access to radio broadcasting. In Taiwan, for example, only 15 percent of the television news reporters are women, while more than half of the radio (Broadcasting Company of China) reporters are female. The national radio systems in Egypt and in France are both headed by women—a milestone that no major national television system has yet reached.[33]

Still absurdly low, the proportion of media jobs held by women does seem to be rising in a number of countries. If the sex ratio among journalism students indicates the future ratio among mass-media employees, even greater changes may lie ahead. Reports from Malaysia, Taiwan, Thailand, and Singapore indicate that in the mid-seventies, half or more of the communications students in a selection of major universities were women. Women made up more than half the students at the prestigious journalism schools of Columbia University and New York University in 1977. Even in Japan, where male dominance of the media is not weakening perceptibly, women students account for one-quarter of those studying journalism or communications at six universities that have media programs. Most journalists enter the field without specialized training in communications, however, so that rising enrollments are not direct harbingers of rising employment figures.[34]

Once employed in the mass media, women often face discrimination in assignments, promotions, and salaries. They also face unusual hurdles in day-to-day operations, some of which are comic in their outlandishness. The first woman hired as a sportswriter for the *Washington Star* newspaper was barred from the local stadium's press room by her own colleagues, until her editor, a former football player, broke its door down on her behalf. A reporter for the Fleet Street News Agency was ordered to leave the British courtroom where she was covering a trial because the presiding judge considered the sight of a woman in trousers an affront to the dignity of his courtroom. Despite obstacles both petty and significant, women continue to enter the communications field in growing numbers.[35]

There is little doubt that employment of women by the mass media has been spurred in the United States by legal action against several prominent organs. Among the institutions that have faced sex-discrimination suits since the mid-seventies are the *Washington Post, Newsday, Newsweek*, the National Broadcasting Company (NBC), and Reuters North America. All the investigations have concluded that women were being discriminated against, and several have resulted in sizable cash awards to the offended party. In 1977, NBC had to pay nearly two million dollars in back pay to women employees. In late 1978, a similar suit against the *New York Times* was settled out of court. Called upon to explain a salary differential of almost four thousand dollars a year between male and female reporters and editors and a job distribution pattern in which men are twice as likely as women to be hired into the six highest-paying job categories (even after correcting for differences in education, length of service, and previous experience), the *New York Times* elected to make compensatory payments (in the form of pension fund contributions) to its aggrieved female employees and pledged to step up its promotion of women into high-level positions.[36]

Most of the organs that have been sued for discrimination have responded by hiring and promoting more women. Sadly, the bene-ficiaries of the improvements are more likely to be women hired from outside than the women who pressed the issue to begin with. Legal action does not always improve women's employment conditions. A climate at least mildly conducive to change is probably prerequisite. In the absence of such a climate, Fujii-TV in Japan responded to having its mandatory female retirement age of twenty-five struck down in court by refusing thereafter to hire women on anything other than a four-year contract.[37]

Greater participation by women in the making of the mass media is undoubtedly a step toward eliminating sex bias in the media's content. But reporters, producers, script writers, directors, and their colleagues operate within a structure that itself limits what an individual can do to produce egalitarian fare. The financial supports of the media have the power to determine what gets on the air or in print (subject, in some cases, to political controls as well), and their views on the proper roles for women affect the way women are portrayed in the media.

In some countries, the state is the sole financial backer of the mass media. In a few of these, the mass media have been enlisted in a campaign to sell sexual equality. In China, popular fiction, films, and theater feature heroines who triumph over adversity and dastardly male chauvinists who either get their come-uppance or finally see the error of their ways; newspapers report the achievements of right-thinking women doing jobs that could make strong men quake; wall posters proclaim "Women hold up half of heaven." A Cuban poster campaign of 1969–70 plastered walls all over the country with slogans such as "Women: The Revolution within the Revolution." In both countries, the mass media reflect the state's commitment to the idea of improving women's status. Many governments, however, seem to take a laissez-faire attitude toward the depiction of women in the media, which are controlled financially or politically by the government. The subject is not really treated as a policy matter except in extreme cases such as hard-core pornography.

When financial support of the mass media is in the hands of commercial interests, its content is determined by a more convoluted but equally purposeful process. The purpose of the words and pictures in commercial media, from the sponsors' point of view, is to give value to the advertising space they surround. This they do by attracting an audience that will then be exposed to the commercial message. Thus, whatever attracts readers, listeners, or viewers is valuable in commercial terms, no matter what its cultural, intellectual, or social value. Three of the popular daily newspapers in Britain regularly feature pictures of naked women on an inside page, and that is a viable commercial policy because it sells papers.

It is no surprise to find that commercial interests are not necessarily consonant with the public interest. In relation to the female half of the public, the dichotomy is particularly large. In a recent survey of housewives in six major cities across the United States, only 8 percent of the respondents thought the advertising image of women as an accurate one.[38] This is striking considering that women are the "target" audience for so much of the mass media's output. Daytime television, for instance, is almost entirely geared toward adult women, as is the advertising it carries.

The serial melodramas that account for more than half of network daytime television got the generic name "soap operas" from the fact that so many of their radio precursors were sponsored by soap manufacturers. Still, half of the soap operas on daytime television are sponsored by Procter and Gamble, the household products manufacturer.[39] Women are the chief consumers of the company's products (and those of its competitors), and it has traditionally been able to reach them with its sales pitch at home, during the day, with the television on.

It must be frustrating to marketers to find a large portion of their captive audience of housebound women suddenly leaving their houses and television sets for paid employment. It makes the target audience more difficult to teach. This is disconcerting for television networks, too, since their advertising space is priced on the basis of how many viewers they can deliver to an advertiser: the smaller the audience, the smaller the advertising income. This relation between commercial media and advertisers may generate resistance to changing roles for women: such changes require rethinking of formulas that have proved successful in the past.

Some advertisers have responded more positively to changes in women's roles, seeing change as an opportunity rather than a threat. They recognize that it is poor marketing strategy to ignore the growing segment of the population made up of women who work outside the home. Therefore, a company like United Airlines, which by 1978 found that 16 percent of its business travelers were women, directs one-quarter of its print-advertising budget specifically toward women. One-third of the bosses who appear on its television ads are female. Sears, Roebuck Company, after noting that 5.2 million U.S. women held blue collar jobs in 1976, featured a line of sturdy work clothes tailored for women in its 1977 catalogue. Other U.S. manufacturers have taken notice of the fact that women in professional and managerial jobs spend $4.6 billion per year on "work" clothes, and have more money to spend on goods and services than their nonearning counterparts.[40]

The commercial messages designed for the more forward-looking sponsors reflect a greater diversity of roles filled by women, and therefore present a more accurate view of women as well as a less demeaning one. But these sponsors, though they acknowledge change, are unlikely to do much to initiate further change; they still have a vested interest in the status quo, though their view of it is more up-to-date than that of many other advertisers. They can also be every bit as exploitive of women as more traditional-minded competitors; some have even tried to exploit for commercial purposes the positive images associated with women's liberation—the most notorious being the "You've Come a Long Way, Baby" theme of the Virginia Slims cigarette company. Yet even though the ads are manipulative by their very nature, this new breed is less damaging to women's self-esteem than the old household-drudge variations. They may even encourage women to view themselves more positively.

Publicly supported media are not entirely immune from the syndromes of commercialism. They are, however, selling a different product for a different sponsor. At their best, it can be said that they "sell" the public interest, at the behest of the public whose representatives control the media. Some of the northern European countries regard a governmental role in sponsorship of the media as clearly preferable to commercial sponsorship alone, because the latter does not give a voice to segments of the population that have no economic clout. Thus, the Norwegian government gives subsidies or grants to many newspapers and press agencies in order to assure a wide spectrum of viewpoints in the press. (One of the great recipients is the Press Service of the Norwegian National Council of Women.) In the Netherlands, any organization with at least 15,000 members can apply for one hour of free television-transmission time per week, provided it does not use the time for any commercial purpose.[41]

It is impossible for the media, print or broadcast, to be neutral in the presentation of values. The only way to guarantee that groups having a particular value system do not suppress all others is to secure access to the media for people who hold diverse views. Where the image of women is concerned, that in itself has revolutionary potential, for one of the most damaging things about women's portrayal in the media has been the apparent lack of options. Even where diversity is encouraged, however, sexism in the media is unlikely to subside as long as discrimination against women is widely tolerated in the real world.

NOTES

1. *Mass Media in Society: The Need of Research*, Reports and Papers on Mass Communication No. 59. Paris: UNESCO, 1970; *Media Report to Women*, March 1, 1978.

2. Margaret de Miraval, "France's Consumer Affairs Minister," *Christian Science Monitor*, February 2, 1977.

3. Yayori Matsui, "Contempt for Women and Asians in the Japanese Press," *Feminist Japan*, February 1978. International issue.

4. Jo Freeman, *The Politics of Women's Liberation*, excerpted in Maurine Beasley and Sheila Silver, *Women in Media: A Documentary Source Book*. Washington, D.C.: Women's Institute for Freedom of the Press, 1977.

5. Sachiko Ide, "Language, Women and Mass Media in Japan," *Feminist Japan*, February 1978.

6. Andrew H. Malcolm, "Support Waning, Women's Movement Knuckles Under in Japan," *New York Times*, July 23, 1977.

7. "Regional Women's Feature Services Taking Shape," UNESCO press release, May 23, 1978.

8. I am indebted to Dr. Elsa Chaney for bringing the story of *Simplemente Maria* to my attention, and for describing the plot and its impact.

9. Cornelia Butler Flora, "The Passive Female and Social Change: A Cross-Cultural Analysis of Women's Magazine Fiction," in Ann Pescatello, ed., *Female and Male in Latin America*. Pittsburgh, PA: University of Pittsburgh Press, 1973.

10. Deidre Carmody, "Women's Magazines are More than Fashionable," *New York Times*, February 14, 1978.

11. *Women Today*, March 29, 1976; *Women's International Network News*, Summer, 1977.

12. Solrun Hoass, "New Women's Magazines," *Mainichi Daily News*, September 28, 1977; Laura Shapiro, "Cosmo: Let Them Eat Quiche," *Mother Jones*, May 1978.

13. Hoass, *op cit.*; M. A. Farber, "Editor Loses Fight for Working Woman," *New York Times*, May 22, 1977.

14. Bob Stanley, "A Tale of Two Magazines," *The IDRC Reports*, June 1978.

15. *Women's International Network News*, Summer 1976.

16. Susan Heller Anderson, "France's Discreetly Feminist Magazine," *New York Times*, January 13, 1978.

17. Armand Defever, "The Role of Radio in Rural Development." Paper presented at the International Seminar: Mass Communication and Development, June 10–25, 1973. Haifa, Israel: Mount Carmel International Training Centre for Community Services; John Maddison, *Radio and Television in Literacy*, Reports and Papers on Mass Communication, No. 62. Paris: UNESCO, 1974.

18. *Ibid.*

19. Manorama S. Moss, "What Extension Educators and the Mass Media Can and Can't Do – A Nutrition Education Project in India," *Development Communications Report*, July 1978.

20. *Ibid.*

21. Carla Clason, "La Campesina," *World Education Reports*, no. 10, December 1975; Susana Amaya, "Radio: School for Millions," *The IDRC Reports*, vol. 7, no. 2. June 1978, p. 16.

22. Clason, *op cit.*

23. Erik Barnouw, *The Sponsor: Notes on a Modern Potentate*. New York: Oxford University Press, 1978; Ellen Proper Mickiewicz, "Watching the Soviets Watch Television," *New York Times*, July 9, 1978.

24. The United Methodist Women's Television Monitoring Project, *Sex Role Stereotyping in Prime Time Television*, July 1976.

25. *Window Dressing on the Set: Women and Minorities in Television*, U.S. Commission on Civil Rights, 1977; *Report of the Task Force on Women in Public Broadcasting*, Corporation for Public Broadcasting, Washington, D.C., 1975; "Monitoring Prime Time," in Beasley and Silver, *op. cit.*; United Methodist Women's Television Monitoring Project, *op. cit.*

26. Gaye Tuchman, "The Symbolic Annihilation of Women by the Mass Media," in Gaye Tuchman, Arlene Kaplan Daniels, and James Benet, eds., *Hearth and Home: Images of Women in the Mass Media*. New York: Oxford University Press, 1978.

27. Robert Sklar, "Just Don't Show the Blood," *American Film*, April 1978.

28. Tuchman, *op. cit.*; Elihu Katz, "Mass Media: Expectations and Performance." Paper presented at the International Seminar, Mass Communication and Development, June 10–25, 1973, Mount Carmel International Training Centre, Haifa, Israel; Kathleen Courrier, review of *Third World Mass Media and their Search for Modernity* by John Lent, *Development Communications Report*, July 1978.

29. Kaarle Nordenstreng and Tapio Varis, *Television Traffic – a One-Way Street?*, Reports and Papers on Mass Communication, No. 70. Paris: UNESCO, 1974.

30. *Ibid.*

31. Rena Bartos, "Madison Avenue Doesn't Try to Insult Women," *Christian Science Monitor*, August 16, 1978.

32. *Royal Commission on the Press: Final Report*, Appendix G, "Selection and Training of Journalists." London: Her Majesty's Stationery Office, July 1977; *Women's International Network News*, January 1976; Yayori Matsui, *op. cit.*

33. *Report on the Status of Women in the CBC*, excerpted in Beasley and Silver, *op. cit.*; *Proceedings of the Asian Consultation on Women and Media*, Center for Communication Studies, Chinese University of Hong Kong, April 1976; Women's International Network News, Spring 1977; *Media Report to Women*, January 1, 1977.

34. *Proceedings of the Asian Consultation on Women and Media*, 1976.

35. Kiki Levathes, private communication, August 1978; Associated Press, "Judge Bars Reporter, A Woman in Trousers," *New York Times*, February 17, 1977.

36. Janice Prindle, "Women, New Math, Old Times," *Village Voice*, March 27, 1978.

37. Keiko Higuchi, private communication, September 1977.

38. *Women Today*, January 9, 1978.

39. C. Gerald Fraser, "A Study of Daytime Network TV Finds it Geared to the Housewife," *New York Times*, July 11, 1977.

40. Barbara Lovenheim, "Admen Woo the Working Woman," *New York Times*, June 18, 1978; *Women Today*, September 5, 1977; Deborah Sue Yaeger, "Many Companies Find Employed Women are a High-Profit Market," *Wall Street Journal*, August 31, 1978.

41. Grethe Vaernø, "Getting Women into Male-Run Media," *Development Forum*, July 1978; Nordenstreng and Varis, *op. cit.*

STUDY QUESTIONS

1. To what degree can a household guest in a foreign country behave like "a member of the family"? Are the expectations of Colombian hosts toward the behavior of their American guests different from your expected behavior within your own family? Are they different from the behavior you would expect of a guest whom you wanted to feel like "one of the family"? Notice that several hosts commented that their guests were "badly brought up." Do you think that this may have been a correct interpretation of their behavior in some cases? For what reason(s)?

2. Compare your own practice of shaking hands with that of the Colombians. How many people do you normally shake hands with when you go to a party where there are lots of people whom you don't know? How often do you shake hands with people whom you see every day? How do you greet friends whom you haven't seen for a week? For a year? How do you interpret a relatively limp handshake?

3. Look in a Spanish language-teaching textbook to see what explanation/ advice is given for the use of *tú* and *usted*. Do they reflect any of the observations reported by the correspondents in the survey? Compare the explanations with those for *tu* and *vous* in a French textbook, *du* and *Sie* in a German textbook, etc. Why do American students of these foreign languages have trouble adjusting to the two forms of saying "you"?

4. Share with your classmates any experiences you have had living with a family in another country. Were there any customs (either yours or theirs) that led to misinterpretation or conflict?

5. Compare *McCall's, Ms., Cosmopolitan*, and *Viva* in terms of the type of woman to which each is designed to appeal. Which do you find the most interesting? Why? Compare your reaction to those of your classmates of the opposite sex.

6. If you watch television regularly, do you agree with Newland's criticism that television presents biased stereotypes of women? If you are not a TV watcher, force yourself to watch it for one whole evening during prime time and see what proportion of the actors (in both shows and commercials) are women, and whether women (and men) are portrayed in stereotypes. What are those stereotypes? Identify the program, character, or situation.

7. If you went to another country, would you expect television programming to reflect the realities of the culture in every respect? What differences, if any, would you expect?

8. Consider the roles of the physician and the patient. What expectations do you hold for the two roles? How is our traditional understanding of these roles being challenged today? Consider the patients' rights movement or the right-to-die issue.

PERCEPTION AND STEREOTYPES

The concepts of perception and stereotyping are demonstrated in two quite different settings for this section. Horace M. Miner's description of "Body Ritual among the Nacirema" is an explicit (and entertaining) exercise of how, through perception, we classify and give meaning to the multiple impressions we have of reality. Miner's imaginary anthropologist helps us to see how our attitudes and actions might be interpreted through an alternate frame of reference. As for the report produced by the Asia Society, it underscores the fact that stereotyping of Asia and Asians in textbooks occurs with greater frequency than we may be aware. It offers the results of a comprehensive study of how Asia is depicted in American school textbooks. The society discovered that despite expert knowledge of the subject matter, with few exceptions, American ethnocentrism left little margin for alternative value systems. It is difficult not to heed the society's conclusions and recognize that major rewriting of the textbooks is a necessity.

(For further discussion on perception and stereotypes, see E. C. Carterette and M. P. Friedman, J. Walz, F. Fitzgerald, *Fair Textbooks* in the bibliography.)

Body Ritual Among the Nacirema

Horace M. Miner

Reproduced by permission of the American Anthropological Association from the *American Anthropologist,* 58 (3), 1956.

The anthropologist has become so familiar with the diversity of ways in which different peoples behave in similar situations that he is not apt to be surprised by even the most exotic customs. In fact, if all of the logically possible combinations of behavior have not been found somewhere in the world, he is apt to suspect that they must be present in some yet undescribed tribe. The point has, in fact, been expressed with respect to clan organization by Murdock (1949:71). In this light, the magical beliefs and practices of the Nacirema present such unusual aspects that it seems desirable to describe them as an example of the extremes to which human behavior can go.

Professor Linton first brought the ritual of the Nacirema to the attention of anthropologists twenty years ago (1936:326), but the culture of this people is still very poorly understood. They are a North American group living in the territory between the Canadian Cree, the Yaqui and Tarahumare of Mexico, and the Carib and Arawak of the Antilles. Little is known of their origin, although tradition states that they came from the east. According to Nacirema mythology, their nation was originated by a culture hero, Notgnihsaw, who is otherwise known for two great feats of strength—the throwing of a piece of wampum across the river Pa-To-Mac and the chopping down of a cherry tree in which the Spirit of Truth resided.

Nacirema culture is characterized by a highly developed market economy which has evolved in a rich natural habitat. While much of the people's time is devoted to economic pursuits, a large part of the fruits of these labors and a considerable portion of the day are spent in ritual activity. The focus of this activity is the human body, the appearance and health of which loom as a dominant concern in the ethos of the people. While such a concern is certainly not unusual, its ceremonial aspects and associated philosophy are unique.

The fundamental belief underlying the whole system appears to be that the human body is ugly and that its natural tendency is to debility and disease. Incarcerated in such a body, man's only hope is to avert these characteristics through the use of the powerful influences of ritual and ceremony. Every household has one or more shrines devoted to this purpose. The more powerful individuals in the society have several shrines in their houses and, in fact, the opulence of a house is often referred to in terms of the number of such ritual centers it possesses. Most houses are of wattle and daub construction, but the shrine rooms of the more wealthy are walled with stone. Poorer families imitate the rich by applying pottery plaques to their shrine walls.

While each family has at least one such shrine, the rituals associated with it are not family ceremonies but are private and secret. The rites are normally only discussed with children, and then only during the period when they are being initiated into these mysteries. I was able, however, to establish sufficient rapport with the natives to examine these shrines and to have the rituals described to me.

The focal point of the shrine is a box or chest which is built into the wall. In this chest are kept the many charms and magical potions without which no native believes he could live. These preparations are secured from a variety of specialized practitioners. The most powerful of these are the medicine men, whose assistance must be rewarded with substantial gifts. However, the medicine men do not provide the curative potions for their clients, but decide what the ingredients should be and then write them down in an ancient and secret language. This writing is understood only by the medicine men and by the herbalists who, for another gift, provide the required charm.

The charm is not disposed of after it has served its purpose, but is placed in the charm-box of the household shrine. As these magical materials are specific for certain ills, and the real or imagined maladies of the people are many, the charm-box is usually full to overflowing. The magical packets are so numerous that people forget what their purposes were and fear to use them again. While the natives are very vague on this point, we can only assume that the idea in retaining all the old magical materials is that their presence in the charm-box, before which the body rituals are conducted, will in some way protect the worshipper.

Beneath the charm-box is a small font. Each day every member of the family, in succession, enters the shrine room, bows his head before the charm-box, mingles different sorts of holy water in the font, and proceeds with a brief rite of ablution. The holy waters are secured from the Water Temple of the community, where the priests conduct elaborate ceremonies to make the liquid ritually pure.

In the hierarchy of magical practitioners, and below the medicine men in prestige, are specialists whose designation is best translated "holy-mouth-men." The Nacirema have an almost pathological horror of and fascination with the mouth, the condition of which is believed to have a supernatural influence on all social relationships. Were it not for the rituals of the mouth, they believe that their teeth would fall out, their gums bleed, their jaws shrink, their friends desert them, and their lovers reject them. They also believe that a strong relationship exists between oral and moral characteristics. For example, there is a ritual ablution of the mouth for children which is supposed to improve their moral fiber.

The daily body ritual performed by everyone includes a mouth-rite. Despite the fact that these people are so punctilious about care of the mouth, this rite involves a practice which strikes the uninitiated stranger as revolting. It was reported to me that the ritual consists of inserting a small bundle of hog hairs into the mouth, along with certain magical powders, and then moving the bundle in a highly formalized series of gestures.

In addition to the private mouth-rite, the people seek out a holy-mouth-man once or twice a year. These practitioners have an impressive set of paraphernalia, consisting of a variety of augers, awls, probes, and prods. The use of these objects in the exorcism of the evils of the mouth involves almost unbelievable ritual torture of the client. The holy-mouth-man opens the client's mouth and, using the above mentioned tools, enlarges any holes which decay may have created in the teeth. Magical materials are put into these holes. If there are no naturally occurring holes in the teeth, large sections of one or more teeth are gouged out so that the supernatural substance can be applied. In the client's view, the purpose of these ministrations is to arrest decay and to draw friends. The extremely sacred and traditional character of the rite is evident in the fact that the natives return to the holy-mouth-men year after year, despite the fact that their teeth continue to decay.

It is to be hoped that, when a thorough study of the Nacirema is made, there will be careful inquiry into the personality structure of these people. One has but to watch the gleam in the eye of a holy-mouth-man, as he jabs an awl into an exposed nerve, to suspect that a certain amount of sadism is involved. If this can be established, a very interesting pattern emerges, for most of the population shows definite masochistic tendencies. It was to these that Professor Linton referred in discussing a distinctive part of the daily body ritual which is performed only by men. This part of the rite involves scraping and lacerating the surface of the face with a sharp instrument. Special women's rites are performed only four times during each lunar month, but what they lack in frequency is made up in barbarity. As part of this ceremony, women bake their heads in small ovens for about an hour. The theoretically interesting point is that what seems to be a preponderantly masochistic people have developed sadistic specialists.

The medicine men have an imposing temple, or *latipso,* in every community of any size. The more elaborate ceremonies required to treat very sick patients can only be performed at this temple. These ceremonies involve not only the thaumaturge but a permanent group of vestal maidens who move sedately about the temple chambers in distinctive costume and headdress.

The *latipso* ceremonies are so harsh that it is phenomenal that a fair proportion of the really sick natives who enter the temple ever recover. Small children whose indoctrination is still incomplete have been known to resist attempts to take them to the temple because "that is where you go to die." Despite this fact, sick adults are not only willing but eager to undergo the protracted ritual purification, if they can afford to do so. No matter how ill the supplicant or how grave the emergency, the guardians of many temples will not admit a client if he cannot give a rich gift to the custodian. Even after one has gained admission and survived the ceremonies, the guardians will not permit the neophyte to leave until he makes still another gift.

The supplicant entering the temple is first stripped of all his or her clothes. In everyday life the Nacirema avoids exposure of his body and its natural functions. Bathing and excretory acts are performed only in the secrecy of the household shrine, where they are ritualized as part of the body-rites. Psychological shock results from the fact that body secrecy is suddenly lost upon entry into the *latipso.* A man, whose own wife has never seen him in an excretory act, suddenly finds himself naked and assisted by a vestal maiden while he performs his natural functions into a sacred vessel. This sort of ceremonial treatment is necessitated by the fact that the excreta are used by a diviner to ascertain the course and nature of the client's sickness. Female clients, on the other hand, find their naked bodies are subjected to the scrutiny, manipulation, and prodding of the medicine men.

Few supplicants in the temple are well enough to do anything but lie on their hard beds. The daily ceremonies, like the rites of the holy-mouth-men, involve discomfort and torture. With ritual precision, the vestals awaken their miserable charges each dawn and roll them about on their beds of pain while performing ablutions, in the formal movements of which the maidens are highly trained. At other times they insert magic wands in the supplicant's mouth or force him to eat substances which are supposed to be healing. From time to time the medicine men come to their clients and jab magically treated needles into their flesh. The fact that these temple ceremonies may not cure, and may even kill the neophyte, in no way decreases the people's faith in the medicine men.

There remains one other kind of practitioner, known as a "listener." This witch-doctor has the power to exorcise the devils that lodge in the heads of people who have been bewitched. The Nacirema believe that parents bewitch their own children. Mothers are particularly suspected of putting a curse on children while teaching them the secret body rituals. The counter-magic of the witch-doctor is unusual in its lack of ritual. The patient simply tells the "listener" all his troubles and fears, beginning with the earliest difficulties he can remember. The memory displayed by the Nacirema in these exorcism sessions is truly remarkable. It is not uncommon for the patient to bemoan the rejection he felt upon being weaned as a babe, and a few individuals even see their troubles going back to the traumatic effects of their own birth.

In conclusion, mention must be made of certain practices which have their base in native aesthetics but which depend upon the pervasive aversion to the natural body and its functions. There are ritual fasts to make fat people thin and ceremonial feasts to make thin people fat. Still other rites are used to make women's breasts larger if they are small, and smaller if they are large. General dissatisfaction with breast shape is symbolized in the fact that the ideal form is virtually outside the range of human variation. A few women afflicted with almost inhuman hyper-mammary development are so idolized that they make a handsome living by simply going from village to village and permitting the natives to stare at them for a fee.

Reference has already been made to the fact that excretory functions are ritualized, routinized, and relegated to secrecy. Natural reproductive functions are similarly distorted. Intercourse is taboo as a topic and scheduled as an act. Efforts are made to avoid pregnancy by the use of magical materials or by limiting intercourse to certain phases of the moon. Conception is actually very infrequent. When pregnant, women dress so as to hide their condition. Parturition takes place in secret, without friends or relatives to assist, and the majority of women do not nurse their infants.

Our review of the ritual life of the Nacirema has certainly shown them to be a magic-ridden people. It is hard to understand how they have managed to exist so long under the burdens which they have imposed upon themselves. But even such exotic customs as these take on real meaning when they are viewed with the insight provided by Malinowski when he wrote (1948:70):

> Looking from far and above, from our high places of safety in the developed civilization, it is easy to see all the crudity and irrelevance of magic. But without its power and guidance early man could not have mastered his practical difficulties as he has done, nor could man have advanced to the higher stages of civilization.

REFERENCES CITED

Ralph Linton, *The Study of Man*, D. Appleton-Century Co., New York, 1936.
Bronislaw Malinowski, *Magic, Science, and Religion*, The Free Press, Glencoe, 1948.
George P. Murdock, *Social Structure*, The Macmillan Co., New York, 1949.

Asia in American Textbooks

The Asia Society

Reprinted by permission of The Asia Society, Inc. (122 East 64th Street, New York, New York 10021).

INTRODUCTION

This study distills the results of an intensive survey of how Asia is depicted in American school textbooks. Conducted by the Asia Society with support from The Ford Foundation, the study considered 306 social studies texts in use in the 50 states as of early 1975. The books came primarily from state and city adoption lists across the country, but since some states and localities do not mandate teaching about Asia, the list was supplemented by additional titles supplied by teachers who were using the books in their classrooms. In this way the Asia Society hoped to conduct as complete a survey as possible of those texts in actual use in American schools.

The books were read by over one hundred experts: scholars of Asian studies, elementary and secondary school teachers with Asian specialization and experience in teaching about Asia, and writers with a special concern about how Americans see Asians.

The study was not the first to analyze attitudes toward Asia in American textbooks, but what distinguishes it from its predecessors is its scope, believed to be the most extensive ever attempted, and even more important, its methodology.

To provide both a common frame of reference for the readers and a tool for quantifying the results, staff of the Society's Educational Resources/Asian Literature Program developed a highly detailed evaluation guide with the assistance of participants in a master's program in

Asian studies for teachers at New York University and revised and refined it several times in consultation with an advisory committee of outstanding leaders in the fields of education and Asian studies.

The questionnaire asked readers to respond to a number of very specific questions on the following elements:

- Accuracy and authenticity
- Underlying assumptions and approaches
- Attitudes toward Asian life and culture and the use of primary Asian sources such as literature, the fine arts, historical documents, case studies, and similar materials (referred to in the evaluation guide as humanistic/human interest materials)
- Style and tone
- Format and illustrations
- Attitudes toward women
- Qualifications of authors and consultants

Readers were asked to document their answers wherever possible by citations from the texts and to indicate how they would rate the books on an overall basis as suitable for classroom use.

Since 34 of the original 306 books turned out to be excerpts from larger units in the sample, the Society did not solicit complete answers on these duplications, although it did receive and tabulate data on the qualifications of authors and consultants for 302 texts—virtually the complete sample. In addition, because not every reviewer answered every question, the number of texts for which information is presented varies from question to question. Data compiled on approaches and underlying assumptions about Asia, for instance, reflected expert opinions on 263 texts; that on the treatment of Asian cultures and the use of primary Asian source materials was based on 260 texts. Every reviewer was asked to report on accuracy, and replies were tabulated for those reports from scholars, 97 in all.

The primary purpose of the study, however, was not to produce a precise numerical profile on the Asian content of American textbooks. It was not even to pinpoint good or bad textbooks, although this indeed was an important consideration. (By far the majority of the texts are a mixture of good and bad.) *Rather, the primary purpose of the survey was to catalog the variety of themes and source materials which can contribute to an understanding of Asia, and on the other hand, those which can distort Asian reality.* It is hoped that this identification will serve as a guide to publishers in the revision and production of new texts, to textbook adoption committees as they select the books that will be used in their schools, and to teachers as they teach about Asia in the classrooms.

It took two years to conduct the survey and compile a full report on the findings, copies of which are on file at both The Asia Society and The Ford Foundation and in limited circulation. In another sense, however, the study has been in the making for nearly 20 years, almost the entire lifespan of The Asia Society.

Founded in 1956 to deepen American understanding of Asia and stimulate thoughtful trans-Pacific intellectual exchange, the Society early undertook two important tasks. One was to produce guides for teachers to books, paperbacks, films, and other supplementary educational materials about Asia. The other was to search out Asian works of literature, find experts to translate them, provide editorial services to translators, encourage the publication of the works in books and literary magazines, and promote their dissemination through readings, conferences, radio programs, and other means.

A logical second step in both these long-term efforts would have been to develop Asian literature selections that might be used to supplement social studies courses on Asia in the elementary and secondary schools. It became apparent, however, that before the Society could create such materials, it must take thorough stock of the social studies texts themselves to find out what was being taught about Asia at each grade level. This report summarizes the findings.

THE ASIA-CENTERED APPROACH

Every textbook approaches Asia with a set of attitudes and assumptions, explicit or implicit, conscious or unconscious. The study also had its own basic point of view—one that it shares with many, if not most, cultural anthropologists: To understand a society one must assume that its cultural system is based upon a coherent set of values—in other words, that commonly held patterns of thought and ways of acting "make sense" to the members of the society. Conveying the reality of the society, then, becomes a matter of describing it in such terms that its people seem "normal" and "logical." Attitudes and actions that may appear to an outsider to be shortsighted, senseless, self-destructive, or even bizarre become rational when viewed from a vantage point within the society.

While this approach avoids the conclusion that the members of another society are strange or stupid, it does not lead to the conclusion that they are "just like us" either. But it does enable us to empathize with the people of that society, to imagine something of the way they feel, think, and look at the world.

One textbook, for instance, employs such an approach in explaining the morning rounds made by Buddhist monks in Thailand. It begins its account by stating that "one of the most common forms of giving is feeding the Buddhist monks, who live on the generosity of the community." The text helps the student to understand this activity as very different from begging in a Western society by going on to say that the monks *do not ask for a contribution, and they receive one in silence. It is rather the giver who states his thanks for the opportunity to gain merit through performing a good deed."* [1]

A textbook employing what we shall call "the Asia-centered approach" does not describe a Japanese home as lacking in the furniture and solid walls with which we are familiar, but tells students that homes in Japan are designed with a simplicity of furnishings and a flexibility of space so that each room can be used in many different ways.

Such a textbook does not recount 19th Century history merely in terms of the Chinese refusal to trade with Europeans or the morality of the opium trade. It also discusses the traditional Chinese tribute system of foreign relations and then describes what followed when *"Europeans rejected the Manchu system of foreign relations."* [2]

Attempting to get beyond the alien and exotic surface of another culture, one textbook employing an Asia-centered approach explains to children that Japanese people prepare and drink tea in a special way and then asks, *"How might you feel if you went to Japan and you were the only person not sitting on the floor to eat?"* Such a textbook helps children to lift their cultural blinders by asking, *"Why is this kind of behavior strange when you think about doing it in the United States, but not when you think about doing it in another country or in a Japanese restaurant?"* It reinforces the child's conclusion by pointing out, *"People have learned to do different things because they live in different places. These things don't seem strange when everyone else does them."* [3]

The Asia-centered approach appears in only 30 percent of the books in the study and predominates in only 18 percent.

THE PROGRESS-CENTERED APPROACH

Far more frequently than the Asia-centered approach, textbooks employ one or another of a cluster of value judgments that can be summarized under the heading of the progress-centered approach. In this view, which was that of 71 percent of the texts in the sample, change is good, necessary, and historically inevitable. "The story of man is one of progress," as one text puts it.

A reader found eight examples from one elementary book on India alone. Among them were the following: *"Its people are changing from old ways of living to new modern ways." "Rural India is changing, though slowly." "Some villagers are learning how to run dairies. They learn how to make the milk safe to drink. Many other villagers go to industrial training schools. They learn to use the machines in India's new factories. They stop being farmers. They begin to lead a new life." "All these things mean that the people of India have a good chance of keeping their freedom during the transition to an up-to-date way of life."* [4]

In *Social Change and History* (Oxford University Press, 1969) the sociologist Robert Nisbet has pointed out that Western thought, following the Greeks, once assumed that social systems are biological organizations that are born, grow to maturity, and die. Since the time of Augustine, the West has tended to believe that cultures and societies grow in a straight line and develop by stages into higher systems. The view that social change is purposeful is no longer confined to the West, however. On the contrary, many Asians now emphasize the importance of development for their own societies. The danger is that the criterion of progress can be applied in such a way that the enduring cultural values of a society—any society—are distorted or neglected. If this happens, tradition (because it is old) may be regarded as existing in quaint juxtaposition with the new rather than interacting with it:

"Rocket experts ride buses alongside Indian mystics. Sacred cows share the streets with automobiles. Indian industries produce tractors, yet millions of peasants still use wooden plows. The contrasts are endless." [5]

Other texts describe modernity as challenging, conflicting with, or contradicting tradition: *"Some of this will become clear as we examine conflicts between the new ways and old in the family, the position of women, and the social classes."* [6]

Some textbook writers find the interaction of past and present simply perplexing: *"Chiyo's youth had been a rather confusing combination of Japanese tradition and Western modernity."* [7]

In citing passages like these from the texts, some readers added that the dichotomy between tradition and change is based on superficial definitions of the two concepts. "Modernity," pointed out a reader of one text, "mentioned in connection with the strivings of Southeast Asian leaders here and there, is characterized implicitly as consisting of tall buildings, electricity, and air-conditioning. . . . The complexity of change is not really brought up at all."

One Way of Presenting Change that Recognizes Continuity   History would seem to indicate that in all societies change has taken place at all times. But in the process, past and present interact; cultural traditions are not destroyed, they are transformed.

The following example from a text assumes a constructive relationship between modernity and tradition: *"Maoism was deliberately invented to replace Confucianism, but in many ways it resembled what was displaced. Anything else would be strange, for Mao was educated in a traditional way until his twenties, when as a young college student he first met Lenin's ideas and began his career as a Marxist. Other Chinese Communist leaders, as well as many of the rank and file, have a similar personal history. Massive carryover from the Confucian past is, therefore, inescapable, even if doctrines have been officially and fundamentally changed."*[8]

Social Institutions as Impediments to Progress   When tradition and modernity are seen as antithetical, traditional social institutions, especially religious ones, become obstacles to the modernizing process, whether economic, social, or political. Readers found these examples, among others, in the texts: *"Religious beliefs and lack of education make progress slow."*[9] *"Thus industrialization and modern agricultural techniques were slow in coming to the Indian subcontinent—partly because of the firm hold tradition has on the way of life of the people."*[10]

The attitude that Asian social institutions are impediments to progress was found by readers in 63 texts. Most of the examples cited by readers centered on Hindu beliefs about caste and animals. The texts tend to regard caste as an obstacle to nationalism or democracy or as a cause of economic deprivation: *"India is a democracy. In a democracy, all men are created equal. The caste system does not fit in with the idea of a true democracy."*[11] *"This system has made life a hopeless nightmare of toil and unspeakable poverty for countless millions of India's people."*[12]

Following this line of thinking, teacher's guides and questions at the end of chapters in student texts frequently suggest that students compare the caste system with racial segregation in the United States.

Many of these texts also lament the Hindu willingness to take the lives of a variety of creatures ranging from cattle and monkeys to snakes and silkworms. A classic expression of the attitude of these texts toward Indian treatment of the cow, for instance, states: *"[Nehru] also had to fight ancient Hindu customs. These customs often hindered India's economic progress. One of these customs were the belief that the cow was a sacred animal. . . . Hindus do not eat beef, and the cattle served no useful purpose."*[13]

In answering questions on accuracy in the texts, scholars heavily criticized discussions of caste and cattle for their failure to reflect the great diversity of views about these elements of Indian culture. The scholars pointed out that these treatments of caste confuse it with class and neglect the fact that castes and their relationship "have been in constant flux" historically and that their underlying principles are "readily adaptable to modern conditions." As one reader argued, "a caste system makes for a division of labor, a high degree of interdependency (and) promotes solidarity by requiring exchanging and distribution of goods and other resources among households of different occupation, caste, and economic class."

How Might a Text Discuss Caste and the Cow?   An exception to the rule, one text was cited as expressing far more accurately the part which the cow plays in the Indian economy. The text included a poem by an Indian, R. K. Narayan:

> "Living, I yield milk, butter and curd, to sustain mankind
> My dung is as fuel used,
>   Also to wash floor and wall;
> Or burnt, becomes the sacred ash on forehead.
> When dead, of my skin are sandals made,
> Or the bellows at the blacksmith's furnace;
> Of my bones are buttons made . . .
> But of what use are you, O Man?"[14]

Two readers argued that a text might discuss caste more profitably by considering how it gives meaning and security to life. They suggested looking at the advantages and disadvantages of a society based on the Indian dharma (duty, seen as function of one's status level) rather than on competition.

The Importance of Economic Wealth and Technology   One of the results of seeing history in terms of "progress" is to place great emphasis on economic conditions and technological advancement. Textbooks tend to speak about nations and people in terms of their material wealth or poverty: *"Like its history and its people, the Japanese government is interesting, but easily the most interesting thing about Japan is its economy."*[15] *"The followers of Zoroaster, from ancient Persia, are called Parsees. Though there are only about 200,000 of them in India, they are important as businessmen."*[16]

The questionnaire did not ask readers to comment on the texts' specific attitudes toward technology, but some readers make a special point of describing a book's tendency to place great emphasis on, or faith in, technology. As evidence, they gave examples like these: *"Modern science, technology, and medicine can provide the means to improve the quality of life for the Indian people."*[17] *"Radio, television and jet airplanes are bringing the billions of people on earth closer together."*[18]

"You can see clearly now that the farmers of East Asia have lagged somewhat behind those in many other lands. But they are not standing still. Here and there, men are learning about new crops and new ways of caring for the old, familiar crops. A few new machines are coming into use. For example, the picture above shows a new way of lifting water to irrigate a rice field. This is Thailand. . . . From such simple beginnings, a new kind of farming and a new way of life may take shape, in time, in East Asia."[19]

"Americans use more machines than any other people in the world. These are found in office buildings, factories, homes, and many other places. With these tools and machines, Americans make many good things for people. Think for a moment of the machines and tools in your home and school. In your home there may be a can opener, a toaster, and a refrigerator."[20]

Readers did not indicate that they thought it was wrong to emphasize the importance of improving the quality of life in Asia. But they reported that the books in which they found these and similar examples showed no awareness that technology can be a mixed blessing, bringing problems as well as advantages.

THE WESTERN-CENTERED APPROACH

Many of the preceding quotations from the texts not only suggest that the proper perspective from which to view a society is how far along it has come on the road to "progress." They also assume that in Asia "progress" by definition must follow the path it has historically taken in the West. The basically ethnocentric character of this point of view has been analyzed in *The Modernity of Tradition* by sociologists Lloyd I. and Susanne Hoeber-Rudolph. They argue that "The myths and realities of Western experience set limits to the social scientific imagination, and modernity becomes what we imagine ourselves to be." This approach is one of a closely related cluster of Western-centered attitudes that occur in 76 percent of the texts and form the exclusive approach of 56 percent of them.

It could be argued that some Asians would share a belief in Western technological, political, economic, or social superiority. Nevertheless it is one thing for an Asian to hold this belief; it is quite another for it to be the only point of view presented to American school students by textbook authors.

"Catching up with the West"   Most frequently (in 99 out of 263 texts) Western ethnocentrism takes the form of portraying Asia as "catching up with the West": *"Once Europe developed machines and mastered the use of power to run these machines, the West forged ahead rapidly. Now, belatedly, the countries of the Orient are trying to catch up."* [21]

"In the twentieth century, the peoples of Asia and Africa have come alive. They have adopted the nationalistic creeds, the democratic ideals, and the modern science of the West, and they have demanded freedom from imperial rule." [22]

"Western civilization developed in Europe among men of the Caucasoid race. This fact tended to give Caucasoids a belief in their own superiority, because they had better ships, weapons, and technology than the non-Caucasoid peoples they conquered. But Western civilization is a cultural factor, not something biological. It can be learned, and is being learned, by people of every race. Western civilization is becoming world civilization. The races of man are competing or, better, cooperating more and more on a basis of equality." [23]

Confusing Westernization with Modernization   In some books (28 in the sample) a Western orientation is reflected in a failure to distinguish "Westernization" from "modernization." In such examples "modernization," "Westernization," and even "industrialization" are used interchangeably, as if they were synonyms. Referring to a photograph in a student text, the teacher's guide, for instance, suggests that the attention of the students be called *"to the fact that the father in the Japanese family is wearing traditional dress, while the other members of the family are dressed in modern clothes."* [24] The reader who cited this example pointed out that "the 'modern' clothes referred to are Western clothes." He added that the kimono worn by the father in the photograph "is no closer to Japanese clothes of a few centuries ago than the Western clothes worn by other family members are to Western clothes a few centuries ago." Both are modern adaptations.

Other readers did not find an explicit identification of "Westernization" with "modernization" but argued that it was often implied, as in a text which said that the Indian government believed that: *"India's enormous problems of illiteracy, poverty, and a very low standard of living could only be resolved by following the currents of industrialization and modernization, courses already travelled by the Western democracies."* [25]

Readers point out that such treatments fail to take into account that Western ideas are actually adapted by Asians, not slavishly copied; that Asians have also borrowed from Asians, and that this has occurred to a far greater extent over a much longer period of time (witness the seminal impact of Chinese and Indian civilizations on most of the rest of Asia); and that Asians have also influenced the West. While texts describe 19th Century Japan as alternately "modernizing" or "Westernizing," for instance, they fail to note that at the same time a passion for "Japonaiserie" was sweeping the arts of Europe.

A Perspective on Japanese Imitation   One reader offered a helpful perspective from which to view Japan, the Asian nation most frequently described as imitating others. "The question of whether or not Japanese culture is all an 'imitation' of China or the West is a tough one to deal with," he said. "It depends on what one means by imitation, and particularly on what value one ascribes to it. At worse, imitation is parrot-like mimicry; at best, it's a truly creative adaptation and eventual assimilation of the high achievements of another.

"The European peoples are so diverse, and they fade off so delicately, in time and geography, into the vast reaches of Asia and the Near and Middle East, that the whole issue of 'imitation' seems never to arise. This is so because mutual influences have been so continuous that they've been almost invisible; and the notion arises that the 'Western' culture is and always has been essentially homogeneous too, and so is all of Asia on into Europe and across the Bering Straits.

"In the meantime, though, Japan is a long way out in the ocean, and whenever she opens herself to foreign influence, she gets caught red-handed stealing goodies from somebody else's island. Of course, the tycoons on the other island are very magnanimous about it, and the more so since they've forgotten what clever imitators they once were themselves; or still are."

Praising and Describing by Western Standards   A very effective method of introducing new material to students is to build on situations with which they are already familiar. Unfortunately, if applied to the study of other societies, this otherwise excellent pedagogical device can easily slide over into ethnocentrism: *"Japanese children study much the same things American children do. English is also taught. Japanese boys and girls even enjoy many of the same sports Americans do, such as baseball, tennis and swimming."*[26] *"Ice cream is a favorite in the United States and is becoming a favorite around the world."* (caption for photograph of Japanese boy with ice cream and baseball glove)[27]

Readers argued that comparisons like these and others they found in the texts assumed American technological, political, economic, sartorial, athletic, or even culinary standards as goals to be met. Some examples can be downright condescending: *"Japanese ocean liners are operated with great efficiency. Their ships which carry passengers to the Orient are quite as comfortable and safe as those of any other nation."* [28]

What readers objected to in these well-intentioned comparisons was the assumption that Asian societies are acceptable to the extent that they are reflections of our own.

Emphasis on Asian Problems—Neglect of Asian Strengths   Although textbooks sometimes use Western yardsticks in an attempt to promote a positive (if sometimes condescending and superficial) portrait of Asia, they more often use these standards to project a picture of technological, economic, political, and social "underdevelopment." Readers were asked by the evaluation guide to note whether the differences between Asian and Western nations were explained in such a way that there is an emphasis on what the Asian societies do not have and whether there was an overemphasis on the poverty of a country or area. The range of examples they offered in return was very great. Some show the very subtle form which Western ethnocentrism can take:

"There was no bread or meat, no milk or fruit, no toast or jelly—just plain oatmeal-like porridge." [29] (From a book on the "emerging" nations)

"Farm families, like Slamet's, do not use knives, forks, or spoons, as you do." [30] (From a book on Indonesia)

By far the majority of the examples, however, depict Asia as a place of unrelieved misery, with insufficient food, flimsy houses, little electricity, a low income level, a short life span, poor health care, few machines, low literacy rates, too many people, and inflexible social and political institutions. Here are some typical examples of what the readers found in 89 out of 263 books:

"In Africa and Asia, millions of people live in small huts that have less protection and less comfort than the huts of Europe in the early Middle Ages. These people do not have any of the conveniences made possible by electricity and gas." [31]

"Most (Indonesian) villagers have no electricity in their homes so they have no radios or television sets for entertainment. They have no books or magazines to read either." [32]

These descriptions are not necessarily inaccurate. But by assuming that the social and material aspects of United States culture are universal norms of the good life, texts describe Asian societies from the perspective of what they *do not* have. The readers' chief quarrel was that this viewpoint offers a very one-sided look at Asian countries. Many of Asia's "huts," for instance, exist in places of year-round warm climate—unlike medieval Europe. In a typical village in Java, where almost half of Indonesia's people live, people might watch dramatic presentations of the *Mahabharata,* the *Ramayana,* or indigenous Javanese epics that last 12 hours at a time, and in many a village every male can play some instrument of the *gamelan* orchestra. Similarly, the following textbook description of regimentation in China gives no hint of the satisfactions that Chinese living in the system may find for themselves:

"In 1958, Mao launched 'The Great Leap Forward.' This was probably the most extreme example of communization in history. China's hundreds of millions of peasants were gathered together on huge farms called communes. They were organized into brigades to work in the fields, ate together in community dining halls, and slept in large dormitories. Before and after work, they were required to attend Communist lectures and drill in the militia. Each commune also had to establish and operate small steel furnaces or other small industries. City people were subjected to similar treatment. Many were sent out to work in the communes or were drafted for labor on huge public work projects."[33]

Perhaps of all the countries, textbook treatment of India most reveals negative attitudes. The stench of rotting garbage and the pall of disease and death hang over many of the passages excerpted from texts by the readers. The following example sums up the grim image that is often evoked: *"Death in India comes in so many more ways: A playful nip from a rabid puppy, a burning fever, a gnawing belly, a leprous hand. . . . Perhaps in no other country is it so easy to talk about life and death, about God and eternal salvation, as it is in India."*[34]

Since textbooks depict India's economic and health conditions with so harsh a brush, it was perhaps all too likely that they would make incorrect or negative inferences about the role of the caste system and the multiplicity of languages in India: *"The village people live in 'another world.' Many of them have barely heard of Gandhi or Nehru. Many of them are sick and cannot read or write. So many different languages are spoken that Indians have a difficult time communicating with one another. Many are terribly poor. The caste system still divides the people, though it has been outlawed by the new government."*[35]

One-sidedness and inaccuracy-by-omission are also at the heart of a textbook discussion of technology and transportation in India: *"Most Indians living in village India find machinery difficult to control or understand. Machines are a mystery. The automobile is a constant source of wonder to Indian peasants. Westerners who ride in cars almost from birth on learn very quickly that in order to stay on a truck as it turns a corner, one must lean into the turn. . . . Many villagers in India so rarely ride in vehicles that they fail to correct for this. . . . In learning to drive an auto, they find it difficult to go around curves smoothly. At 35 to 60 miles per hour, they are constantly overturning autos, trucks, and buses because they find themselves going off the road and jerking the wheel in order to frantically make the last-second adjustments necessary to stay on the road."* Having set forth the "problem," the textbook offered the following "solution": *"Time and practice, of course, solve this problem. Americans started with slow-moving Model-T Fords and, as a nation, over the years built and became adept at driving cars traveling at sixty to eighty mile-an-hour speeds on modern four-lane freeways. Indians are being thrust into the automobile age without a corresponding Model-T phase."* [36]

Stated the reader who found this example, "The implication is that Indians are completely unable to handle technology. It is not mentioned that India is the sixth largest industrial power. Furthermore, Indians are able to keep automobiles running which would be on the scrap heap elsewhere."

Charges of one-sidedness as well as inaccuracy were also leveled by readers against treatments of 19th Century Japan and China, which are often portrayed as stagnant until contact with the West.

Readers particularly objected to the inaccurate treatments they found of the People's Republic of China. The following example is typical of the out-of-date economic information they discovered in many textbook discussions of China: *"The beggars at left illustrate the hunger of China's people. Given all these conditions, disease spreads quickly. The Communist government has been unable to solve these problems that have long plagued the nation."* [37]

"Communes are a failure . . . there is good reason to believe that the average Chinese is not getting enough food to keep healthy, and in many cases even enough food to keep alive." [38] (This same text, which was published in 1974, also said that China was "poor in petroleum.")

While some texts do report economic progress made by the People's Republic of China, they frequently describe it grudgingly: *"The communist Chinese have tried to combine these small farms into large agricultural cooperatives, with modern machinery and methods. So far, however, these methods have not been entirely successful. But progress has been made, and agricultural production in China has increased."* [39]

Economic desperation is seen by the texts as the rationale for acceptance of political restrictions, which are sometimes described as having been achieved through tricks and deceptions rather than motivated by social goals: *"Everyone would live happily ever after. While these were mainly empty promises, they found sympathetic ears in a country where poverty and war had destroyed all other hope. . . . The*

*newly 'liberated' peasants were organized into 'mutual aid teams.' The
peasants were lured by promises of what they longed for.*"[40]

Using Different Yardsticks   The eradication of poverty, hunger,
disease, and social injustice are worldwide goals. No reader quarreled
with discussion of these problems where they exist provided the texts did
not concentrate on them to the exclusion of the positive side of Asian
life. But readers did object to the assumption of American social or
economic standards behind the discussions of Asian deprivations: *"If you
were a Brahmin, could you go to a movie with a Kshatriya? Think of
some Americans who started life as farm boys or poor city boys, and
became presidents of the United States. . . . Could this happen in India
under the caste system?"*[41]

*"The (Chinese) government has not shown a great effort to improve
the living standard of the individual."*[42]

Charging "gross unfairness," the reader who cited the second of these
passages said, "I am afraid that the author means Western, American
standards of living when he uses that term." Similar examples were found
in other texts which emphasized the absence of cars in China without
regard for the fact that two cars for every family is not the national goal
of the Chinese themselves.

Readers argued that using standards such as life span or number of
cars can produce a favorable picture of the United States and a dismal
one of many countries in Asia. However, concentration on the problems
of our society, such as pollution and high consumption of irreplaceable
sources of energy, could easily reverse the image. Indeed it is ironic that
these standards should be used to derogate Asia just when we are
beginning to wonder whether they are fully valid for us. Reports from
readers, questioning whether it is right to continue to glorify the use of
the car and electricity, pointed up how texts lag behind recent public
opinion.

Readers also discovered that the picture of Asia set forth in the texts
was sometimes even more unflattering by comparison with that of the
West because Europe or America had been painted in unrealistically rosy
tints: *"At a time when Europe was rapidly entering the modern age and
new nations were rising, Japan was still living under feudalism."*[43]

Remarked the reader, "This attitude is taken for granted by a lot of
people and by a great many Japanese indeed. Nonetheless, I think it's
unfair. Japan in, say, 1800 seems to have been a good deal more lively
and 'progressive' (if this is what one wants) than is generally supposed;
and Europe and America were a good deal more grubby than we care to
remember."

How Might a Text Discuss a Technologically Less Developed Society in a Sympathetic Way? It is possible to compare our way of life with that of technologically less advanced societies in a way that does not make them (or us) sound inferior. It is even possible to show that very positive values exist in such societies. One textbook does this so well that we quote it at length:

"The standard of living in rural Southeast Asia, from our point of view, might seem only slightly above subsistence level. We would find it difficult to live without running water, refrigerators, package foods, and the host of conveniences surrounding us. The typical one or two room dwellings made of bamboo and palm leaves would strike us as interesting to visit but impossible to live in. The privacy valued by most Americans is not part of the Southeast Asian peasant's life. Life is simple and, consequently, needs are not so great. The competitive drive which so dominates our urban, industrialized society is largely lacking in the peasant society of Southeast Asia. It is interesting that even most of the games played by young people are non-competitive in nature.

"Due to the relatively small size and interdependent nature of the village, rural life tends to be typified by harmonious community relations. They include a democratic election of village offices, communal plowing and land ownership, and various forms of mutual aid. Nearly an entire village participated in the dedication of a new house in a small village in Northern Thailand recently. Hunters went into a jungle and shot a wild boar which they contributed to a village feast. Most of the members of the village came to pay a visit to the owner of the house to wish him well and sample some of the special treats he had prepared. It was an occasion largely foreign to our experience, but one with which our early forefathers had more in common. In fact, it was not totally unlike an Amish barnraising in our own country today."

"Again, in another place, the same text explains the differences between life with machines and life surrounded by nature without making either seem less satisfying from a human point of view:

"Many of us in America have grown up in a highly controlled environment. Modern machines have eased the burden of physical labor; lighting and heating systems enable us to alter the pattern of hot to cold, light to darkness; and modern modes of transportation and communication have vastly reduced conceptions of time and space. Our industrialized, highly mechanized world view greatly conditions our behavior and attitudes. . . . While modernity is beginning to change life in many parts of rural Southeast Asia, these societies are still largely traditional. The forces of nature which determine the successful rice harvest are to be placated rather than controlled, and the major values of the human

community are still centered about the family and religion. The most important celebrations revolve around the agricultural calendar, significant occurrences in family life such as weddings and funerals, and the major religious events of Buddhism, Islam, or Hinduism. "[44]

Europeans and Americans in Asia   Some textbooks not only describe Asia from a Western point of view but also magnify the historic role of Americans and Europeans. Readers reported that 48 books in the sample either discuss Asia primarily in terms of its contact with the West, so that it is seen as merely a stage on which some of the drama of Western history unfolds, or give a disproportionate amount of attention to the West by comparison with Asia. So-called "world" history books are particularly susceptible to this flaw. Two-thirds of the world's people live in Asia. Yet the average amount of text devoted to it in the 42 "world" histories in the survey is 15.6 percent.

But most frequently the glorification of Europe and America takes the form of showing Westerners as helpers in Asia, bringing technology, government, and security to the area. The colonial period, the occupation of Japan after World War II, and the assistance rendered to Asia through AID, the Peace Corps, and our military establishment are usual topics for textbook writers who, in the judgment of the evaluators, discuss only the Western contributions to Asian life and fail to mention any Asia initiatives and strengths at all.

"During the many years the British occupied India, new ideas and ways were introduced. The British contributions to India were railroads, schools, and a European form of government. Under British rule, the people of India also learned a little about manufacturing." [45]

"The occupation authorities instituted many significant changes in Japanese life. Japan was given a democratic constitution, guaranteeing the people the right to participate in their government. Women were given the vote. . . . Schoolbooks were rewritten to teach Japanese children the ways of democracy. The Japanese people have taken enthusiastically to their new form of government, and to the new freedom in their personal lives." [46]

"With Western help, American surplus food, and improved transportation, the devastating famines of a few decades ago are currently being thwarted. . . ." [47]

"Red China is using its growing power throughout the region. . . . If they (nations trying for democratic forms of government) fail, much of the Far East will be closed to the people of the free world. American soldiers and arms have been sent to Southeast Asia to help keep South Vietnam free of communism." [48]

None of the readers argued that Western contacts with Asia be ignored or that humanitarian motives are not also operating along with those of self-interest in our postwar activities in Asia. They do believe, however, that a more balanced view would lessen the impression of Asia the weak and America the powerful.

Textbooks might achieve balance in their description of the Western presence in Asia by considering Asian experiences under colonialism and United States military and economic aid in the period following World War II. The books might discuss Asian initiatives toward development as well as Western ones.

Why Learn about Asia?   The emphasis on Asian weaknesses and deficiencies in the majority of American texts might lead one to suspect that in the eyes of many textbook writers, a discussion of Asia is merely a device to teach students, by comparison, the blessings of the American way of life. Such indeed was the explanation given by one teacher's guide that explained its objective as enabling the pupil *"to appreciate the basic American values which make the United States distinct from other nations."*[49]

The readers had no quarrel with this purpose as a valid educational goal for American schoolchildren. They merely questioned whether it should be carried out in the context of teaching about other societies. Must the United States be praised at the expense of other peoples?

Readers also found explicit references in 33 of the books to another argument for studying Asia, that of American self-interest: *"If we are wise, we shall realize that nothing important can happen in any part of the world (even Asia) without in some way affecting us. It will make a difference to us whether Asia has peace.*

"We may not care to get mixed up in the problems of government in India or Southeast Asia, but it will be to our interest that those who do have responsibility for those things shall be our friends, and that the native people of those distant lands shall be able to live peacefully and happily with as democratic a government as they are able to manage."[50]

"First, by helping the less-developed nations raise their standards of living, we are creating future customers for American goods and those of our European allies. Second, most of this country's leaders believe that people who are well fed and well clothed are more capable of resisting the influence of communism."[51]

It may be true that some part of Asia is vital to our security. It is undoubtedly true that a peaceful and prosperous Asia is a better customer for American business. It is also undoubtedly true that the world is becoming increasingly interdependent. All these points may make excellent arguments for selling technical and military assistance programs in Asia to Congress and the American taxpayer. But readers argued that quotations like those cited above present Asia in a Western-centered, rather than Asia-centered, context.

ASIA AS INSCRUTABLE OR EXOTIC

The progress-oriented and Western-centered approaches are not the only ones which fail to present Asian reality fully. Regarding Asia as inscrutable—once a common attitude among Westerners—also fails dramatically the first criterion for interpreting a society: to reveal it as it is to its members. One teacher's guide suggested that Asia might be depicted initially as strange to stimulate student interest. But, as the reader commented, "the goal should be to demystify Asia."

Presenting Asia as exotic also fails to reflect the full humanity of its people by making them seem alien and "other than" us. In a textbook on the Philippines, for instance, one ethnic group, the Moros, is described solely in terms of its colorful dress. In an anthropology text for younger children, the student's first introduction to any Asians is to a group of headhunters: *"India, where the Nagas live, is in Asia. Asia is the largest of all the continents. About half of the world's people live in Asia."*

Breathtakingly juxtaposing a familiar situation (having neighbors) with the fearfully different, the textbook then asks the student: *"How would you like to have headhunters for neighbors?"*[52] It goes on, in a description of a Naga village, to suggest that the child would be scared silly by the sight of human skulls hanging all over the place.

Another text emphasizes the strangeness and exoticism of Hindu religious practices (and errs in the use of *Brahma,* the name of an individual Hindu deity, instead of the correct, *Brahman,* meaning the universal spirit):

"They worshiped thousands of gods and offered bloody sacrifices to them. They became fatalistic about life, passively accepting the evils about them. Fanatical holy men achieved fame by half-starving themselves or by performing incredible feats like lying for years on a bed of nails. In such ways they hoped to free their souls from the burden of flesh and to become one with Brahma."[53]

Readers reported, however, that textbooks only relatively rarely spoke of Asia as inscrutable or exotic.

Scrutinizing the "Inscrutable"   Mysticism is one of the aspects of certain Asian cultures most bewildering to Westerners. It is possible, however, to present it in such a way that it becomes approachable. The following discussion from a text shows how this might be accomplished:

"Though we may find it hard to take mysticism and asceticism seriously, more than half the human race has done so. Indian transcendental ideas spread to China and Southeast Asia, and influenced Christianity as well. Such a career requires us to adjust our usual habits of thought and ask ourselves what we would do and how we might behave if it really were true that reality lay behind the world of sense. How do you know that it does not? How do you know that the Indian mystics were not on the right track after all, and that it is we moderns who are chasing after illusions? Many people in our time have asked themselves this question. Many people in every age of the past, from the time when such ideas first clearly came to be formulated, have been fascinated by these questions. It would be absurd to scoff and pay no attention, or refuse to take seriously ideas that sustained one of the world's greatest and most successful civilizations." [54]

ECLECTICISM

The fact that many Asians are progress-oriented while retaining many of their own cultural values suggests that there are times when a text might profitably adopt a multivalued approach to Asia. Even a Western-centered point of view might be used, provided that it is carefully labeled as such and presented as one of several that can be taken toward Asia. Obviously, one of the others should be Asia-centered. If a text employs more than one perspective consciously, we shall call its approach "eclectic." While many, if not most, of the texts unconsciously—and thus, uncritically—adopted several basic approaches, only 14 out of the 263 titles were truly eclectic in this sense. The core of the method is described in the following excerpt from a reader's report:

"In Volume I, the (Indian) culture seems quite rational. Given Hindu assumptions, the whole system seems to make so much sense that many students are quite attracted to the model. But then in Volume II, especially during the section on 'development,' students begin to question the assumptions of Volume I. They see that there is a plurality of value systems at work in India and many of the values are difficult to reconcile to each other. How does one digest dharma, karma, and caste together with egalitarianism, social revolution, and technological progress?"

Teachers sometimes use the technique of "values clarification" as a way of introducing questions of value into the classroom without inculcating any specific set of values. As a reader pointed out, however, the danger is that with such an approach, another culture is not studied for its own sake but is used as a tool of student self-discovery. "If a student is asked to clarify his or her attitudes toward the question of violence (e.g., was peasant violence during the Chinese Revolution justified)," he argued, "the student will naturally appeal to the value base of his own culture in clarifying this question. The point here is not that confronting such a question may not be a useful thing to do (which it is) but whether confronting it tells you anything significant about Chinese values (which it doesn't.)"

How "Values-Clarification" Can be Eclectic   One reader reported that a text did indeed present an Asian culture as rational within its own context by providing exercises in which the students were asked to examine the feelings of the people within the culture before making a cross-cultural comparison. For instance, it asked them to compare the meaning of "a good life" as the Japanese parents in the text saw it with how the young people saw it. Only then were the students to compare their own view with that of the young Japanese.

TALKING ABOUT ASIANS
AND THE ASIAN EXPERIENCE

To overcome the barriers in the way of understanding another society, a text should avoid focusing exclusively on "important" people such as heads of state (or at least the public, political side of such people), or upon "typical" people such as "farmers" or "city dwellers." It should make the effort to relate such abstractions as problems, forces, events, and movements to individual people and the concrete reality of their everyday lives. It should let the people speak for themselves—and allow students to think for themselves without becoming involved in judgments about what is good and bad in the lives they are studying. That texts must center on peoples and their cultures was a fundamental point of view behind the evaluation study.

With such an approach, for instance, a textbook on Japan shows how (in the words of one reader) "at a TV factory, the employees sing a company song at the start of each work day . . . how many students, even in grade school, attend special afternoon classes to prepare for college entrance examinations . . . and how religion, music, and calligraphy play some small part in the lives of the people."

In discussing the Korean war, another book deals with questions of foreign policy and the conduct of war, but relates all of these issues to real individuals. In addition to revealing the personalities and philosophies of the military and civilian leaders of the age, it provides a movingly real account of the plight of the ordinary foot soldier and even the noncombatant.

A text encourages understanding of what is being attempted in the People's Republic of China by quoting three statements from Mao Tse-tung: "Of all the things in the world . . . people are the most precious." "Our duty is to hold ourselves responsible to the people." "Anyone should be allowed to speak out, so long as he means to be helpful."[55]

Literature, art, music, dance, drama, philosophy, religion, and other primary expressions of the human experience provide excellent devices to present a people and their culture vividly and concretely, as do such materials as journalistic pieces, letters to the editor, historical and political documents, case studies, and photographs of people.

Readers were asked to rate books on how Asian life was discussed and to what extent actual Asian sources were included. Of the 260 texts for which responses were received on this topic (termed "humanistic/human interest approach and content" in the evaluation guide), readers found that only 43 were centered on people and their culture; only 23 books actually included primary sources. Far more frequently, readers found the books to be negative or inadequate in their treatment of Asian peoples and their cultures.

NEGATIVE AND ETHNOCENTRIC TREATMENT OF ASIAN CULTURAL ACHIEVEMENTS

Considering the strong emphasis on change and progress in American textbooks and the insistence of many that tradition and modernity are incompatible, it is not surprising that textbooks often treat Asian cultures negatively, regarding them as hindrances to progress or as primitive trappings that will become outmoded when change has taken place. One reader characterized a book on India as suggesting that pride in its cultural achievements is "preventing India from changing rapidly enough to keep its people from starving."

The readers found many examples in the texts in which Asian art forms are referred to as "strange" or as lacking what ours have. One textbook, for instance, describes Indian and East Asian music in the following terms:

"Hindu music is confined largely to popular songs and to accompaniments for the famous temple dances. Drums, cymbals, wooden flutes, and many stringed instruments have been used for centuries. Because it lacks harmony and relies solely on melodies that are so different from our own, Hindu music, like that of most East Asian countries, seems strange to Western ears."[56]

Many students would probably never experience Indian music or other Asian art forms as strange unless prompted to do so. On the contrary, there is strong evidence that art forms of other cultures are particularly accessible to children, especially younger ones. While some older students might find Asian art forms unfamiliar (a preferable word), there is no reason that this has to be the lasting effect. But when the first and only impression of some aspect of an Asian culture is one of "strangeness," why should anyone want to explore it further?

Other ethnocentric and in effect negative treatments of Asian art forms are to be found in textbook characterizations of Japanese plays as moving *"too slowly for Westerners"* [57] or of Afghan singing as *"a monotonous groan with a kind of growl quality."* [58]

Ironically, textbooks also adopt the opposite outlook. They describe Asian artists and art forms in terms of ours: *"Kalidasa, who lived in the 400's A.D., has been called the Indian Shakespeare. He wrote three plays, the most famous of which is* Sakuntala. *The story, a romantic one, concerns. . . ."* [59]

"As with Christian churches during the Renaissance, wealthy Buddhist monasteries employed numerous painters and sculptors. They have left us with many figures of Buddha, usually carved but also shown in fine fresco paintings such as those in the Ajanta caves. In style the paintings somewhat resemble the work of early Italian Renaissance artists." [60]

"Asoka's services to Buddhism compare to Constantine's to Christianity." [61]

If sensitively done, these comparisons might have potential for a positive initial introduction to a new art form, but the textbooks from which the readers took these examples go no further than the Western-oriented references. The problem with these facile analogies—beyond their superficiality—is that they fail to relate Asian arts and thinkers, and their achievements, to their own cultures and thus fail to say anything very meaningful about them. Like all descriptions of Asia in Western terms, they are essentially ethnocentric in character.

FAILURE TO PROVIDE ASIAN SOURCES

Some texts signal their awareness of the need to use Asian sources in teaching about Asia but fail to include such sources or explain how to go about finding them. Teacher's guides suggest that students prepare a Japanese tea ceremony or write *haiku,* for instance, but fail to provide instructions on how to go about these activities. More seriously, however, some texts use Western sources instead of Asian ones. Probably the most widespread example is the inclusion of works by Pearl Buck and Rudyard Kipling in the Chinese and Indian literature sections of some textbooks. But the "Pearl Buck-Rudyard Kipling syndrome" has many symptoms. One takes the form of presenting a Western author as if he or she represented an Asian point of view. Other symptoms are the dependence, exclusively or primarily, on Western authors or documents and the failure to list Asian authors in bibliographies. Readers' comments leave no doubt as to the distortions such treatment can create:

" 'Shooting an Elephant' is authentic Orwell, not authentic Burma. It tells how he felt about the Burmese and how he thought the Burmese felt toward him."

"The author . . . has a tendency to quote from Western writers when characterizing India; e.g., there are a number of quotations from Mark Twain and one from H. G. Wells. I would like more quotations from Indian writers and ordinary people to make India come alive."

"It's interesting that many novels are suggested out of Western literature. These include: *A Tale of Two Cities, Drums along the Mowhawk, Hornblower and the Hotspur, Celia Garth, The Three Musketeers,* and *A Bell for Adano.* In spite of the fact that there are many excellent Asian novels available in English translation, nothing comparable is suggested, unless you count *Anna and the King of Siam,* which is offensive to most Thai people."

"Where outside commentators are quoted—in the teacher's guide—only Americans are doing the commenting; e.g., J. Anthony Lukas and C. L. Sulzberger of *The New York Times.* Political cartoons in the text come from the United States, England, and the Netherlands, not from Indian newspapers."

How Might Asians' Voices be used in the Texts?   One reader praised the artistic, philosophical, and literary selections he found in a book on Confucian China as serving not only to "establish the existence of artistic activity in China," but also to "elucidate and make real the other subjects, such as historical events and social structure, being discussed."

In another book on China, proverbs were cited frequently throughout. The enthusiastic reader pointed out that they were "always pertinent, always shedding new light on the subject under discussion or bringing some difficult conglomeration of facts and events into a comprehensible pattern."

Traveler's Tales   To impart a vivid dimension to a discussion of life in an Asian country, textbooks sometimes employ what might be called "the traveler's tale." The problem with eyewitness accounts by foreign visitors, however, is that the authors are more concerned with their own impressions than with trying to convey the Asian experience:

"I had to assume the lotus position by tucking my feet under myself and sitting calmly. The session lasted only 15 minutes, but it was difficult to concentrate on nothingness. . . . At the time I did not realize enough about true Zen to have the experience of satori." [62]

Remarked the reader who found this example, "From the standpoint of an American first visiting Japan, the author's reactions are pretty standard and quite authentic. But they are also quite out of place in a textbook on Japan."

The essence of entertaining travel writing is to convey a sense of the distance one has come from the familiar. One tends to exploit the potential for amusement or excitement in the unfamiliarity of the surroundings. First-time impressions are very different from those experienced by someone who has grown up in a culture.

In addition to presenting an inaccurate view of a culture, the use of "travelers' tales" usually precludes the utilization of actual Asian accounts.

Westernization of Asian Sources   By retelling Asian myths, legends, folktales, or history, textbooks also in effect Westernize Asian sources. If sensitively and authentically done, a retelling can be effective, especially if the vocabulary and writing style would otherwise be too advanced for the textbook's grade level. All too often, however, texts present retellings as actual Asian sources; fail to provide identification, so that it is impossible to know whether the story is authentically Asian; rewrite history in a condescending manner; or change the concept and story line. In a description of Commodore Perry's arrival in Japan, for instance, one textbook does not draw upon actual Japanese accounts in translation. Instead it presents the following fictionalized, Westernized version:

"On July 7, 1853, the crews of some Japanese fishing boats in Tokyo Bay saw a strange sight. Into the mouth of the bay steamed a squadron of warships flying a foreign flag. The Japanese fishermen were speechless with amazement, for they had never seen a vessel propelled by steam." [63]

The Japanese myth of creation in its accepted version has been available in English translation for over 75 years and readily accessible in a standard anthology for more than 10 years, yet two recent textbooks, in remarkably similar versions, retell the myth, transforming its male and female deities Izanami and Izanagi, into a single unnamed masculine figure reminiscent of Neptune or Jupiter; turn "the floating bridge of heaven" on which they stand in the original version into a rainbow;

eliminate the delightful dialogue between the two deities; and portray them as producing not "countries," as in the authentic version, but merely the islands of Japan. Yet both textbook versions are accompanied by a Japanese painting from the Museum of Fine Arts in Boston which depicts both Izanami and Izanagi thrusting down "the jewel spear of Heaven" into the waters to produce the first island, Ono-goro-jima. One wonders whether students ever notice the inconsistency and what they think about it.

THE USE OF CASE STUDIES

Textbooks often advocate case studies of an individual, a family, or a village as an effective way of presenting social studies concretely. In fact, case studies are frequently the only attempt a textbook will make to focus on a people and their culture. Out of the sample of 260 texts, readers reported that case studies appeared in 75. Unfortunately, in only 8 of these was an Asian-centered approach dominant and only 3 scored "dominant" on the use of actual Asian sources.

Far more frequently textbook case studies are inventions, replete with "fanciful misinformation," as one reader put it. They are filled with situations, dialogue, and attitudes that either have been made up outright or seem to have been very loosely constructed from scholarly evidence and presented as fact.

One textbook contains an account of a civil service examination in Confucian China. The character is named Cheng She Kit, which the reader characterized as "a hodgepodge of Mandarin and Cantonese," and the text describes in detail how Cheng *"cut a piece from the stick of ink,"* [64] mixed it with the water on his palette, and then proceeded to take his examination, writing out each passage as it was read by the examiner, and then writing an explanation for it. Commented the reader, "It is wholly inaccurate, from the way Chinese ink is used to the way the examinations were conducted, as any one who has read a single book on China might know."

Readers also faulted the case studies for the general lifelessness and robot-like character of their people. In effect, they appeared reminiscent of the Dick and Jane robots the American schoolchild frequently meets when first learning to read. ("See, Jane, see. Run, Dick, run.") Such characters talk and question in a cardboard way and live in families typically consisting of a brother and sister heroine, "Mother," "Father," and "Little Brother." Such characters, if they do not utterly bore the students, can give the false impression that case-study characters are typical of people in the country.

Asia through Western Eyes   Although it is possible to present authentic Asian data but color it with a Western point of view, readers suspected that many case studies were invented because they seemed to reveal more about the ways in which Americans see Asians than about how Asians see themselves. One book, for instance, tells the story of Sachin, an Indian untouchable, who goes to the city, makes good with top grades and a well-paying job, and then returns to his village wearing a Western suit and shiny new shoes, only to be rejected and left standing in the dust by the caste-conscious people of his village. The reader commented that "going out with a few girls" is "nice and American" but not the way things are usually done in India. But the reader found it plainly incredible that the people where Sachin worked would not be aware—or at least curious—about his caste, and that Sachin himself would not know what to expect of the villagers when he returned home. The tenor of the story is far more that of a Horatio Alger plot gone sour than that of an actual Indian experience.

Another book uses the device of boy and girl twins to introduce village life in Thailand. But the reader argued that had the writer really been familiar with Thailand, she would have introduced a brother and sister with one or two years' difference in age, so that she could have presented the Thai social relations of status and reciprocity, in which, in the case of family members, the younger automatically owes obedience to the older and the older has a natural obligation to protect the younger.

Still another book on Pakistan talks about a youth's preference for tight jeans and his hope for "good grades," and has a Pakistani bride saying "I do."

Many of the case studies fail as genuine projections of the Asian experience because they are used exclusively or primarily to convey an aura of backwardness, deprivation, and material poverty. In short, the studies portray Asians from the standpoint of how far they have come along the road of Western progress. The following example from a textbook on Japan illustrates the bias that often occurs when a village, a family, or an individual is described in terms of possessions familiar to Americans that it may or may not have: *"All the Nakamuras sleep in one bedroom divided by a screen. The road to the house is not paved. There is a growing list of appliances in the Nakamura home—an electric refrigerator, stove, toaster, and color television. Yet the bathroom is far from modern. The toilet is primitive, and there is no shower."*[65]

Ethnocentrism in the form of explicit comparisons with the United States also enters into some of the progress-oriented case studies. One book makes the point with pictures: A woman in an American laundromat is pictured alongside a painting of Indian women doing their washing in a stream. Another book compares the situation of a Japanese farmer with what can only be described as that of an upper middle class American: *"Sekine... owns only 1.5 acres of land–hardly more than a 'backyard' in American terms, but an average-size farm in overcrowded Japan."*[66]

The insistence on "learning new ways" and the condescension of the "white man's burden" combine in another typical "case study" to suggest a strong ethnocentric flavor and the overwhelming likelihood that the "study" is actually the figment of a textbook writer's mind. The book describes how an American girl and her businessman father are seeing Bangkok's canals by boat and run into a Thai youth with the improbable (for a man) name of Siri. Unlike most Thais, who won't talk politics with strangers, Siri speaks of *"the threat of Communist China"* and says that the Thais *"have little defense against the huge army of China."*[67] Reports the reader, "The American, acting in an almost patronizing and certainly 'let me, the American, help you' manner, tells Siri that he and his group of men can get him a scholarship to learn modern ways so that Thailand will have educated leaders."

The progress-centered case study as seen through American eyes with a cast of unreal people, is vividly illustrated by two characters which appear most frequently in textbook discussions of India. One, whom we'll call "Toothless Ram," is pathetically backward and poverty-stricken. The following excerpts from different texts show him in two typical appearances: *"Ram is a toothless little man who lives in a small village in India. He is a poor tenant farmer. He cannot read or write, but he is no different in this respect from millions of others. At 42, he looks and feels like an old man. He and his wife had seven children, but only three, two sons and a daughter, are still alive. Both of his sons are married and live with him. He is worried because his daughter is not yet married."*[68]

"Arun cannot read or write. . . . For the past few years he has had a bad cough in his chest. He went to the village doctor and paid him three rupees or 42 cents for treatment. The doctor rubbed his chest with a large red stone and told him the coughing would stop. It never did, but Arun has not been back to the doctor because he does not want to spend more money."[69]

"Enlightened Ram," on the other hand, is the mirror opposite of "Toothless Ram." He is in favor of progress, modernity, and Western ways. He is impatient with his countrymen who cling to old ways and are slow to change: *"Ram is a farmer who is now living in a small village near Bombay. One of the government advisers came to discuss the new method of rice growing. . . . Even his own father warned him against changing his ways. 'Take whatever God gives you,' he said. 'Don't ask for too much.' "*

However, he agrees to try the new agricultural methods, and: *"Many years later, Ram looked back on the changes he had made. He had learned to use fertilizer. He was now borrowing tools from the village's new cooperative. He was buying good seed. He was using a new plow and sickle that were better than the ones his father and grandfather used. All of this puzzled Ram's father. He remarked, 'You are getting everything— good seed, fine fertilizer, and good tools—as if a spirit is bringing all these to you.' "*[70]

Sometimes the issue is not one of technology but of social customs: *"This was the home Krishna was expected to return to. But after six years of being away, he was no longer sure that he was suited to live under the rules of the family. For some time he had run his own life, and he thought it would be hard to take orders from the older members of the family. He wanted to choose his own career and his own wife. This was not acceptable to his grandfather's way of life."*[71]

While there might be some Indians who resemble "Toothless Ram" or "Enlightened Ram," in the textbooks both Rams are caricatures.

OTHER DIMENSIONS OF ADEQUACY AND ACCURACY IN THE TEXTS

Treating an Asian topic superficially and imposing a Western framework on it are essentially forms of inaccuracy. Scholar-readers also found inaccuracies in fact, such as "The practice of suttee was common through Asia" and "Bengal is a province"; in the use and definition of foreign terms, such as *Hinayana* instead of the correct *Theravada* Buddhism and *hara-kiri* instead of the preferred *seppuku*; and in the identification of illustrations and photographs.

The unattractiveness of some formats is another dimension of the inadequacy of many texts. Exactly 50 percent of the 168 readers who replied to a question on whether the format was initially appealing to the eye said that the poverty of the design of the book did not invite children to read onward.

Illustrations tend to perpetuate stereotypes and cliches about Asia. The inevitable pictures of the Taj Mahal, of beggars, and of cows in the streets abound in books on India, while Japan is represented with the usual delicate women in kimonos, the tea ceremony, gardens, and shrines, as well as overcrowded subways, student riots, and traffic jams in Tokyo. "There seems to be no middle ground," remarked a reader. In general, illustrations and photographs give no indication also of the ethnic diversity of many Asian nations.

There were also instances of sexism in the stereotyping of women's roles and the neglect of women as characters in the case studies.

The tone of the terminology used reinforces many of the Western ethnocentrisms apparent in the texts. One book says that *"to a remarkable extent the Japanese citizen can say what he thinks, read what he wishes, and write what he believes."*[72] Why should this be remarkable unless one assumes that Asian countries in general should model their behavior on American patterns? Another text likens colonial countries to *"problem children"* in a hurry to grow up. But the most prevalent offenders are such terms as *"underdeveloped," "backward," "primitive," "tradition-bound," "superstitious," "old-fashioned," "static," "unchanging," "have-nots"* and *"new nations"* as applied to the countries of Asia. Continued use of cold war language, even in very recent texts, is revealed by such habitual phrases as *"Communist China"* or *"Red China,"* instead of the relatively value-free and correct designation, The People's Republic of China, and by such rubrics as *"Communist challenge"* or *"the ruthless imperialism"* of China.

Readers also took exception to the number of instances in which Asia was referred to Europocentrically as the *"Far East"* or *"the Orient,"* a term whose root meaning is "the East." Sometimes Asian and African societies are lumped together under the designation *"non-Western."* Terminology like this encourages American (or European) students to develop a belief in the centrality of their own culture.

Still another dimension of ethnocentrism, readers reported, is revealed in the use of such condescending terms as *"the friendly, fun-loving Filipinos"* and *"the happy, gentle Thais,"* which suggest a childlike nature in need of guidance, if not domination.

Expert knowledge is no insurance that Western biases will not creep into the formulation of American textbooks on Asia, nor does all Asian experience qualify an author to take on the responsibility of interpreting an Asian culture to American students. Nevertheless it is noteworthy that of 302 texts on which replies were tabulated to questions concerning the qualifications of authors and consultants, only 24 percent listed authors and consultants credited with Asian expertise. Fewer than one percent of the membership of the Association for Asian Studies, the leading professional organization in the field, were involved in the production of any of the texts. Moreover, of those few experts who did participate in the formation of the texts, only a fraction were specialists in the humanities.

Overall Ratings   Basing their judgments on the variety of factors set forth in the evaluation guide, readers were asked to give overall ratings of the books they reviewed. Out of 261 books for which these evaluations were received, 63 were designated either as "excellent, should be highly recommended" or "can be used, but has some problems." Reports from readers indicated that 118 books should not be used without revision and an additional 80 were declared to be so inadequate that they should be replaced by new texts. On any given topic there appear to be at most 4 usable titles. Most of the material on Asia judged to be suitable is produced for the high school student. Of 16 elementary books given "suitable" ratings, only one series of basic texts received consistently good marks. Twelve books on the junior high level and 35 on the high school level were seen as usable by readers.

PLAN FOR ACTION

The Asia Society has concluded from the reports of the readers that the majority of textbooks in common use in American elementary and secondary schools do not come close to reflecting what thoughtful educators have long been recommending for teaching about other societies: a recognition of these societies' unique aspirations, lifestyles, systems of values, and modes of thinking.

More than 70 percent of the books emphasize the importance of progress, a yardstick which, if applied uncritically, can neglect or distort the persistent themes and continuities inherent in all cultures. The result in many texts is that Asian traditions are regarded as irrelevant to the present or thought of as obstacles to modernization.

Three-fourths of the texts approach Asia from a Western-centered point of view. They assume Westernization and modernization are one and the same and talk of Asia as "catching up" with the West. They describe it in terms of what it possesses—or lacks—by comparison with us. They discuss the material poverty of Asian nations without pointing out the satisfactions of life for Asian peoples.

The role of Americans and Europeans in Asian history is also magnified in the textbooks, and in world histories, a disproportionate amount of space is given to America and Europe.

An even larger percentage of the texts fail to discuss Asians as individuals, to depict the concrete reality of their everyday lives, and to include authentic Asian sources or at least bibliographies of these sources.

Inaccuracies of fact and definition are frequent, and illustrations and terminology perpetuate Western ethnocentrism, stereotyping, and conde-scending attitudes toward Asian peoples. Few Asian specialists are involved as authors or consultants in the preparation of the texts and of those who are, a very small proportion hold credentials in the humanities.

If the texts are characteristic of social studies curricula across the country, then serious questions should be raised about the effectiveness of the entire post-World War II movement for "international" education or "global" studies.

The Asia Society intends to disseminate the findings widely to the general public, teachers, publishers, writers, textbook selection committees, state education departments, teacher training programs, and government agencies. A list of outstanding texts was drawn up as a result of the evaluation survey, and is currently available to anyone requesting it.

Through the Association for Asian Studies and other professional organizations, the Society will work to enlist the concern and involvement of specialists in Asian studies, particularly in the humanistic disciplines, and assist them in the preparation and distribution of papers on frequently misrepresented topics, such as caste and cattle in India. It will also use the findings on the individual texts to assist publishers in the revision of texts and the preparation of new ones.

NOTES

1. *Thailand,* p. 41, Ginn, 1966.
2. *China,* p. 107, Houghton Mifflin, 1972.
3. *Communities We Build,* p. 51, Follett, 1973. Teacher's guide.
4. *The Indian Subcontinent,* pp. 1, 90, 93, 117, Allyn & Bacon, 1971.
5. *India: Focus on Change,* p. 1, Prentice-Hall, 1975.
6. *Global History of Man,* p. 444, Allyn & Bacon, 1974.
7. *Women of Asia,* p. 2, Cambridge, 1974.
8. *The Ecumene,* p. 744, Harper & Row, 1973.
9. *The Social Studies and Our World,* p. 325, Laidlaw, 1974.
10. *People in a Changing World,* p. B 105, Laidlaw, 1974.
11. *How People Live in India,* p. 80, Benefic, 1973.
12. *The Human Achievement,* p. 543, Silver Burdett, 1970.
13. *You and the World,* p. 300, Benefic, 1968.
14. *India,* p. 81, Prentice-Hall, 1975.
15. *Diversity of Ideas,* p. 94, Harper & Row, 1972.
16. *How People Live in India,* p. 49, Benefic, 1973.
17. *Exploring World Cultures,* pp. 178-179, Ginn, 1974.
18. *The Earth,* p. 5, Globe, 1971.
19. *A World View,* p. 133, Silver Burdett, 1968.
20. *Communities around the World,* pp. 35-36, Sadlier, 1971.
21. *The World Today,* p. 528, Webster McGraw-Hill, 1971.
22. *Living World History,* p. 201, Scott Foresman, 1974.
23. *Geography and World Affairs,* p. 30, Rand McNally, 1971.
24. *Living in Places Near and Far,* p. 104, Macmillan, 1969. Teacher's guide.

25. *Class and Caste in Village India,* p. 38, Addison-Wesley, 1969.
26. *Exploring a Changing World,* p. 474, Globe, 1968.
27. *Three Billion Neighbors,* p. 49, Ginn, 1965.
28. *Eastern Lands,* p. 402, Allyn & Bacon, 1968.
29. *Voices of Emerging Nations,* p. 14, Leswing, 1971.
30. *The Story of Indonesia,* p. 27, McCormick-Mathers, 1965.
31. *World Cultures Past and Present,* p. 315, Harper & Row, 1964.
32. *The Story of Indonesia,* p. 10, McCormick-Mathers, 1975.
33. *Past to Present,* p. 683, Macmillan, 1963.
34. *India: Today's World in Focus,* p. 38, Ginn, 1968.
35. *Exploring a Changing World,* p. 481, Globe, 1968.
36. *India: Focus on Change,* p. 63, Prentice-Hall, 1975.
37. *Eastern Lands,* p. 396, Allyn & Bacon, 1968.
38. *World Geography,* pp. 426, 429, Ginn, 1974.
39. *People in a Changing World,*p. A 71, Laidlaw, 1974.
40. *China: Development by Force,* pp. 20, 27, Scott Foresman, 1964.
41. *The Indian Subcontinent,* p. 62, Allyn & Bacon, 1971.
42. *China,* p. 72, Oxford, 1972.
43. *The Story of Japan,* p. 44, McCormick-Mathers, 1970.
44. *The Third World: Southeast Asia,* pp. 23, 19, Pendulum, 1973.
45. *The World around Us,* p. 136, Harcourt Brace Jovanovich, 1965.
46. *The World Today,* p. 585, Webster McGraw-Hill, 1971.
47. *Inside World Politics,* p. 231, Allyn & Bacon, 1974.
48. *Exploring the Non-Western World,* p. 227, Globe, 1971.
49. *Communities around the World,* p. 8, Sadlier, 1971. Teacher's guide.
50. *Eastern Lands,* p. 363, Allyn & Bacon, 1968.
51. *World Geography Today,* p. 540, Holt, Rinehart and Winston, 1971.
52. *Inquiring about Cultures,* pp. 80-81, Holt, Rinehart and Winston, 1972.
53. *Past to Present,* p. 51, Macmillan, 1963. Teacher's edition.
54. *The Ecumene,* p. 132, Harper & Row, 1973.
55. *The Social Sciences: Concepts and Values,* p. 317, Harcourt Brace Jovanovich, 1975.
56. *The Human Achievement,* p. 553, Silver Burdett, 1970.
57. *Exploring World Cultures,* p. 376, Ginn, 1974.
58. *The Story of Afghanistan,* p. 39, McCormick-Mathers, 1965.
59. *Men and Nations,* p. 171, Harcourt Brace Jovanovich, 1971.
60. *Record of Mankind,* p. 223, D.C. Heath, 1970.
61. *A Global History of Man,* p. 472, Allyn & Bacon, 1974.
62. *Japan and Korea,* p. 91, Oxford, 1972.
63. *East Asia,* p. 113, Silver Burdett, 1970.
64. *The Story of China,* p. 50, McCormick-Mathers, 1968.
65. *China-Japan-Korea,* p. 196, Cambridge, 1971.
66. *Japan,* p. 53, Scott Foresman, 1971.
67. *Your World and Mine,* p. 388, Ginn, 1969.
68. *Exploring a Changing World,* p. 681, Globe, 1968. Teacher's guide.
69. *Exploring the Non-Western World,* p. 316, Globe, 1971.
70. *People and Cultures,* p. 278, Noble and Noble, 1974.
71. *South Asia: People in Change,* p. 29, Addison-Wesley, 1975.
72. *Japan, Ally in the Far East,* p. 27, Laidlaw, 1967.

STUDY QUESTIONS

1. Compare Miner's account of "Body Ritual among the Nacirema" with the treatment of Asian cultures in the textbooks cited by the Asia Society. Do you see any similarities? How do you react to having your own cultural practices portrayed this way? Do you feel that it is a valid approach?

2. At what point do you realize who the "Nacirema" really are? Can you identify what the shrine, the charm box, and the various rituals represent?

3. Consider some other aspect of American culture, such as the ownership, use, and care of the automobile and its importance in American life. Describe it from the point of view of an imaginary anthropologist. Does it cause you to see these values and practices in a different light?

4. When you think of India, what associations immediately come to mind? Can you identify the source(s) of these impressions?

5. Go to a public library and see if you can get two or three of the textbooks listed in the Asia Society bibliography. Without referring to the article or to the page reference in the bibliography, look through each and try to determine for yourself whether the texts interpret Asia in terms of Western standards.

6. Get two or three textbooks that deal with Africa and evaluate them in terms of the same criteria that the Asia Society uses in evaluating textbooks on Asia. What are your findings? What general observations can you make about them?

7. What is your own personal definition of "progress"? Do you feel that "progress," as you define it, is universally good and worthy of striving for by all societies?

8. After viewing several prime-time television programs, show how the programs do or do not reflect changes in our perception or stereotypes of certain roles. Consider, for example, the portrayal of students, blacks, lawyers, and foreigners who are guests in our country.

Bibliography

Adler, Nancy J. "Re-entry: Managing Cross-Cultural Transitions," *Group and Organization Studies*, 16, 3 (1980), 341–356.

Adler, Peter. "The Transitional Experience: An Alternative View of Culture Shock," *Journal of Humanistic Psychology*, 15, 4 (1975), 13–23.

Argyle, Michael, Adrian Furnham, and Jean Ann Graham. *Social Situations*, Cambridge University Press, New York, 1981.

Asia in American Textbooks: A Survey Conducted by the Asia Society, The Asia Society, Inc., New York, 1976.

Barnlund, Dean C. *Public and Private Self in Japan and the United States*. The Simul Press, Tokyo, 1975.

Barrett, G., and B. Bass. "Comparative Surveys of Managerial Attitudes and Behavior," in Jean Boddewyn (ed.), *Comparative Management*, New York University Press, New York, 1970.

Batehelder, Donald, and E. Warorer. *Beyond Experience, an Experimental Approach to Cross-Cultural Education*, Vermont, 1977.

Bilmes, Jack, and Stephen Boggs. "Language and Communication, The Foundations of Culture," in A. Marsella et al. (eds.), *Perspectives on Cross-Cultural Psychology*, pp. 47–76, Academic Press, New York, 1979.

Bochner, Stephen. *Cultures in Contact*, Pergamon, New York, 1982.

Boucher, Jerry D. "Culture and Emotion," in A. Marsella et al. (eds.), *Perspectives on Cross-Cultural Psychology*, pp. 159–178, Academic Press, New York, 1979.

Brislin, Richard W., S. Bocher, and W. J. Lonner (eds.). *Cross-Cultural Perspectives on Learning*, John Wiley, New York, 1975.

Brislin, Richard W., and Paul Pederson. *Cross-Cultural Orientation Programs*, Gardner Press, New York, 1976.

Carterette, Edward C., and Morton P. Friedman. *Handbook of Perception*, vol. 10 (Perceptual Ecology), Academic Press, New York, 1978.

Casse, Pierre. *Training for the Cross-Cultural Mind*, SIETAR, Washington, D.C., 1979.

Condon, John C., and Fathi Yousef. *Introduction to Intercultural Communication*, Bobbs-Merrill, Indianapolis, 1975.

Condon, John C., and Mitsuko Saito (eds.). *Intercultural Encounters with Japan*, The Simul Press, Tokyo, 1974.

Darrow, Kenneth, and Bradley Palmquist. *Transcultural Study Guide*, Volunteers in Asia, Stanford, CA, 1975.

Dodd, Carley H. *Dynamics of Intercultural Communication*, Wm. C. Brown, Dubuque, Iowa, 1982.

Druckman, Daniel, Richard M. Rozelle, and James C. Baxter. *Nonverbal Communication: Survey, Theory, Research*, Sage Press, Beverly Hills, CA, 1982.

Eddy, William B. (ed.). *Handbook of Organization Management*, Marcel Dekker, New York, 1983.

Fair Textbooks: A Resource Guide, U.S. Commission on Civil Rights, Publication 61, December 1979.

Fieg, John P. *The Thai Way: A Study of Cultural Values*, Meridian House International, Washington, D.C., 1976.

Fieg, John, and John G. Blair. *There Is a Difference: Twelve Intercultural Perspectives*, Meridian House International, Washington, D.C., 1975.

Fisher, Glen H. *Public Diplomacy and the Behavioral Sciences*, University of Indiana Press, Indiana, 1972.

Fisher, Glen H. *International Negotiation*, Intercultural Press, Yarmouth, Maine, 1980.

Fitzgerald, Frances. *America Revised*, Little, Brown, Boston, 1979.

Framework for Development Education. Prepared by the Joint Working Group on Development Education of Private Agencies in International Development (PAID) and now known as the American Council of Voluntary Agencies for Foreign Service, INTERACTION: The American Council for Voluntary International Action, INTERACTION, New York, April 1984.

Gorden, Raymond L. *Living in Latin America*, National Textbook Co., 1974.

Goulet, Denis. *The Uncertain Promise: Value Conflicts in Technology Transfer*, Overseas Development Council, Washington, D.C., 1977.

Grove, Cornelius Lee. "Improving Intercultural Learning through the Orientation of Sojourners," *Occasional Papers in Intercultural Learning*, AFS International, No. 1, New York, June 1982.

Hall, Edward T. *Beyond Culture*, Anchor Books, Garden City, 1977.

Hamnett, Michael. "Oceania: Cross-Cultural Adaptation," in Landis and Brislin (eds.), *Handbook of Intercultural Training*, vol. 3, pp. 181-195, Pergamon Press, New York, 1983.

Hanvey, Robert G. *An Attainable Global Perspective*, Center for War and Peace Studies, New York, n.d.

Harmes, L. S. *Intercultural Communication*, Harper & Row, New York, 1973.

Harris, Philip, and Robert Moran. *Managing Cultural Differences*, Gulf Publishing Company, Houston, Texas, 1979.

Harris, Philip, and Robert Moran. *Managing Cultural Synergy*, Gulf Publishing Company, Houston, Texas, 1982.

Hartung, Elizabeth A. "Cultural Adjustment Difficulties of Japanese Adolescents Sojourning in the U.S.A.," *Occasional Papers in Intercultural Learning*, AFS International, No. 5, New York, November 1983.

Hoopes, David, and Paul Ventura. *Intercultural Sourcebook: Cross-Cultural Training Methodologies*, SIETAR, Washington, D.C., 1979.

Hoopes, David S. (ed.). *Readings in Inter-Cultural Communication*, Regional Council for International Education, University of Pittsburg, Pittsburgh, 1972-.

Huston, Perdita. *Third World Women Speak Out*, Praeger (for the Overseas Development Council), New York, 1979.

"Japan," *Science Digest*, November 1981, 66-77.

Kohls, L. Robert. *Survival Kit for Overseas Living*, Intercultural Press, Yarmouth, Maine, 1979.

Landis, Dan, and Richard Brislin (eds.). *Handbook of Intercultural Training*, vol. 3, Pergamon Press, New York, 1983.

Marsella, Anthony, Roland Tharp, and T. J. Ciborowski. *Perspectives on Cross-Cultural Psychology*, Academic Press, New York, 1979.

Olsson, Micael. "Meeting Styles for Intercultural Groups," *Occasional Papers in Intercultural Learning*, AFS International, No. 7, New York, February 1985.

Osgood, C. E., W. H. May, and Murray S. Miron. *Cross-Cultural Universals of Affective Meaning*, University of Illinois Press, Urbana, 1975.

Ouchi, William. *Theory Z*, Avon Books, New York, 1982.

Parker, Orin. *Cultural Clues to the Middle Eastern Student*, American Friends of the Middle East, Inc., New York, 1976.

Pascale, Richard T., and Anthony Anthos. *The Art of Japanese Management*, Warner Books, New York, 1981.

Patai, Raphael. *The Arab Mind*, Scribners, New York, 1973.

Pick, A. D., and H. Pick, Jr. "Culture and Perception," in Edward C. Carterette and Morton P. Friedman (eds.), *Handbook of Perception*, vol. 10, pp. 19–39, Academic Press, New York, 1978.

Prosser, Michael. *The Cultural Dialogue*, Houghton Mifflin, Boston, 1978.

Prosser, Michael H. (ed.). *Intercommunication among Nations and Peoples*, Harper & Row, New York, 1973.

Raban, Jonathan. *Arabia through the Looking Glass*, Wm. Collins Sons, Glasgow, 1979.

Ramsey, Robert M. "A Technique for Interlingual Lexico-Semantic Comparison: The Lexigram," *TESOL Quarterly*, 15, 1 (March 1981), 15–24.

Ramsey, Sheila J. "Nonverbal Behavior: An Intercultural Perspective," in Molefi Asante (ed.), *Handbook of Intercultural Communications*, Sage Press, Beverly Hills, CA, 1979.

Ramsey, Sheila, and Judy Birk. "Preparation of North Americans for Interaction with Japanese: Consideration of Language and Communication Style," in Landis and Brislin (eds.), *Handbook of Intercultural Training*, vol. 3, pp. 227–259, Pergamon Press, New York, 1983.

Reeves, Richard. *American Journey*, Simon and Schuster, New York, 1982.

Rhinesmith, Stephen H. *Bring Home the World*, AMACON, A division of the American Management Association, New York, 1975.

Robinson, Gail Nemetz. *Issues in Second Language and Cross-Cultural Education*, Heinle and Heinle, Boston, 1981.

Rogers, Everett M., and F. F. Shoemaker. *Communication of Innovations: A Cross-Cultural Approach*, Free Press, New York, 1971.

Ruffino, Roberto. "An Assessment of Organized Youth Mobility in Europe," *Occasional Papers in Intercultural Learning*, AFS International, No. 3, New York, March 1984.

Samovar, Larry A., and Richard E. Porter. *Intercultural Communication: A Reader*, 4th ed., Wadsworth Publishing Co., California, 1984.

Scherer, Klaus Rainer, and Paul Ekman. *Handbook of Methods in Nonverbal Behavior Research*, Cambridge University Press, New York, 1982.

Seelye, Ned. *Teaching Culture*, National Textbook Co., Skokie, 1976.

Singer, Marshall. "Culture: A Perceptual Approach," in Larry A. Samovar and R. Porter (eds.), *International Communication: A Reader*. Wadsworth Publishing Co., California, 1972.

Smart, Reginald. "Using a Western Learning Model in Asia: A Case Study," *Occasional Papers in Intercultural Learning*, AFS International, No. 4, New York, June 1983.

Spindler, George D. *Doing the Ethnography of Schooling*, Holt Rinehart, Winston, New York, 1982.

Steiner, Shari. *The Female Factor: Women in Western Europe*, Intercultural Press, Yarmouth, Maine, 1977.

Stessin, Lawrence. "Culture Shock and the American Businessman Overseas," *Exchange*, 9, 1 (1973).

Stewart, Edward C. *American Cultural Patterns: A Cross-Cultural Perspective*, University of Pittsburgh, Pittsburgh, 1972.

Suleiman, Michael W. "The Arabs and the West: Communication Gap," in Michael H. Prosser (ed.), *Intercommunication among Nations and Peoples*, Harper & Row, New York, 1973.

Triandis, Harry. *The Analysis of Subjective Culture*, John Wiley, New York, 1972.

Triandis, Harry, and Richard Brislin (eds.), *Handbook of Cross-Cultural Psychology*, vols. 1–5, Allyn and Brown, Boston, 1980.

Triandis, Harry, and Jures D. Draguns (eds.). *Handbook of Cross-Cultural Psychology*, vol. 6, Allyn and Bacon, Boston, 1980.

Walz, Joel. "Colonialistic Attitudes toward the French-Speaking World in American Textbooks," *Contemporary French Civilization*, fall 1980, pp. 87–104.